THE RETURN OF Jesus

The Time May Be Much Closer Than You Think

ROBERT HART

The Return of Jesus

Published by:
Northpark Media
425 Glenmont Ct
Atlanta, GA 30350

Cover design and layout by Bridgett Joyce.

Published in the United States of America

ISBN paperback: 979-8-9883603-0-8

ISBN hardback is: 979-8-9883603-2-2

ISBN Kindle: 979-8-9883603-1-5

Library of Congress number applied for

All Scriptures are from the *New American Standard Bible* 95 version unless otherwise noted.

Reference material from:
The Jewish Study Bible
Jewish Publication Society
Tanakh Translation

Contents

Preface...xi

Introduction..xii

Chapter 1: God Keeps Time Differently from Us........................1

What is coming for the saints?

Understanding "the day of the Lord." Is it good or bad?

The saints reigning with Jesus on earth.

How long is "the day of the Lord?"

The "Seventh Day" in Hebrews 4.

Why should we study prophecy?

Chapter 2: Tribulation Versus Wrath 15

Three theories about Jesus' return.

Why would the Lord want His bride, the body of Christ, to endure the great tribulation?

Who is kept from "the hour of testing that will come upon the whole world?"

Why does God allow His children to endure persecution, afflictions, and suffering?

Who is the "great multitude no one could count" in Revelation 7?

When is it announced in heaven that God's wrath has come?

Timeline of Major Events of the Day of the Lord.

The sword, famine, and pestilence; what do these have to do with our world today?

More Understanding about the day of the Lord.

Will the saints know when the Lord's return is near?

The day of the Lord comes as a thief in the night.

Does Scripture teach that some things must take place first before the Lord will return?

Some details revealed in Scripture about the day of the Lord that you may not know.

Chapter 3: Sealed Prophecies 43

The End Time

Some prophecies have been sealed up by divine decree.

Have we reached the point when Scripture indicates these prophecies would be unsealed?

Why Jerusalem is important.

The Times of the Gentiles

The Thousand Year Reign of Christ, is it literal or metaphorical?

What does Scripture tell us about the millennial reign?

What is the "First Resurrection" and who has a part in it?

What is the "Second Resurrection" and who does it involve?

Chapter 4: Keep On the Alert 63

When does Jesus Return?

Will there come a time when it is too late?

Is tribulation different from wrath?

Does your current view produce “good fruit” or complacency?

One rapture or two?

The one who would save his life will lose it.

Chapter 5: Differing Views of The Lord’s Return 93

Three Primary Schools of Thought

Pre-Tribulation

Is there Biblical support for a huge revival after the rapture?

Test all things, hold fast what is good.

Mid-Tribulation

Does God protect His saints from His wrath?

The second resurrection and the judgment of the unsaved.

How does God protect His Saints?

Reassurance for Christians

Post-Tribulation

When does the rapture occur?

A look back two thousand years ago

Will a special group of saints reign with Jesus on earth?

Chapter 6: Unfulfilled Prophecies 151

Can Jesus return at any moment?

Unfulfilled prophecies that must be fulfilled before Jesus comes back.

Over the past two thousand years, have there been examples of these prophecies that were fulfilled?

Dual fulfillment of prophecy.

Events dealing with Iran (Persia).

Words concealed and sealed up until the time of the end.

Is who controls Jerusalem an end time sign?

How long is a generation?

The final "seven" of Daniel 9:27.

Who is Javan?

Chapter 7: The Antichrist 183

The Final Beast

Beasts are kings or rulers.

Defining characteristics of the antichrist.

Who is presently restraining the antichrist?

First appearance of the antichrist-beast.

Who are the two witnesses in Revelation 11?

Seven Heads and Ten Horns

The antichrist will war against the saints.

The False Prophet or Helper of the Antichrist

The Statute Dream of Nebuchadnezzar

Daniel provides further information about the antichrist.

The Antichrist and the Ten Horns.

The antichrist is destroyed

Chapter 8: Seventy Sevens 227

A Little-known Key to Unlocking Prophecy

Seventy years of exile for Israel to Babylon

Daniel's Realization and His Prayer

A New Prophecy About a New "Seventy of Sevens"

A Day for a Year Prophecy

The Angel's Declaration

The Meaning of this Prophecy Was Hidden Until it was Fulfilled

The Hebrew Word for "Seven."

The events that would unseal the meaning of Daniel's prophecy have now occurred.

The Decree to Rebuild Jerusalem Found in Nehemiah.

Chapter 9: The Millennial Reign 241

The Great Harlot is Judged Before the Rapture

Nations Must Be Judged While They Still Exist

When Are Men Judged?

What Does the Bible Teach About the Thousand-Year Reign of Christ on Earth?

Who Comes to Life to Reign with Christ?

When Do the Rest of the Dead Come to Life?

Who does Jesus Rule Over "With a Rod of Iron?"

Will people be having children during the thousand-year reign of Jesus on earth?

Different Life Spans

The "Prince" in Ezekiel 44

Water Flowing from the Sanctuary

Is Zechariah 14 Referring to the Millennial Reign?

Chapter 10: Jewish Feasts 265

How Do Jewish Feast Days Relate to End Time Events?

The Feast of Passover

The Feast of Weeks (Pentecost)

The Feast of Trumpets

The Day of Atonement

The Feast of Tabernacles

Chapter 11: Israel's Future 273

Is God finished with Israel?

The Remnant

Why would God show favor to the Jews?

God Will Use Israel to Exalt His Name in All the Earth

Chapter 12: Takeaways 289

Appendix 1.. 295

How are we saved?

Appendix 2 303

Do you sometimes doubt your own salvation?

Are we supposed to know for certain that we are saved and will have eternal life?

Appendix 3.. 319

Other "a day for a year" applications.

1290 days after the sacrifices ceased until the Abomination that causes desolation is set up.

The year 688 AD and the Dome of the Rock.

Comparing the pattern of the Levitical code of Sabbath rest for the land to the prophecy.

Is the seventieth-seven counted different from the prior sixty-nine sevens?

Appendix 4.. 337

Signs at the opening of the sixth seal

Appendix 5.. 343

America in the End Times

The man of lawlessness, the antichrist

Do we find America referenced in the Scripture concerning the time of the end?

The antichrist, the beast, and ten kings aligned with him.

A very wealthy place will be "burned up with fire in one hour."

All the merchants of the world sell their goods to this place.

God's people are told to "come out of her."

Is there Biblical precedent for God's deliverance of His people.

Appendix 6.. 361

Compare Revelation 18 and Jeremiah 51

Parallels between ancient Babylon and the harlot, Babylon the Great in Revelation.

Appendix 7.. 371

Scriptures referenced by section

About the Author.. 377

Preface

This book serves as a comprehensive study of prophecy in the Bible, focusing on what God intends for His children in the last days leading up to and including the return of Jesus, and what comes afterward. It shows why it is crucial that we be prepared for these times. It will include Scriptures from both the Old and New Testaments, and even sometimes lengthy portions, in order to achieve a fuller understanding of these prophecies.

To understand biblical prophecy, we need the indwelling guidance of the Holy Spirit. This is the case anytime we desire to understand God's Word, and especially with regard to prophecy. Throughout the following chapters it is assumed you have Jesus Christ dwelling within you providing leadership and guidance as you as you seek understanding in challenging passages in Scripture. However, we acknowledge that we need the Lord to open our eyes to the truth contained in His Word. In appendix 1 in this book, I recommend reading about how we are saved if are not sure that you have been born again as a child of God through faith in Jesus Christ.. Furthermore, if you possess faith but find yourself doubting your own salvation, I encourage you to read appendix 2 before embarking on this book's journey. It is helpful to pray and ask the Father to enlighten the eyes of your understanding and make His Word clear to you. I will join you in praying this on your behalf.

The Word tells us that since prophecy is Scripture, it will be profitable for us to study it, just as we do other portions of God's Word. It informs us all prophecy is God's doing, and did not originate with man, **"for no prophecy was ever made by an act of human will, but men moved by the Holy Spirit spoke from God" (2 Peter 1:20–21).**

Introduction

I began authoring this book back in 2013, and most of the content was completed by 2016. However, I did not feel any urgency to publish it, so I left it untouched for years. Every now and then I revisited the manuscript, making additions or edits, only to let it sit months before returning to it. It wasn't until late first quarter of 2023 I felt a strong urge to finish editing and publish the book. I dedicated six to eight hours daily, six days a week to completing the task. Then, during this time the Lord revealed something to me that I had never seen in my fifty-plus years of studying these topics. This revelation led me to rewrite the first chapter. As a result, in the first chapter of this book, I state that I do not find it implausible that the Lord may return as soon as September or October of 2031. Of course, this means the seven-year period representing the seventieth-seven of the prophecy from Daniel 9:24-27 would begin in late summer of 2024. I provide my reasons for these conclusions based on Scripture in the pages that follow.

There are three potential responses to the information contained in this book. At the two extremes are fear and panic on one end, and complacency and indifference on the other end. Neither of these responses is warranted or proper. In between is a mind and heart set on trusting God, purposing to remain steadfast in faith, persevere, and endure until the end. Even more crucial however is that if the time really may be as short as you will see could be the case, we must be praying for those we love who are not disciples of Jesus to be drawn to Him by God's grace and be saved.

This book is primarily written to those who are believers in Christ Jesus as their Lord and Savior and who believe that the Bible is inspired by God. Believing the Scriptures to be "God-breathed" means understanding that the writers only wrote what He put in their hearts to write. The Bible informs us that all Scripture is authored by God, and that it is truth and is authoritative: "**All Scripture is inspired by God and profitable for teaching, for reproof, for correction, for training in righteousness; [17]so that the man of God may be adequate, equipped for every good work" (2 Timothy 3:16–17).**

In recent decades, a disturbing trend has emerged in many evangelical churches. Much of the teaching on prophecy related to the last days as revealed primarily in the books of Revelation and Daniel has been ignored or dismissed. In the few instances where it has been taught, the overwhelming message has been that Christians will not have to face the great tribulation, but rather that the rapture will rescue them before it begins. This perspective, contrary to centuries of mainstream church teaching, has led to a sense of complacency and naivety among many Christians who are ill-prepared to face trials, suffering, and persecution.

I am deeply concerned about this trend. I believe in maintaining love and unity in the body of Christ, and yet I believe that many Christians have been misled by an incomplete and distorted understanding of biblical prophecy. While I am aware that my message may challenge and even contradict the views that some have long held dear, I am committed to being faithful to the truth as revealed in Scripture, no matter how unpopular it may be. For you the reader, I encourage you to remember the Bible encourages us to "test all things" and to "hold fast to what is good" **(1 Thessalonians 5:21, NKJV).** Therefore, it is important to approach these discussions with an attitude of humility and a willingness to learn from one another. I encourage you not to take my word or interpretation of anything, but as Paul admonished all Christians, to examine the teachings contained herein (or from any preacher) to ensure it lines up with scripture.

Among other things, you can expect to see clearly from Scripture the following things in this book:

1. What evidence is there in the Bible that Jesus might return in late summer of 2031.
2. Why the final seven-year period could begin in late summer of 2024.
3. Why the great tribulation may begin in spring of 2028.
4. What the Scripture says you should do to avoid having to endure the great tribulation.
5. Why some believers will have to endure the great tribulation.
6. When and where Scripture shows that Jesus returns to rapture (gather) the saints.
7. That some saints, but not all, are kept from "the hour of testing that will come upon the whole earth, and what Scripture says you can do to be kept from this hour of testing.
8. How and when the saints are rescued by Jesus from God's wrath.
9. How we (the saints) will know for sure that His return is near.
10. Whether Jesus' reign on earth for a thousand years is literal or symbolic.
11. That there are two resurrections (apart from Jesus' resurrection) and what the difference is between them.

12. Is there going to be an individual who is the antichrist? If so, how can we recognize him?

13. When does God's wrath begin?

14. Can Jesus presently return at any moment?

It is essential to recognize that one of the key reasons we study prophecy about the Lord's return is *to avoid being misled, to purify ourselves,* and *to prepare our minds to endure trials and tribulation with perseverance*. We must also be vigilant not to be weighed down with the worries of life, lest that day catch us off guard like a trap. Prophecy, being a part of Scripture, is meant to encourage, edify, and exhort the body of Christ, His saints. In this book, my focus is almost exclusively on what the Scriptures teach about prophecy related to the last days. While acknowledging the existence of historical theology and the shift in perspective that has taken place in recent times, my concern is to keep the foundational issues centered on the Word of God, rather than the doctrines or traditions of men. In the following pages, I will present a compelling case based on careful study of the Scriptures that the traditional understanding of prophecy related to the last days has been ignored and replaced by a modern interpretation that is not in line with what the Scriptures actually reveal to be true regarding Jesus' return and the saints having to suffer through the great tribulation.. I will examine the roots of this shift in perspective, present evidence from Scripture and history, and offer a more comprehensive and balanced view of what the Bible teaches about the end times. My aim is to provide readers, and especially fellow teachers of the Scriptures, with a solid biblical foundation for understanding prophecy and to inspire them to be discerning and faithful in their interpretation of Scripture, independent of the influence of human doctrines or traditions. My aim is not to divide or criticize, but rather to challenge and equip fellow believers to be discerning and prepared for the challenges that lie ahead, perhaps very soon. I recognize that this may be a difficult message for some to receive, but I believe it is necessary for the spiritual health and vitality of the body of Christ. I urge my readers to approach this book with an open mind and a willingness to reexamine their beliefs in the light of Scripture. Additionally, it can be like trying to drink water from a fire hose to attempt to read this type of material like a normal book. I suggest trying to read it in small sessions to better digest what the Scripture is informing us about.

It is my hope and prayer that this book will contribute to a deeper understanding of biblical prophecy related to the last days and that it will inspire believers to be vigilant, discerning, and faithful in the face of trials, suffering, and persecution. May the truth revealed in Scripture guide and strengthen us as we navigate the challenges of these times and may our love and unity in the body of Christ prevail as we seek to honor and follow the Lord Jesus Christ, our Savior and King. Like me, you probably have taken part in conversations with others who have lamented the changes taking place around us, and you already know that the world is changing very quickly and not for the good. I expect that in your heart you are already thinking the time for our Lord's return must be growing near.

I have authored this book for two important reasons. Firstly, my primary reason for writing this book is my deep concern for my fellow brothers and sisters in Christ. I do not want any to be deceived or complacent about what lies ahead. As I mentioned earlier, I believe that the time of the Lord's return may be extremely near, and I will use Scripture to demonstrate how Jesus rescues us from the wrath to come. However, it is important to distinguish between wrath and tribulation or trials. As you continue to learn about God's plans for us, His beloved children, I urge you to keep Jesus' own words in mind: **"When you hear of wars and rumors of wars, *do not be frightened*; those things must take place; but that is not yet the end" (Mark 13:7, emphasis mine).** Jesus Himself exhorts us not to be fearful, even amid tumultuous events.

Second, I believe the Lord intended for me to author this book, and it has been my sincere desire to faithfully follow the Lord's guidance and complete the course of the path He has set before me. Over five decades of studying God's Word and observing the world, I've become keenly aware of the growing lawlessness and immorality in our world. This evil has escalated, some might say exponentially, particularly in the past decade. As a result, I feel compelled to share the things God has put on my heart because the time is short.

If we have an incorrect understanding of how God is going to orchestrate events leading up to the return of Christ, it could set us up for disaster, even the abandonment of our faith. Some popular books that are fiction depict a scenario in which the Lord returns, and a "rapture" rescues all the saints, so none of them must experience the great tribulation and persevere in their faith until the end. However, believing in such a scenario can leave us ill-equipped to face the trials and suffering that Scripture tells us are coming. We need to purpose beforehand to be steadfast in our faith, so we may endure to the end.

Consider the words of the Lord Jesus in Matthew 13: **"The one on whom seed was sown on the rocky places, this is the man who hears**

the word and immediately receives it with joy; yet he has no root in himself, but endures only for a while. For when tribulation or persecution arises because of the word, immediately he stumbles" (Matthew 13:20, 21).

Consider this, if you study the Scripture I expose you to in this book, what is the worst that can happen? Even if you disagree with my conclusions, you may nevertheless become more devoted to living in a holy manner, and more committed to praying for those you love. If I am right, hopefully you become fully prepared for what lies ahead, and ultimately hear "well done, my good and faithful servant, enter into my rest."

A word of caution is in order. I am not predicting a date for Jesus' return. There have been notable examples of people over the centuries who have predicted a date for the Lord's return, only to find themselves and those who followed them disillusioned and confused. A group called the Millerites, who were followers of William Miller, a Baptist preacher, sold or gave away their belongings, anticipating the Lord's return between March 21, 1843 and March 21, 1844. Needless to say, when the predicted dates came and went, they were disheartened.

Similarly, the Jehovah's Witnesses have made several failed predictions about the return of Jesus. In 1914, they predicted that Jesus would return to earth, but when this did not happen, they revised their prediction to suggest that Jesus had returned invisibly. They made similar predictions in 1925 and again in 1975, and you need not be told how these turned out. Others have made predictions as well, all of which proved to be premature.

However, I am emphatically stating that I am not saying you should count on it happening in the time frame I suggest. I am saying it is reasonable to think that Jesus may return in the September-October period of 2031. He will not return then unless the individual spoken of in 2 Thessalonians 2:3-12 is apparent to Christians in the three-and-a-half-year period immediately beforehand. If on the other hand, this individual is apparent, then you can count on the Lord's return soon. According to Scripture, for the unbelieving world, "God will send upon them a deluding influence so that they will believe what is false" (From 2 Thessalonians 2:11). The result will be they will not expect it, and it will come on them "like a thief in the night." Rather, my point is *if indeed* His return is to be in this period, then believers who are consistently studying the Scriptures and striving to live according to them will increasingly perceive signs indicating that the event is approaching. The Scriptures confirm this to be the case, as you will discover. Moreover, Scripture indicates a unique seven-year period will precede the moment of His return and it could begin in late summer of 2024. I believe the final 42 months of this time will be the great tribulation period that Jesus spoke about. The events that will occur during that period will be unmistakable to those who belong to the Lord. This said, if we are truly disciples of Christ Jesus, and if He is returning soon, you and I will know it for the signs will become increasingly clear as the day draws near.

I invite you to see if I am mistaken and in error in some of this. If so, perhaps the Holy Spirit will reveal that to you, and you can share it with me. I would not be the first to have been mistaken, and perhaps you will bring to my attention Scripture that I have overlooked that will alter my view.

If you believe I am in error, please reach out to me at **robert@jesus-returns.net**, but be prepared to substantiate your view with Scripture. In this book, I have made a conscious effort to avoid targeting individuals by name. However, I have not hesitated to use Scripture to address erroneous teachings. My intention in authoring this book is rooted in love and concern, and I hope that those who read it will respond in kind, refraining from personal attacks and engaging in a spirit of mutual respect and understanding.

chapter ONE

God Keeps Time Differently from Us

"With the Lord, a day is like a thousand years,

and *a thousand years are like a day"* **(2 Peter 3:8, emphasis mine).**

Imagine the following scenario:

- Mark and Ava were not certain if they had actually heard it, or if they had felt it in their spirits. They turned to look at each other, both recognizing the familiar sound of a loud trumpet blast. As they looked up, their eyes took in a breathtaking sight - a brilliant light emanating from the clouds illuminating the entire sky. They knew what this meant. The time they had been anticipating, the day they had been waiting for, had finally arrived. They had endured unimaginable tribulation and hardships for several years, witnessing many of their closest friends sacrifice their lives rather than deny their faith. They had been prepared to do the same. But now, in this moment, they were filled with pure joy! The moment for which they had yearned and prayed was here! The Lord was returning to gather His saints to Himself! At that very moment, they began to feel themselves being lifted into the air, a sensation of awe and wonder washing over them.

What is Coming for the Saints

This is often the image that comes to mind when people think of *the day of the Lord:* a moment of glorious reunion and the fulfillment of long-held hopes and prayers. In simple terms, this is telling us of a time when Jesus comes and sends His angels out over all the earth and the seas to gather His saints to Himself. It begins with the dead in Christ being raised from the dead and clothed with their immortal bodies, followed by believers who are still alive on earth being transformed and clothed with immortal bodies as well. Both groups are caught up to meet Jesus in the air, and taken to heaven, marking the start of "the day of the Lord." Then, in heaven, believers celebrate the marriage supper of the Lamb, a long-awaited event. Regardless of how we view the timing of the gathering of the saints, we know from Scripture that the Lord comes to gather all of us, His saints, and take us to be with Him. We also have the assurance that Jesus rescues us from the wrath to come.

Understanding "The Day of the Lord"

I referred to "the day of the Lord" above. For believers, it is when the Lord returns to take us to heaven to be with Him. But for unbelievers, it is when the God pours out wrath and retribution on those who remain on the earth: "***the day of the Lord is coming*, Cruel, with both wrath and fierce anger, To lay the land desolate; And He will destroy its sinners from it" (Isaiah 13:9 NKJV).**

So, *the day of the Lord* is characterized as incredibly good for one group, but unbelievably bad for another. We read in 1 Thessalonians 4 and 5 about how we will know the beginning of this day because **"*the day of the Lord* will come just like a thief in the night" (1 Thessalonians**

5:2). This verse gives us the starting point for the day of the Lord. Looking back to the end of chapter four, we see clearly the context tells us this is about the time when the Lord comes to gather His saints to Himself**: "For the Lord Himself will descend from heaven with a shout, with the voice of the archangel and with the trumpet of God, and the dead in Christ will rise first. Then we who are alive and remain will be caught up together with them in the clouds to meet the Lord in the air, and so we shall always be with the Lord (1 Thessalonians 4:16–17).**

Consider this next verse about "the day of the Lord": "**But *the day of the Lord* will come like a thief, in which the heavens will pass away with a roar and the elements will be destroyed with intense heat, and the earth and its works will be burned up" (2 Peter 3:10).** This verse taken together with the verses above from 1 Thessalonians might persuade one to think that when the Lord comes to gather His saints, we are taken to heaven, and that is the end of all life on the earth, for it appears that the earth is at that moment burned up and destroyed with intense heat. But you will see as we examine the Scriptures further that there is much more that is still to happen on "the day of the Lord." We read in Revelation 19 the following: **"From His mouth comes a sharp sword, so that with it He may strike down the nations, and *He will rule them with a rod of iron* (Revelation 19:15, emphasis mine).** If Jesus is to rule over the nations with a rod of iron, it begs the question, "When will He rule, and for how long?" When we read chapters nineteen and twenty of Revelation, we learn that Jesus comes back from heaven with His armies and destroys the antichrist (referred to as the "beast") by casting him and the false prophet into the lake of fire.

The Saints Reigning with Jesus on Earth

Then Satan is bound and thrown into the abyss for *a thousand years*. Jesus then begins to reign, and His saints reign with Him: "[4]**And I saw thrones, and they sat on them, and judgment was committed to them. Then I saw the souls of those who had been beheaded for their witness to Jesus and for the word of God, who had not worshiped the beast or his image, and had not received his mark on their foreheads or on their hands. And they lived and reigned with Christ for a thousand years" (Revelation 20:4,NKJV).**

Where does this take place? It takes place on the earth, and He is reigning over the nations. We can be confident of this when we read the following from Revelation 20: "**Now when the thousand years have expired, Satan will be released from his prison and will go out to deceive the nations *which are in the four corners of the earth,* Gog and Magog, to gather them together to battle, whose number is as the sand of the sea" (20:7-8, NKJV, emphasis mine).** This passage confirms that after a thousand years, Satan gathers *the nations on the earth* for a war against the Lord and His saints. God sends fire from heaven to destroy these who join Satan to war against His son and the saints, and Satan is himself then cast into the lake of fire where the beast and the false prophet are also.

How Long is "The Day of the Lord?"

So, as we reflect on the promises about that day, it is worth asking how the term "day" is defined in the Bible, especially regarding this particular day, *the day of the Lord.* In 2 Peter 3:8 we read a thought-provoking statement: **"But do not forget this one thing, dear friends: With**

the Lord, a day is like a thousand years, and a thousand years are like a day." (2 Peter 3:8) Understanding the context in Scripture is paramount if we are to fully grasp what the Lord is telling us. We read before a passage that comes just two verses later here: "**But *the day of the Lord* will come like a thief, in which the heavens will pass away with a roar and the elements will be destroyed with intense heat, and the earth and its works will be burned up (2 Peter 3:10).** God intentionally placed this information about the time called "the day of the Lord" right after the verse telling us *"A day is like a thousand years, and a thousand years are like a day."* It indicates *one of many things that will happen on that day.* This event spoken of here is the time when God destroys the armies which Satan has gathered to war against His son Jesus, when he is released from the abyss *after being bound for a thousand years*. During the interim, Jesus and His saints were reigning over all the nations on earth. Because this Scripture refers to "the day of the Lord" we know this is occurring on this day, for which we now have *the endpoint*. We remember that we learned this day begins when Jesus comes to gather His saints. Taken together, we now understand that the "day of the Lord" *begins* when Jesus gathers His saints and the *endpoint* of the day is a thousand years later, when God burns up the present heavens and the earth and creates a new heaven and a new earth. In between, Jesus is on earth, reigning over it with His saints. Thus, we understand that "the day of the Lord" is a thousand years long.

For the next few pages, it will help to keep in mind this strange concept concerning "the day of the Lord," for it will help explain a few otherwise difficult conundrums which we encounter in Scripture. Moreover, as we examine Scripture, we will learn that it is the "seventh day," one which follows six others that are also a thousand years long.

Let me provide an example. When God created Adam and put him in the Garden of Eden, He gave him the freedom to eat from any tree in the garden except one. He warned him about the consequences of eating from that tree: "**The Lord God commanded the man, saying, "From any tree of the garden you may eat freely; but from the tree of the knowledge of good and evil *you shall not eat*, for *in the day* that you eat from it *you will surely die*" (Genesis 2:16–17, emphasis mine).** We know from the Genesis account that the serpent deceived Eve and she ate from the tree and gave the fruit to Adam, and he ate as well. Did Adam die *in that day* on which he ate from the tree? Some would argue that he died spiritually in that very day. But when did he die physically? Genesis 5:5 informs us he lived to be nine hundred and thirty years old. After eating from the tree and being expelled from the garden, he fathered children and lived quite a long life. He lived *almost a thousand years*. However, in the sense that "a day is like a thousand years," Adam died just as God had warned him that he would, "*in the day*" that he ate from the tree, because the "day" in this context was equivalent to a thousand years.

According to my research including but not limited to the appendices that E.W. Bullinger compiled in 1901 to the Companion Bible, Adam was created roughly four thousand years before the birth of Christ. In the Companion Bible, there is a chronological chart that puts the creation of Adam at 4004 BC. The origin of this chronology is credited to John Ussher, the Archbishop of Ireland in the seventeenth century. Ussher's work, titled "Annales Veteris Testamenti," was published in the early 17th century and aimed to establish a chronology of biblical events.

Given that Jesus was crucified when He was approximately thirty-three, we are approaching two-thousand years from the time of his crucifixion. Thus, we have four "days" each of "one-thousand years" that have elapsed from the creation of Adam to the birth of Jesus, and we are about to reach the completion of two more "days" of one-thousand years each from the crucifixion of Jesus to the present time. Scholars argue that Jesus was crucified between 30 AD and 33 AD, so the completion of two more thousand-year "days" falls between 2030 and 2033, at which point we will have reached the completion of six thousand-year "days" since the creation of man.

The "Seventh Day" in Hebrews 4

God rested on the *seventh day* after completing His work of creation in six days. We can see there is a parallel between this and the six days of one thousand years from Adam until the present time. This is an interesting concept to ponder as we consider the passage of time according to the Bible. What comes on the seventh day?

Consider the following verses from Hebrews in light of the concept that "a thousand years is like a day": **"For He has said somewhere concerning *the seventh day*: 'AND GOD RESTED ON THE SEVENTH DAY FROM ALL HIS WORKS'; and again in this passage, 'THEY SHALL NOT ENTER MY REST.' Therefore, since it remains for some to enter it, and those who formerly had good news preached to them failed to enter because of disobedience, He again fixes a certain day, 'Today,' saying through David after so long a time just as has been said before, 'TODAY IF YOU HEAR HIS VOICE, DO NOT HARDEN YOUR HEARTS.' For if Joshua had given them rest, He would not have spoken of another day after that. So there remains *a Sabbath rest* for the people of God" (Hebrews 4:4–9, emphasis mine).** Here Scripture informs us there *remains a Sabbath rest for the people of God,* and this incredibly unique day is itself not just twenty-four hours long. It bears resemblance to the "day" God told Adam "He would surely die" if he ate the fruit of the tree of the knowledge of good and evil was not just twenty-four hours long. The "day" being referred to by the previous passage in Hebrews, "Today, if you hear His voice," is about entering God's "Sabbath rest," for we are told it *still remains* for us to enter it. This seventh day is "the day of the Lord," and like the six days preceding it, is one-thousand-years long. It begins when Jesus comes to gather His saints. It continues as the millennial reign of the Lord Jesus on earth. It ends when God burns up the present heavens and earth, and destroys Satan, and then creates a new heaven and a new earth. Then God makes His dwelling here on earth with us, in the new Jerusalem, which is now in heaven, is brought down to earth.

Soon there will come a time that will not be called "Today" any longer, for it will be *the day of the Lord.* At that point, it will be too late to enter His rest. Therefore, it is crucial to be sure you enter His rest *before* the day of the Lord arrives. The purpose of this book is to emphasize the importance of paying attention to this exhortation, and others like it, so we will not be caught unaware. Remember what Jesus told us regarding His return: **"What I say to you I say to all, 'Be on the alert!' " (Mark 13:37) .**

The coming of the day of the Lord, the beginning of *this seventh day,* which starts with the gathering of the saints (the rapture), may be much closer than you think. This day is also *the Sabbath rest of the Lord,* which we read about in Hebrews chapter 4. After the rapture, the saints are then taken to heaven for the marriage supper of the Lamb. They will subsequently return with the Lord Jesus to reign with Him on earth. If this interpretation is correct, this momentous event could occur within the next ten years, and the years leading up to the Lord's return are going to be tumultuous. It is crucial to be aware of what lies ahead, so that we can be prepared. Jesus Himself admonished, **"Be on guard, so that your hearts will not be weighted down with dissipation and drunkenness and *the worries of life*, and that day will not come on you suddenly like a trap" (Luke 21:34).**

This *seventh day* that Scripture speaks of, the day of the Lord, is *one-thousand-years* long and immediately follows the completion of the six *one thousand-year days*. The approaching start of this seventh "day," also called Jesus' millennial reign, wherein believers come to life and reign with Jesus for a thousand years, is discussed throughout this book and in much detail in chapter 9, citing Scriptural evidence. This event may arrive soon, perhaps as soon as the early 2030's. One indication of its nearness will be if the "man of lawlessness, the son of perdition" is revealed. Christians the world over would begin to suddenly experience great difficulties; i.e., persecutions and afflictions, for many resulting in death. If that happens, this tribulation period for Christians is projected to last approximately three and a half years, constituting *the latter half* of a seven-year period. At some point during the first forty-two months of this seven-year time, the man of lawlessness, the individual Scripture calls the beast, who is the antichrist, is to be revealed to believers. The remainder of the world will be completely deceived and will not understand what is going on. Scripture informs us that many people **"will be purged, purified and refined, but the wicked will act wickedly; and none of the wicked will understand, but those who have insight will understand" (Daniel 12:10).** This seven-year period could therefore potentially commence within the next twelve to twenty-four months. For example, if the Lord is to return in 2031, then the seven-year period preceding it would begin sometime in 2024, most probably in the fall.

Three Theories About Jesus' Return

Three different theories about the Lord's return related to this seven-year time will be examined in detail considering Scripture in this book. One theory is that the Lord returns at the start of the seven years for His saints, and then comes again a second time at the end of the seven-year period. Those who subscribe to this first theory also hold to the belief that during the seven-year period, many who were initially "left behind" in the first rapture will repent and become believers in Christ. As a result, these will be included in the kingdom of God when, they believe, Jesus comes again a second time at the end of the seven years and raptures those new believers who were left behind the first time.

Another theory holds that He comes somewhere in the middle of this period, and the last teaches that the Lord will return for His followers near the conclusion of the seven-year period. In all three theories, it is acknowledged that there are saints on the earth during at least some portion of the seven years. Likewise, all acknowledge that the final three and a half years will be a time containing great difficulties for those on earth. However, referring to the final three and a half years as a time when "great difficulties" are in store is a significant understatement of the gravity and magnitude of what is to come. If our Lord's return is really as close as ten years away, we will soon discover one way or another which of these theories about the rapture of the saints is correct. My interpretation of the prophecies about Christ's return aligns with the third theory, but we will examine Scriptures which are used to support each one.

Why Should We Study Prophecy?

To gain insight into God's plans for us, it is crucial to study the prophecies in Scripture that unveil these revelations. The question arises, "Why study prophecy, especially pertaining to the end times, the "last days?" Revelation 1:3 tells us, **"Blessed is he who reads and those who hear the words of the prophecy, and heed the things which are written in it; for the time is near" (Revelation 1:3).** Scripture also attests that **"no prophecy was ever made by an act of human will, but men moved by the Holy Spirit spoke from God" (2 Peter 1:20–21).**

Some have the attitude that studying Scripture on prophecy and the return of Christ is pointless as it would not change how they currently live. However, what if a thorough study of God's Word on these subjects leads to a more sober and prayerful walk in your daily life? If you become convinced that His return *is this close,* would you be praying fervently for the salvation of your loved ones, and for yourself if you are unsure of your own salvation? Could it not equip and motivate you to share these truths with those you love so they will not be caught off guard? Ecclesiastes 7:4 reminds us that "the mind of fools is focused on worldly pleasures." While it is not wrong to enjoy the good things that God has provided in our lives, He warns us about loving the things of the world. Studying the last days and the return of Jesus could lead to a deeper devotion to Christ and a greater concern for the eternal destiny of your loved ones. The alternative is too significant to ignore.

Are you comfortable in your Christian life, enjoying the blessings of your family, your home, your friends, and your church? Take a moment to imagine scenes of Ukrainian families, huddled in basements and bomb shelters because of sudden invasion by Russia, with no basic necessities like toilets, heat, and sufficient food and water, and the constant fear of injury or death by a missile blast. Conflicts in Syria, Yemen, and elsewhere are not dissimilar. What does this have to do with the last days and the return of Christ? The connection becomes clear as you delve into God's Word on these topics.

Even if you approach the prophecies about the end times with a very different perspective than mine, I strongly believe that journeying with me through the Scriptures on these topics will be a blessing to you. God preserved these prophecies for a reason, intending for us to be impacted by them just as much as any other part of His Word. Will you be changed by a mindful study of them? I believe you can count on it. Will you be more devoted to prayer? Will your life be more intentionally directed toward Jesus as you look forward to His return? Or will you be like the mockers described in 2 Peter 3: 3-4, dismissing the promise of His return and continuing to live unchanged? "**Know this first of all, that in the last days, mockers will come with their mocking, following after their own lusts, and saying, 'Where is the promise of His coming? For ever since the fathers fell asleep, all continues just as it was from the beginning of creation'" (2 Peter 3:3–4).**

Is it not worth turning our attention to these prophecies to avoid becoming like these mockers we are warned about? We are told that a great "falling away" is one of two signs that must precede His return. This is *the apostasy*. This abandonment of the faith is happening presently, and the indications are that it is accelerating. A Pew Poll reported by UPI on December 14, 2021 indicated the number of Americans who identified as Christian dropped 15% over the previous 14 years. We will examine the apostasy and another requirement for His return. According to

Scripture He cannot come at any moment until these two events have occurred. Those who presently say Jesus can come at any moment are failing to understand what He meant when he said He will come as a thief in the night. Still explaining the answer to His disciples' question about the signs of His return, Jesus continues: **"For then there will be a great tribulation, such as has not occurred since the beginning of the world until now, nor ever will. Unless those days had been cut short, no life would have been saved; but for the sake of the elect those days will be cut short."** (It clearly reads as though the elect are still there, enduring tribulation.) **"Then if anyone says to you, 'Behold, here is the Christ,' or 'There He is,' do not believe him. For false Christs and false prophets will arise and will show great signs and wonders, so as to mislead, if possible, even the elect" (Matthew 24:21-24).** He warned us about false prophets, *and false Christs*. The hallmark of false prophets in the Old Testament was that when the true prophets of God were warning people about grave events ahead, the false prophets were saying, "oh no, you need not worry." By studying prophecy that pertains to our time, we can avoid being deceived by false prophets.

chapter TWO
Tribulation Versus Wrath

Why God Might Allow the Church to Endure Tribulation

Regardless of which theory about the rapture you believe to be true, it is evident from Scripture that there are saints on earth during the great tribulation. For them, the scenario we envisioned previously together of being caught up to meet the Lord in the air will eventually become their reality. Since we know from many Scriptures there are saints on the earth when the antichrist is present, a question we will explore through Scripture is "How do these saints end up in the great tribulation?" A second related question is "Why do these saints end up in the great tribulation?" We see in Scripture images of hail with fire falling from the sky, demonic locusts that torment men for months making them want to die, waters turned bitter, and something like a burning mountain falling from the heaven into the sea. In addition, we have the knowledge that the antichrist wars against and kills many if not almost all of the saints on earth during this period. For these saints who are present, is this punishment? Why would God allow this to happen to His children?

I recently had a conversation at dinner with a renowned Bible teacher and prolific author. We were discussing the different views of the last days before Jesus returns and the timing of the rapture. He asked, "Why would the Lord want His bride, the body of Christ, to endure the great tribulation?" We could similarly ask, "Why does God allow His children to suffer trials, persecutions, and afflictions?" To understand these tough questions, we must make an important distinction between God's wrath and the great tribulation, which for the saints in question brings trials, persecutions, and afflictions.

We see from multiple places in Scripture that *some saints will have to endure the great tribulation,* according to Jesus' words in Mark: **"For those days will be a time of tribulation such as has not occurred since the beginning of the creation which God created until now, and never will" (Mark 13:19).** Consider the following Scripture from Revelation in which Scripture informs us about the antichrist-beast: **"It was also given to him *to make war with the saints and to overcome them,* and authority over every tribe and people and tongue and nation was given to him" (Revelation 13:7, emphasis mine)** A couple of verses later, Jesus states: "**If anyone is destined for captivity, to captivity he goes; if anyone kills with the sword, with the sword he must be killed. *Here is the perseverance and the faith of the saints*" (Revelation 13:10, emphasis mine).** We learn from these verses that the saints are present during the great tribulation, and they have been given over to the antichrist. As noted, some theorize that the rapture has already occurred, taking all the saints to heaven. They further theorize that the saints being referred to here are new believers, who repented and came to faith after the first rapture. For this to be true, these people *would have had to repent of their sins* and trust God for their salvation. Keep this fundamental truth in mind, and we will revisit this point again later.

Who is Kept from the Hour of Testing that Will Come upon the Whole World?

In Revelation, we find messages from Jesus to each of seven different churches. To one of those, the church in Philadelphia, Jesus said (along with other things) the following: **"Because you have kept the word of My perseverance, *I also will keep you from the hour of testing*, that hour which is about to come upon the whole world, to test those who dwell on the earth. I am coming quickly; hold fast what you have, so that no one will take your crown" (Revelation 3:10–11, emphasis mine).** To another one of the seven churches, the one in Smyrna, the Lord said, "**Do not fear what you are about to suffer. Behold, the devil is about to cast some of you into prison, so that you will be tested, and you will have tribulation for ten days. Be faithful until death, and I will give you the crown of life" (Revelation 2:10).** (The ten days just spoken of here by Jesus was in this case, a literal ten days, not ten thousand years. Later in this book I cover how Scripture gives us an indication of when a passage is literal or is using a metaphor or symbol to mean something else.) For neither of these two churches did Jesus have words of reproof; to one He said, "I will keep you from the hour of testing," and to the other He said, "You will be tested, and you will have tribulation for ten days; be faithful until death." Jesus gave none of the other churches any promise of being spared the hour of testing. Instead, they each received stern words of reproof and warnings of what He would do to them if they did not repent. Only *one in seven* was to be kept from the hour of testing; let us keep this in mind also as we examine the next portion of Scripture.

Why does God allow His children to endure persecution, afflictions, and suffering? We were considering the question of why God would allow His church, His bride, to endure tribulation and suffering before He returns. We know that some saints will have to endure this period. To understand part of God's purpose for this, we can look to the Scriptures, specifically 2 Thessalonians 1:4-10. In this passage, the apostle Paul speaks proudly of the Thessalonian believers for their perseverance and faith amid persecutions and afflictions. He explains that their suffering is a plain indication of God's righteous judgment, showing that they are considered worthy of the kingdom of God, for which they are suffering. This passage informs us that enduring suffering and persecution serves a purpose in demonstrating the worthiness of believers for the kingdom of God. It also demonstrates that God is just in dealing out retribution to those who afflict His people: **"therefore, we ourselves speak proudly of you among the churches of God *for your perseverance and faith in the midst of all your persecutions and afflictions which you endure*"** (While this was a message to Christians in the church in Thessalonica, it will become clear that it applies equally to us in our time, and it goes on to address the Lord's return for His people.) **"This is a plain indication of God's righteous judgment *so that you will be considered worthy* of the kingdom of God, for which indeed you are suffering. For after all it is only just for God to repay with affliction those who afflict you, and to give relief to you who are afflicted and to us as well when the Lord Jesus will be revealed from heaven with His mighty angels in flaming fire, dealing out retribution to those who do not know God and to those who do not obey the gospel of our Lord Jesus** Paul is focusing the hearts of these believers on the kingdom of God and Jesus' coming by telling them their suffering is an indication they are worthy of it. It seems clear in verse 10 of this passage that the persecution and suffering that Paul refers to in his writing is connected to the anticipation of the Lord's return. How much more will the suffering of His people be cause for the anticipation of His coming in the great tribulation period right before His return? About those who afflict His people and refuse to believe in the gospel of Jesus, it says they will "**pay the penalty of eternal destruction, away from the presence of the Lord and from the glory of His power, when He comes to be glorified in His saints *on that day,* and to be marveled at among all who have believed—for our testimony to you was believed (2 Thessalonians 1:4–10).** Scripture informs us of this same principle in Philippians, telling us to be "**in no way alarmed by your opponents—which is a sign of destruction for them, but of salvation for you, and that too, from God. For to you it has been granted for Christ's sake, not only to believe in Him, but also to suffer for His sake" (Philippians 1:28–29).** When we suffer for our testimony for Christ, it is a blessing; it is not punishment. To suffer for Him has been granted to us by God, just like He granted that we believe in Him and receive salvation; both are His blessing: **"Blessed are those who have been persecuted for the sake of righteousness, for theirs is the kingdom of heaven" (Matthew 5:10).** We also read in 1 Peter: "**But even if you should suffer for the sake of righteousness, you are blessed. And do not fear their intimidation, and do not be troubled, (1 Peter 3:14)** We will find many Scriptures like this as we examine further what to expect in the last days.

Who is The Great Multitude that no one could count in Revelation 7?

I pray that the eyes of our understanding will be opened regarding what lies ahead. God even reveals that there is a number that must be complete which He has set of His children who must be killed for their faith in Him and His Word, and for the testimony of Jesus. Only once that number is complete will He judge and avenge their blood on those on the earth. Revelation 6:9 we read that the souls under His altar are shown to be crying out to Him, asking, "How long, O Lord, before you judge and avenge our blood on those on the earth?" **9 When He opened the fifth seal, I saw under the altar the souls of those *who had been slain for the word of God and for the testimony which they held.* 10 And they cried with a loud voice, saying, "How long, O Lord, holy and true, *until You judge and avenge our blood on those who dwell on the earth?"* (Revelation 6:9-10).** God responds that **"they should rest a little while longer, until *both the number of their fellow servants and their brethren, who would be killed as they were, was completed*" (Revelation 6:9-11).** These souls had been resting, for they were told to rest a little while longer. Perhaps resting alludes to their being "asleep in the Lord." I believe these souls in heaven, under the altar, had gotten there *by being slain for the Word of God and for the testimony which they held.* There is no indication that any other souls were there, other than those who had been *killed for the Word of God and for the testimony they held.* Also, only their souls were present; they had not yet received their immortal bodies. So, we have no evidence or indication of a rapture having occurred up until this point. God reveals that He intends for others to be killed as they were, until a number has been completed. This, you will see, happens in the great tribulation in such substantial numbers that it produces what Scripture calls "a great multitude which no one could count." When the question was asked, where did they come from, the answer was the following: "These are the ones who come *out of* the great tribulation." These who make up this great multitude were also in heaven. Revelation 7 provides us with more understanding: **"After these things I looked, and behold, a great multitude which no one could count, from every nation and all tribes and peoples and tongues, standing before the throne and before the Lamb, clothed in white robes, and palm branches were in their hands [...] Then one of the elders answered, saying to me, "These who are clothed in the white robes, who are they, and where have they come from?" I said to him, "My lord, you know." And he said to me, "*These are the ones who come out of the great tribulation*, and they have washed their robes and made them white in the blood of the Lamb (Revelation 7:9,13-14).** Note that it says these came out of the great tribulation, not before it. As is the case with the "souls under the altar" in Revelation 6, we still have no evidence or indication that the rapture had occurred. These who make up this great multitude, like the souls under the altar, we may reason, got there by dying for their testimony and for the Word of God. These are the ones God indicated had to be killed for their testimony even as the first ones under the altar had been killed. Why would God do this? According to his Word, he does this first, to prove we are worthy of the kingdom of heaven, and second, to show He is just when He deals out retribution,. So, we have two reasons (among others) why He would allow His bride, the saints, to go through the great tribulation. We are told they are blessed because of this. It is part of God's plan.

The first theory which has the Lord coming twice for His saints, once before the great tribulation and once afterward, is called a pre-tribulation rapture theory. It postulates a great coming to faith of those "left behind" that would be necessary to comprise "a great multitude that no one could count" coming out of the great tribulation. Advocates of this pre-tribulation theory assert that the Lord would not subject His bride, His saints, to the suffering of the great tribulation, and many state that the great tribulation is God's wrath. They point to verses that say, "He has not appointed us to wrath," and that "Jesus rescues us from the wrath to come." Therefore, they say, He must come and rapture the saints before the beginning of the great tribulation. Yet the verses we read explaining these two reasons why saints endure tribulation, suffering, and persecution directly contradict that reasoning. I believe it will become clear as we examine more Scripture that tribulation and afflictions are different from God's wrath. Moreover, one group of saints certainly will be subjected to the great tribulation. If, as they say, the great tribulation is God's wrath, why would He not rescue these saints as well? We have seen that God has a purpose for having His saints endure suffering and tribulation. We also are told plainly, "He has not appointed us unto wrath." (1 Thessalonians 5:9) His wrath has not yet come, either at the point in Revelation 6 where the souls are shown under the altar in heaven, crying out for God's justice, or later when we see the great multitude no one could count that came out of the great tribulation in chapter seven. Shortly, we will see from Scripture exactly the point where it is announced in heaven that His wrath comes.

Is tribulation God's wrath? You will see that Scripture clearly states the tribulation that believers endure is not synonymous with God's wrath. Scripture tells us He rescues us from His wrath. What is tribulation exactly? This passage of Scripture in Matthew 24 gives us more insight about tribulation **"You will be hearing of wars and rumors of wars. See that you are not frightened, for those things must take place, but that is not yet the end. For nation will rise against nation, and kingdom against kingdom, and in various places there will be famines and earthquakes. But all these things are merely the beginning of birth pangs. Then they_will deliver you to tribulation and will kill you, and you will be hated by all nations because of my name. At that time many will fall away and will betray one another and hate one another. Many false prophets will arise and will mislead many. Because lawlessness is increased, most people's love will grow cold. But the one who endures to the end, he will be saved" (Matthew 24:6–13).** Pay special attention to verses 10 and 12. Jesus says, "that many will fall away" and "most people's love will grow cold." Another purpose of this tribulation and suffering, in addition to those already discussed, is to purge and purify the people of God. Again, we read in Daniel: **"Many will be purged, purified and refined," (Daniel 12:10).** If you are not prepared, you are at greater risk and you could be one who falls away.

The Announcement in Heaven that God's Wrath has Come

Where in Revelation is it announced *in heaven*, not by men on the earth, that God's wrath has come? This distinction is important, because men, in their fear and terror, say **"to the mountains and to the rocks, 'Fall on us and hide us from the presence of Him who sits on the throne, and from the wrath of the Lamb; for the great day of their wrath has come, and who is able to stand?'" (Revelation 6:16–17).** This was *the cry of man*, not an announcement from the Lord, or one of His angels. But the time when it is announced *in heaven that the wrath of God has come* is not declared until Revelation 11:18, where the twenty-four elders who are on their thrones before God announce that "**"the nations were enraged, and *Your wrath came*, and the time came for the dead to be judged, and the time to reward Your bond-servants the prophets and the saints and those who fear Your name, the small and the great, and to destroy those who destroy the earth" (Revelation 11: 16-18).** We will examine this moment in more detail, but rest assured, this was after the rapture, the gathering of the saints.

We saw that Jesus highlights the perseverance and faith of the saints in Revelation 13:10. In verse 7 just before this, He has told us that the beast, the antichrist will make war with the saints, and will overcome them. In summary, there are multiple purposes of the trials and suffering that the saints must endure during the tribulation, just as the saints have done over the centuries. Sufferings and trials are meant to demonstrate the perseverance and faith of the saints, to purge and purify the body of Christ of those who are not truly believers, to show we are worthy of the kingdom of God, and to prove that God is just in dealing out retribution to those who do not know God. We confirmed the presence of saints during the great tribulation. We continue to reflect on the fact that if all the saints were taken to heaven in the rapture before the great tribulation, these saints who are present would have to be new believers who repented and received salvation after the rapture. We will continue to examine this latter possibility, because we will find evidence in Revelation stating that the rest of mankind did not repent. Further, nowhere in Revelation do we find a single statement telling us that anyone did repent and receive salvation. I would think that if such a massive work of God occurred that a multitude no one could count repented and came to faith in Jesus after all believers had been removed from the earth, we would be told of it in Scripture. While this message may not be easy to accept, I encourage you to read and examine the Scripture to verify the truth of these statements.

Dear brothers and sisters in Christ, I humbly urge you to consider a perspective that might challenge some of our long-held beliefs about the return of Jesus. As we strive to deepen our faith, it is crucial to approach this topic with an open mind and a willingness to reevaluate our understanding in light of new insights. I remind you, it is possible the Lord *might* return in the first part of the next decade, the 2030's, as you have seen. *If* the Lord is going to return in the early 2030's, then during the forty-two-month period just before He comes to gather His saints, there will come a time such as never has been since the beginning of creation nor ever will be again. Prior to this forty-two-month period there will be an equal amount of time in which a great deception will come upon the unbelieving world. When could this great deception begin? I believe it could begin as early as late summer of 2024. As noted before, if Jesus is going to return in 2031 for example, then seven years prior to 2031, or in 2024, the last week of the seventy weeks of Daniel 9:24-27 would begin. Am I asserting that these things will surely happen in this time frame? No, I am not. However, if it is a possibility that the time frame is as I have suggested, we should be learning from Scripture the signs that signal this prophesied period of time. We are told to learn from the parable of the fig tree as we look to understand when our Lord might return: **"[29]Then He told them a parable: "Behold the fig tree and all the trees; [30]as soon as they put forth leaves, you see it and know for yourselves that summer is now near." (Luke 21:29–30)** While we know that no man knows the day or the hour, Jesus told us we will know when the time is near. *If* the time of the Lord's return is to be in the early 2030's, then seven years prior to His coming things will really accelerate, and the beginning of this seven-year period is almost upon us. If Jesus' return is to be this soon, one of two things will occur. Either the rapture will occur, in 2024 or soon after, and none of this will be your concern if you follow Jesus. Or it will not occur, and if major things are happening that are unmistakable considering Scripture, we might realize that the first part of this seven-year period is upon us and is minimal compared to what is yet to come. If this proves to be true, we must take the exhortations in Scripture seriously to endure to the end. After reading this book, if you find you agree with most of what you have read, I suggest you may want to obtain a paper copy of it, rather than relying on having a digital version for reference in coming years. I have concerns that there may come a time when authorities may decide that certain elements are no longer to be tolerated and it is not inconceivable that extreme censorship of all things Biblical or Christian could be implemented. The elimination of these documents and related materials from our digital devices could easily be implemented from all sources connected to the internet and we could just one day find our resources no longer there.

It is crucial that we understand that Scripture tells us God has a purpose for allowing our suffering and persecution. If we reject the teaching of Scripture regarding this aspect of what is to come, I fear our minds will not be open to what God reveals to us and how to prepare our hearts to persevere and endure.

A Timeline of Major Events of the "Day of the Lord"

If the Lord is to return in the next ten years, here is a broad overview of the major things we will examine, in order, which will be confirmed by Scripture in the following chapters:

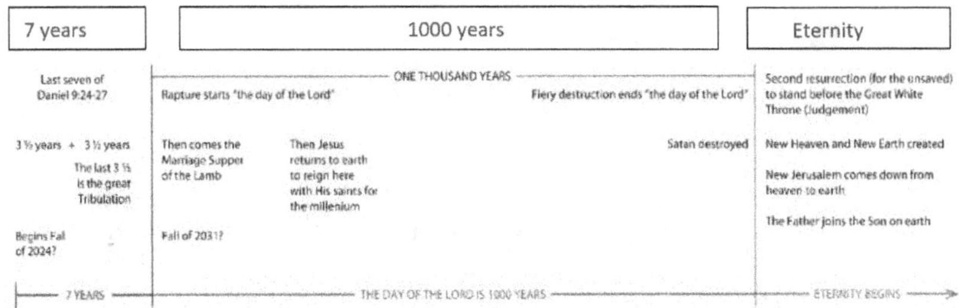
7 years
1000 years
Eternity
Last seven of Daniel 9:24-27
ONE THOUSAND YEARS
Rapture starts "the day of the Lord"
Fiery destruction ends "the day of the Lord"
Second resurrection (for the unsaved) to stand before the Great White Throne (Judgement)
3 ½ years + 3 ½ years
The last 3 ½ is the great Tribulation
Then comes the Marriage Supper of the Lamb
Then Jesus returns to earth to reign here with His saints for the millenium
Satan destroyed
New Heaven and New Earth created
New Jerusalem comes down from heaven to earth
The Father joins the Son on earth
Begins Fall of 2024?
Fall of 2031?
7 YEARS
THE DAY OF THE LORD IS 1000 YEARS
ETERNITY BEGINS

1. Either the Lord will come as is theorized by those who have a pre-tribulation view of the rapture, within the next one to three years, or He will not. At that point, we are at or in the seven-year period prior to His return. (*If* Jesus is coming in the early 2030's.) I earnestly hope He does. I present Scripture further on to show why He may tarry.

2. The lawless one, also known as the son of perdition or the antichrist, will be revealed, and he will deceive the unbelieving world. This is the beast, the final world ruler. This will be during this period of seven years, the last three and a half of which will be when the saints are handed over to him.

3. A great tribulation, such as never has been nor ever will be again, will comprise the final forty-two months.

4. Jesus will send His angels over all the earth to gather His saints, beginning "the day of the Lord." This marks the beginning of what we saw is the "seventh day" (of a thousand years), the "day of the Lord."

5. To begin this day, the dead in Christ will rise first, and then those believers who are alive and remain at this moment will join them.

6. All will be taken up into the air and changed in a twinkling of the eye, clothed in their new immortal bodies.

7. The Lord Jesus and His angels will take the saints to heaven for the "marriage supper of the Lamb," which may last for a short time.

8. It is during this brief period while the saints are in heaven that the wrath of God will be poured out on those who remain on the earth. Not everyone remaining on earth will perish; some will survive.

9. After the marriage supper of the Lamb, Jesus will return to earth accompanied by his saints. He will war against the antichrist and his armies, and cast him and the false prophet into the lake of fire.

10. Satan will be bound and shut up in the abyss during Jesus' millennial reign.

11. Jesus will begin His thousand-year millennial reign on the earth and His saints will reign with Him. He will reign over all nations, peoples, tribes, and families.

12. At the end the of the thousand years, Satan will be released for a short season, to deceive the nations, and gather them for war against Jesus and His saints one final time.

13. God will rain fire down from heaven on the armies who join Satan against Jesus, and Satan will be cast into the lake of fire forever, where the beast and the false prophet are also.

14. Then, in the final event still to occur on "the day of the Lord"

God will burn up the present heavens and earth with fire and intense heat, and He will create a new heaven and a new earth. He then will bring down the heavenly Jerusalem to earth and make His dwelling on earth with His son and all the saints.

15. The second resurrection will occur in which all the rest of the dead who are unsaved will arise to come before the great white throne judgment (GWTJ).

16. Finally, we will begin eternity with the Father and the Son in the city God built here on the new earth.

This timeline will be further elucidated and confirmed by Scripture in the following chapters.

Sword, Famine, and Pestilence; What do these have to do with our world today?

Consider this profound passage from Revelation 6:8: **"I looked, and behold, an ashen horse; and he who sat on it had the name Death; and Hades was following with him. Authority was given to them over a fourth of the earth, to kill with *sword* and with *famine* and with *pestilence* and by the wild beasts of the earth" (Revelation 6:8) (emphasis mine).** Sword, famine, pestilence…

I began authoring this book in 2013, and it has been mostly finished since 2016, but I had not felt prompted by the Lord to publish it. I asked Him to give me clear directions as to when to release this study, and I felt led to reflect on the themes of the *sword, war, and violence* and how we may be beginning to see signs of those in our world today.

First, regarding the *sword*: in August 2021, China's increased military aggression toward Taiwan began to raise concerns. Japan warned China against aggression toward Taiwan, indicating that they would intervene to assist Taiwan if China attacked them. China's response was chilling, telling Japan "that it would be their undoing if they did so." It is possible that military action by China against Taiwan could draw America into the fight to defend Taiwan. Now, two years later in 2023, China and Russia are showing signs of becoming allies. China has just recently succeeded in persuading some countries to purchase oil in their currency, the yuan, rather than in the dollar. This shift shows signs of accelerating with more countries doing the same. Russia recently launched the world's largest submarine, one which contains nuclear missiles and nuclear bombs on underwater drones with the ability to travel 6000 miles (about twice the width of the United States) underwater directed by AI (artificial intelligence). In February 2022 Russia invaded Ukraine. Are we on the precipice of a new global war among the world's superpowers? All of this is in addition to increased tensions in the Middle East involving Iran. We should expect more war if the time is near.

Next, the Lord caused me to reflect on *famine.* July 2021 was marked by a record-breaking heat wave extending from southern California all the way up the west coast into British Columbia, Canada. Lake Meade, the reservoir behind the Hoover Dam, decreased to a fill level of 1040.8 feet (about 317.24 m), its lowest level since the lake was constructed in the 1930s. This water source is a main source of water for Los Angeles. It is also critical to supply irrigation for much of the farming done in the southern California region that supplies fruits and vegetables to the entire country. This heat wave is depleting lakes, rivers, and aquifers well beyond their ability to recharge. This is happening all around the world. California is currently experiencing one of the worst droughts in history, and the Colorado River basin is in a record drought. The world's population continues to grow, and yet our water resources are not increasing. Are we at the limit of our planet's ability to provide food and water for our ever-increasing population? These conditions will intensify if the time is near.

Lastly, He prompted me to think about *pestilence*. Since early 2020 the world has been dealing with a global pestilence called COVID-19. Already, mutations of this virus have occurred and spread in India, the United Kingdom, and now in the United States, as well as Russia and other nations. The ease with which these new mutations such as the Delta and then the Omicron variant have spread is more than double the transmissibility of the initial COVID-19 virus. Some observers predict that we could soon be on the threshold of an outbreak of pestilence that will be many times more lethal than the death rate of COVID-19. These reflections on the sword, famine, and pestilence could have been made at about any time in history. However, if the Lord is coming soon, as He might, then these occurrences will all increase significantly in the years ahead.

If you believe in Jesus and have submitted to Him as Lord and Savior, your eternal future is assured. But *if you do not stand firm until the end, then you were deceiving yourself and were not saved in the first place*. However, we need to know what is going on in the world and the significance according to Scripture of what is happening. We must remember that God is in control and that everything that is happening is according to His plan. We know that Jesus is coming back soon, and we must be prepared. You and I need to be praying for our loved ones who do not know Jesus as their Savior, living our lives in a way that honors Him and brings glory to His name, and sharing the love of Jesus with those around us and helping to meet their physical and spiritual needs. The time is short, and the days are evil, but the light of Jesus shines brighter in the darkness. Let us not be complacent, **"For the waywardness of the naive will kill them, And the complacency of fools will destroy them" (Proverbs 1:32).**

We live now in a time in which wickedness, depravity, immorality, violence, and lawlessness are increasing and *at an accelerating pace*. How long will God tolerate this? Scripture has answers to the questions about what will come and what we should do to respond. Jesus said, **"These things I have spoken to you, so that in Me you may have peace. In the world you have tribulation, but take courage; I have overcome the world" (John 16:33).**

You will see as we examine Scripture that as the saints are taken to be with the Lord, the wrath and retribution of God are simultaneously poured out on the rest of mankind on earth during the very first part *the day of the Lord* that extends for a thousand years. Following the pouring out of the wrath of God, Jesus returns from heaven to earth with His saints after a brief time perhaps as soon as 45 days after the rapture), waging war against the antichrist-beast and his armies. He destroys the beast and the false prophet, casting them into the lake of fire. Jesus then establishes His reign on earth, often referred to as the millennial reign of the Lord. We will examine Scripture about the millennial reign period in detail together in chapter 9.

Let us read about the thousand years of His reign as described in Revelation 20: **"And I saw thrones, and they sat on them, and judgment was committed to them. Then I saw the souls of those**

who had been beheaded for their witness to Jesus and for the word of God, who had not worshiped the beast or his image, and had not received his mark on their foreheads or on their hands. And they lived and reigned with Christ for a thousand years. But the rest of the dead did not live again until the thousand years were finished. ***This is the first resurrection.*** **Blessed and holy is he who has part in the first resurrection. Over such the second death has no power, but they shall be priests of God and of Christ, and shall reign with Him a thousand years" (Revelation 20:4–6,NKJV, emphasis mine.** In verses 7 through 9, we learn that after the thousand years, Satan is released, and he gathers the nations *on the earth* to war against the Lord and His saints.

It is evident from this Scripture that this reign of Christ is taking place on earth. We can also learn from reading the end of the previous chapter, Revelation 19:11-21, that Jesus has returned from heaven with His armies clothed in fine linen, white and clean (which represents the saints), and put an end to earthly kingdoms, establishing His reign over them on earth. Revelation 11:15 further confirms that His reign is over the kingdoms of the world, and it begins at that moment, which marks the start of the day of the Lord: **"Then the seventh angel sounded; and there were loud voices in heaven, saying, 'The kingdoms of the world have become the kingdoms of our Lord and of His Christ; and He will reign forever and ever'" (Revelation 11:15).**

How Does Jesus Return?

Does He come twice? The next verses state quite plainly that He returns after the tribulation of those days to gather his saints: ***"But immediately after the tribulation of those days*** **THE SUN WILL BE DARKENED, AND THE**

MOON WILL NOT GIVE ITS LIGHT, AND THE STARS WILL FALL from the sky, and the powers of the heavens will be shaken. [30]**"And then the sign of the Son of Man will appear in the sky, and then all the tribes of the earth will mourn, and they will see the SON OF MAN COMING ON THE CLOUDS OF THE SKY with power and great glory.** [31]***"And He will send forth His angels with A GREAT TRUMPET and THEY WILL GATHER TOGETHER His elect from the four winds, from one end of the sky to the other."*** **(Matthew 24:29–31)**.

As touched on briefly, one possibility that is advanced by some teachers is that *Jesus comes twice*, once prior to the great tribulation, and again right after it. We have just verified that He does come after it. These teachers would say the gathering referred to by Jesus in the passage above is the second time He comes. We will examine the Word and let it speak to several possibilities.

Woven throughout Scripture, we find prophetic proclamations of Jesus' coming, and of the coming Kingdom of God. The analysis in these chapters seeks to study and clarify how and when we might arrive in the Kingdom, and what this kingdom might look like. To gain a fuller insight into these things, however, we must examine a number of eschatological prophecies or declarations from God about the end times. My hope is that we can shine the light on whatever seems confusing and find God's purpose for us in this pursuit. Let us bear in mind that "All Scripture" (including prophecy) "is profitable" and thus continue our study of what the Lord says about the return of Jesus Christ.

I challenge you to investigate the Scriptures in this chapter and in those that follow.

More Understanding about the Day of the Lord

The phrase "the day of the Lord" in Scripture can be perplexing and often cause confusion. Is it the day the Lord returns for His saints? It is not just a single day. As we delve into this topic, we will discover that "the day of the Lord" has discrete implications for believers and for unbelievers. It encompasses a multitude of events and is not limited to a mere twenty-four hours.

On the one hand, we see that "the day of the Lord" can refer to the return of Jesus to gather His saints, which is also commonly called His second coming. This day commences with the Lord descending from heaven with a shout, accompanied by the trumpet of God, visibly appearing for all to see in the clouds, escorted by His holy angels. It is at this moment that the dead in Christ are raised, and we, as believers, are caught up to meet the Lord in the air. For the saints, this day is a day of great rejoicing.

On the other hand, we also saw in the previous chapter that at the end of the day of the Lord, the earth and the works that are in it will be destroyed by fire. This phrase, "the day of the Lord" is used in Scripture on more than twenty-two separate occasions, and almost all point to something dreadful. Notably, Isaiah, Ezekiel, Amos, and Zephaniah each mention it twice, with five in the book of Joel, and the Apostle Paul references it four times in his epistles. It occurs elsewhere as well. For the unbelieving world, this day begins with God's wrath coming upon them.

The Scriptures suggest that for unbelievers, the day of the Lord does come upon them when they are least expecting it: [9]"**Behold, *the day of the Lord* comes, Cruel, with both wrath and fierce anger, To lay the**

land desolate; And He will destroy its sinners from it. [10]For the stars of heaven and their constellations Will not give their light; The sun will be darkened in its going forth, And the moon will not cause its light to shine. [11]"I will punish the world for its evil, And the wicked for their iniquity; I will halt the arrogance of the proud, And will lay low the haughtiness of the terrible. (Isaiah 13:9–11 NKJV).

These passages show us that "the day of the Lord" connotes quite different things for the saints than it does for the unbelieving world. For those who follow the Lord, it will be a day of joy, but for all others it will be an incredibly sad day indeed.

A Thief in the Night

Will we, as saints, know when the day of the Lord is near? The answer is yes, and we find confirmation in multiple Scriptures. One of those is the following passage, which may surprise you, as many teachers use 1 Thessalonians 5:1-2, that "the day of the Lord so comes as a thief in the night," to suggest we will not know the time and that it will come as a complete surprise.

[1] "But concerning the times and the seasons, brethren, you have no need that I should write to you. [2] For you yourselves know perfectly that *the day of the Lord* so comes as a thief in the night." (1 Thessalonians 5:1-2)

At first glance, that interpretation may seem plausible, but if we read more carefully the next verses shed light on the matter: **"For when they say, "Peace and safety!" then sudden destruction comes upon them, as labor pains upon a pregnant woman. And they shall not escape."** Here, the reference to "they" is referring to unbelievers, who will be caught off guard. Sudden destruction comes on "them," and they will not escape. **"But you, *brethren,* are not in darkness, so that this Day should overtake you as a thief" (1 Thessalonians 5:1-4).** Now it becomes clear that the people who will be taken by surprise on the day of the Lord are not the saints. The reference to "brethren" is talking about God's children. It says this day will not overtake us like a thief; we will be watching for it and earnestly waiting for it.

This passage clearly states that while one group (they) will be caught off guard, another group (you, brethren) *will not be surprised.* The saints will be expecting this event and be ready for it. In fact, when Jesus was asked by His disciples about the signs of His return, He gave them a detailed reply, which we will examine. After telling them what to look for, He said "no man knows the day or the hour." But Jesus went on immediately to say, **"Now learn the parable from the fig tree: when its branch has already become tender and puts forth its leaves, you know that summer is near; so, you too, when you see all these things, recognize that He is near, right at the door" (Matthew 24:32–33).** Some believe Jesus is referring to Israel because of the reference to the fig tree. But in Luke Jesus says almost the same thing, but adds something. **[29]Then He told them a parable: "Behold the fig tree and all the trees; [30]as soon as they put forth leaves, you see it and know for yourselves that summer is now near" (Luke 21:29–30).** I do not believe He was prophetically referencing Israel here, but rather He was indicating that while we would not know exactly the day or the hour, we would recognize the season, and know He was near, right at the door. So, as saints, we will have an awareness of the approaching day, and should be vigilant and prepared for His coming.

What Must Take Place First?

While some passages in Scripture leave the impression that we could expect His return at any moment, such as the use of the phrase "a thief in the night," we must carefully consider other passages that provide additional context. For example, in 2 Thessalonians 2 we learn that certain events must occur before His return: **"Let no one deceive you by any means; for that Day will not come unless (First) *the falling away comes first*, and (Second) *the man of sin is revealed, the son of perdition*, who opposes and exalts himself above all that is called God or that is worshipped, so that he sits as God in the temple of God, showing himself that he is God." (2 Thessalonians 2:2-3)** (The man of sin who must be revealed, is the antichrist, also called "the beast" in Revelation. Words in parentheses are mine.) Some teachers discount this Scripture, claiming that Paul was merely comforting a group of believers in the church he founded at Thessalonica who were afraid they had missed the rapture. In alleging this to be the case they indicate that this Scripture need not be heeded by future generations of believers. While it may be the case that some in the early church in Thessalonica may have had this fear, that does not change the clear message of this Scripture which like all others was inspired by God, and did not come about from man's own thoughts.

It is important to be aware of these specific events mentioned in Scripture that must take place before His return. While there is a sense of His imminent return, we must not overlook the prophetic signs that are described in Scripture as prerequisites for His coming.

Some Details Revealed in Scripture about the Day of the Lord

According to Scripture, the earth will have survivors who live through the period when the wrath of God is poured out on the earth at the beginning of the day of the Lord. (More detail on these survivors is provided in later chapters.) These survivors are not disciples of Jesus, as the saints are rescued before this time and taken to heaven. The saints receive their immortal bodies when they rise from the dead in the first resurrection, and those who are still alive on earth are also gathered to meet Jesus in the air and put on their immortal bodies. All the saints, now immortal, are taken to heaven for the marriage supper of the Lamb. The rest of mankind can and will die, but men will begin to live extraordinarily long lives. If someone does not live to be at least one hundred years old, they will be thought to be accursed, as we shall see in Scripture.

During the millennial reign of Jesus on earth from Jerusalem the saints will reign with him. Many believe that Jesus distributes His saints throughout the earth as His co-rulers. Scripture tells us the period of Jesus' reign will be a thousand years. The destruction of the earth and mankind is believed to mark the end of His reign on the day of the Lord, rather than at the beginning. This understanding is based on the scriptural reference to the destruction happening "in the day of the Lord." Therefore, it is reasoned that the "day of the Lord" must be a thousand years in duration. Otherwise, there would be no nations for Him to rule over.

There will be a new temple of God in Jerusalem, likely the fourth temple (I give reasons for this statement later), and Jesus is the one who will build this temple. This temple will be the center of worship, and a river will flow from its sanctuary, with trees on either side whose leaves will have special healing properties.

During the thousand-year reign of Jesus on earth, there will be unprecedented peace and harmony. As foretold in Scripture, the wolf will graze alongside the lamb, and wars will cease. At the very beginning of the thousand years, Satan will be bound, thrown into the abyss, and prevented from deceiving the nations. It will be a glorious time when the Lord Christ will be reigning on earth, and people are living in safety alongside one another. Even unbelievers will experience greatly extended lifespans.

Moreover, Israel will finally come to possess all the land that God promised Abraham His servant He would give to his descendants. Jesus, also known as the Branch, will build a new temple in Jerusalem. Jesus will Himself once again enter and exit this temple. These prophetic events can be found in Scripture, revealing the immense blessings and fulfillment of God's promises during this extraordinary period of Jesus' reign on earth.

At the end of this glorious thousand-year reign, God has declared that Satan is to be released from his prison. Satan will go out to deceive the nations on the earth, and he will succeed. He will gather the nations to make war against the Lord Jesus and His saints, surrounding Jerusalem. But God will intervene and destroy these rebels with fire from heaven, and Satan will come to his end, being cast for eternity into the Lake of Fire, where the beast and the false prophet were cast at the beginning of the thousand years.

Scripture says every man's work will be tried by fire. The end of the thousand years is the time when that will occur. The second resurrection occurs, and all the rest of the dead, who are the unbelievers, are raised to stand before Jesus at the great white-throne judgment. The saints have already been judged and declared righteous, having been given by faith the righteousness of Christ in exchange for our sin which He took upon Himself on the cross. Judgment will take place and everyone who is not a faithful disciple of Christ Jesus will perish. When God creates the new heaven and a new earth, God the Father brings down the heavenly city Jerusalem to earth, and the Most High will make his dwelling here with His children. The Father and the Lamb will be the light of the city, so there will be no need for a sun or moon to light it.

Now you have an idea of where we will be going as we examine Scripture together.

chapter THREE
Sealed Prophecies

The End Time

Some portions of prophecy found in Scripture have been sealed up by decree from heaven until the end time according to chapter twelve of Daniel: "[9]**He said, "Go your way, Daniel, for these words are *concealed and sealed up until the end time*" (Daniel 12:9).** When will God unseal what has been concealed and sealed up?

These are the words of the angel Michael, who, along with the angel Gabriel, is one of the only two angels specifically referred to by their names in Scripture; Gabriel and Michael are both found in Daniel. Gabriel was also sent to Mary to inform her that she would become the mother of the Son of God. What this Scripture indicates to us in the twenty-first century is that some of the prophetic words of the Holy Scripture given to Daniel in the sixth century before Christ Jesus were "sealed up until the end time." Therefore, it follows that attempts to explain these prophecies by scholars, theologians, and others prior to "the end time" would necessarily be futile because they have been "sealed up" according to the angelic decree. Perhaps not just prophecies given to Daniel, but others as well have been sealed up until the end time. If we are not in the end time now, then efforts to discern the clear meaning of these prophecies will still prove to be futile. So, men of God, godly Bible teachers, theologians from renowned seminaries and universities, and scholars alike have been thwarted in all attempts to unseal these prophetic words until the end time when God will unseal them for His saints. The question is this: are we now in the time of the end? If so, when did it begin and what does God's Word tell us to indicate that we may be in the time of the end?

When Will These Prophecies Be Unsealed?

I believe we are in the time of the end based on this passage: "[24]**and they will fall by the edge of the sword, and will be led captive into all the nations; and *Jerusalem will be trampled under foot by the Gentiles until the times of the Gentiles are fulfilled*" (Luke 21:24, emphasis mine).** The verse above appears only in Luke's account of Jesus' answer to the disciples when they asked about His statement that the temple would be torn down, and not one stone left upon another. We turn to Matthew for confirmation that the context of this Scripture also informs us of the signs that will precede the return of the Lord Jesus at the end of the age, since Matthew and Mark record the same conversation as that of Luke. But we read in Matthew what is obvious from reading the entire account of Jesus' response: **"[3]As He was sitting on the Mount of Olives, the disciples came to Him privately, saying, 'Tell us, when will these things happen, and what will be the sign of Your coming, *and of the end of the age?*'" (Matthew 24:3, emphasis mine).** Thus we have clear confirmation that in addition to speaking about the destruction of the temple and Jerusalem, which occurred about 69 AD, Jesus was also informing them about His return when He comes back to gather His saints.

Eight verses after the passage in Luke about the "times of the Gentiles being fulfilled," we read another of the Lord's statements: **[32]"Truly I say to you, this generation will not pass away until all things take**

place" (Luke 21:32). Now it is apparent that the generation of those who heard Him teach all these things pertaining to His return have long since died, so He must have been referring to a different generation. Ask yourself, "what generation could He have been referring to?" I suggest Jesus is referring to the generation that will be on earth *when Jerusalem is "no longer trampled under foot by the Gentiles,"* marking the end of "the times of the Gentiles" and the beginning of a new time, "*the time of the end*." I believe our generation is the one Jesus referred to in His answer. The following is my thinking regarding why I believe our current generation will not pass away before Christ Jesus returns.

Why Jerusalem Is Important

First, we are informed by the passage in Luke that Jerusalem is key when looking for the end of an age, one referred to as "the times of the Gentiles." Scripture speaks extensively about the city of Jerusalem being the place where God has chosen *for His name to dwell*: **[5]"But you shall seek the LORD at the place which the LORD your God will choose from all your tribes, to establish *His name there for His dwelling,* and there you shall come" (Deuteronomy 12:5, emphasis mine); " [11]then it shall come about that *the place in which the LORD your God will choose for His name to dwell*, there you shall bring all that I command you: your burnt offerings and your sacrifices, your tithes and the contribution of your hand, and all your choice votive offerings which you will vow to the LORD" (Deuteronomy 12:11, emphasis mine); " [9]but if you return to Me and keep My commandments and do them, though those of you who have been scattered were in the most remote part of the heavens, I will gather them from there and will bring them *to the place where I have chosen***

***to cause My name to dwell*" (Nehemiah 1:9, emphasis mine); "7They have burned Your sanctuary to the ground; They have defiled *the dwelling place of Your name*" (Psalm 74:7, emphasis mine) "'12May the *God who has caused His name to dwell there* overthrow any king or people who attempts to change it, so as to destroy this house of God in Jerusalem. I, Darius, have issued this decree, let it be carried out with all diligence!'" (Ezra 6:12, emphasis mine).**

Jerusalem is the only place on earth that the Lord God has chosen to be *the dwelling place of His Name*. It has been called the City of David, as King David reigned from Jerusalem. The significance of this city is evident as God has promised to bless those who pray for the peace of Jerusalem: **"6Pray for the peace of Jerusalem: 'May they prosper who love you'" (Psalm 122:6).**

However, despite its glorious history under the reigns of King David and King Solomon and the construction of the first temple in Jerusalem, eventually God gave the city into the control of a Gentile nation, Babylon, after many warnings to Israel regarding their disobedience, about six centuries before the time of Christ. This marked the beginning of a prolonged period of Gentile domination over the city where God's name dwells, the holy city, lasting for over 2500 years – a staggering two and a half millennia!

The Times of the Gentiles

Only in 1967, after the conclusion of the Six Days War, did Israel regain sovereignty over Jerusalem. This means that by the time Jesus spoke about it, Jerusalem had already been under Gentile control for over six centuries and would continue in that state for another nineteen centuries, until 1967.

Could it be that the "times of the Gentiles" have ended? Are we now in the midst of the "end time"? It seems plausible, considering that God has returned Jerusalem to the control of Israel after more than 2500 years of Gentile domination over His Holy City. This is a momentous event, as it signifies that prophecies that were concealed and sealed up for centuries may now be unveiled.

It is worth noting that prior to 1967, interpretations of these concealed and sealed prophecies, offered by godly, well-intentioned, and scholarly individuals, may be questionable at best, and are unreliable. This is because Daniel 12:4 tells us that the words of Daniel are sealed up and concealed until the end, and this may apply to other end-time prophecies as well.

Therefore, it is crucial for us to seek understanding from the Holy Spirit and approach the study of end-time prophecy with open hearts and fresh eyes, recognizing that we may now have access to previously concealed insights as God's saints. Let us encourage one another to diligently seek truth and examine the Scriptures dealing with various end-time subjects, such as "the day of the Lord," the antichrist, the beast, the false prophet, the return of Jesus for His saints, and the thousand-year reign of Jesus on the earth, among others. We will look at some prophecies of Scripture that have already been fulfilled (at least partially) and some that remain to be fulfilled. Please understand that I approach this from the perspective that what I suggest is what Scripture is saying to me. I quote the Scripture, relate it to other Scripture, and encourage and invite others to use Scripture to show me if I seem to be in error in my thinking. I believe by reasoning with one another from the Scriptures, we become like the Bereans, who were called noble because they daily examined the Scriptures together: **"[11]Now these were more noble-minded than those in Thessalonica, for they received the word with great eagerness, *examining the Scriptures* daily to see whether these things were so" (Acts 17:11, emphasis mine).**

The Thousand-Year Reign of Christ

I interpret Scripture literally, unless Scripture itself indicates that it should be understood as a symbol or metaphor. Let me provide an example from **Revelation 20:6: "Blessed and holy is the one who has a part in the first resurrection; over these the second death has no power, but they will be priests of God and of Christ and will reign with Him for a thousand years."**

There is a school of thought that suggests this passage should not be taken literally. Some proponents of this view argue that Jesus began His reign when He rose from the dead, and that the reference to a thousand years is symbolic, representing a long but indeterminate period of time. They point to other Scriptures, such as **Psalm 50:10**, which says, **"For every beast of the forest is mine, the cattle on a thousand hills."** Their argument is that God's ownership of the cattle extends beyond just a literal thousand hills, as God owns everything in the world. This particular verse is an example of synechdoche, a literary device in which a part of a greater whole is referred to but represents the whole. The use of this device here does not suggest that anytime a thousand is referred to it is non-specific or metaphorical.

While it is true that God's ownership is not limited to a literal thousand hills, some argue that this does not necessarily mean that the reference to a thousand-year reign of Jesus is metaphorical. To understand the meaning of this passage, it is important to carefully examine the Scriptures that address this topic and consider the context surrounding it. As a believer, I was taught and initially accepted this metaphorical interpretation for many years. However, upon closer examination of the Scriptures myself, I began to question this view.

I include Scripture from Revelation 20 here for reference: "[1]**Then I saw an angel coming down from heaven, having the key to the bottomless pit and a great chain in his hand. [2]He laid hold of the dragon, that serpent of old, who is the Devil and Satan, and bound him for a thousand years; [3]and he cast him into the bottomless pit, and shut him up, and set a seal on him, so that he should deceive the nations no more till the thousand years were finished. But after these things he must be released for a little while. [4]And I saw thrones, and they sat on them, and judgment was committed to them. Then I saw the souls of those who had been beheaded for their witness to Jesus and for the word of God, who had not worshiped the beast or his image, and had not received his mark on their foreheads or on their hands. And they lived and reigned with Christ for a thousand years. [5]But the rest of the dead did not live again until the thousand years were finished. This is the first resurrection. [6]Blessed and holy is he who has part in the first resurrection. Over such the second death has no power, but they shall be priests of God and of Christ, and shall reign with Him a thousand years" (Revelation 20:1–6, NKJV).**

In verse 6, we read about the concept of a thousand-year reign of Jesus on earth, commonly known as the millennium. Some interpret this passage metaphorically, suggesting that the thousand years symbolize a lengthy period of time, and that Jesus began His reign after His resurrection from the cross. However, when we carefully examine the context of this passage, we find that it is connected to events that cannot have happened yet.

In Revelation 19, just a few verses before Revelation 20:6, we read about the beast (the antichrist) and the false prophet being thrown into the lake of fire (Revelation 19:20). Then in Revelation 20:1-3, we see an angel coming down from heaven who binds Satan and throws him for a thousand years into the abyss, preventing him from deceiving the nations. Following this, we see thrones and judgment being given to those who had been beheaded for their testimony of Jesus and the word of God, and they come to life and reign with Christ for a thousand years (Revelation 20:4-6).

These events, such as the binding of Satan and the reign of Christ with His saints for a thousand years, are distinct from the events surrounding the cross. There is no mention of a beast (king) demanding that people to take a mark on their hand or forehead, or causing beheadings for not worshiping him, which suggests that the events described in Revelation 20:1-6 are not related to the cross or events that occurred prior to it. While some might argue that kings like Herod demanded to be worshipped in Jesus' day, we have no evidence of such a king being "cast into the lake of fire, along with the false prophet" by Jesus, who is to have His armies, the saints with Him when He does this.

Let us take a look now at the next section of Revelation 20: "[7]**Now when the thousand years have expired, Satan will be released from his prison [8]and will go out to deceive the nations which are in the four corners of the earth, Gog and Magog, to gather them together to battle, whose number is as the sand of the sea. [9]They went up on the breadth of the earth and surrounded the camp of the saints and**

the beloved city. And fire came down from God out of heaven and devoured them. [10]The devil, who deceived them, was cast into the lake of fire and brimstone where the beast and the false prophet are. And they will be tormented day and night forever and ever" (Revelation 20:7–10, NKJV).

This passage speaks of Satan being released from his prison after the thousand years, and deceiving the nations on earth once again before being ultimately thrown into the lake of fire *where the beast and the false prophet are also*. These who he deceives join him and he wages war *against Jesus and His saints on earth.* These events are not reflective of the cross, indicating that the thousand-year reign of Jesus mentioned in Revelation 20:6 is a future event that is yet to come, and *it takes place on earth, not in heaven*.

Clearly, is important to carefully consider the context and sequence of events. The passage in Revelation 20:6, along with the surrounding verses, indicates a literal thousand-year reign of Jesus on earth after the events described in Revelation 19, which are distinct from events related to the cross or prior to it.

In these Scriptures above, all of which deal with what Jesus does upon His return and a specific thousand years, we learn the following:

1) The beast and the false prophet are thrown into the lake of fire, ending the reign of the beast (the antichrist) and his followers on the earth.

2) Satan is bound and thrown into the abyss and sealed for a thousand years, during which time he is prevented from deceiving the nations. The beast and the false prophet had just

been thrown into the lake of fire when this happened.

3) When the thousand-year period is complete, Satan will be released for a brief period and will come out to deceive the nations once again, gathering them together for a war on earth against the saints and the beloved city.

4) Fire comes down from heaven and devours those who joined Satan in his rebellion against Jesus and the saints.

5) The devil is at this point thrown into the lake of fire and brimstone, where the beast and the false prophet were thrown at the beginning of the thousand years. (See Revelation 19:20 above)

6) Souls of those who were beheaded for their testimony of Jesus and their faith during the great tribulation when the beast and the false prophet were on the scene come to life and reign with Jesus for this same thousand-year period.

The beast and the false prophet were not cast into the lake of fire at the cross. People were not beheaded for refusing to take the mark of the beast at the cross, nor did souls who were beheaded for their testimony of Jesus come to life and reign with Him on the earth at the cross. In an attempt like this to interpret prophetic Scripture as a metaphor, which is instead meant to be understood literally, all the interpretations become very subjective and variable, and a matter of personal opinion. Therefore, unless a Scripture indicates clearly that it is symbolic or a metaphor, I look for a literal interpretation.

Let me provide an example of where symbols *are used*, and the meaning follows soon after: at the beginning of Revelation in chapter 1, John turned and saw *the seven lampstands*. Now read what Jesus says to him:

"[12]Then I turned to see the voice that was speaking with me. And having turned I saw *seven golden lampstands*; (Revelation 1:12) [...][16]In His right hand He held seven stars, and out of His mouth came a sharp two-edged sword; and His face was like the sun shining in its strength" (Revelation 1:12,16). Just a few verses later, Scripture reveals the meaning of these strange images: **"[20]As for the mystery of the seven stars which you saw in My right hand, and the seven golden lampstands: the seven stars are the angels of the seven churches, and *the seven lampstands* are *the seven churches*" (Revelation 1:20, emphasis mine).** The significance of this is that Scripture almost always tells us what figurative language means, either in close proximity to where we find it or by looking for the same usage of an image elsewhere in the Word where it does tell us the meaning. Sometimes Scripture does have metaphorical, symbolic meaning and even dual meanings. For example, Jesus said John the Baptist was Elijah, but that Elijah was still to come. Note the following Scriptures, both spoken by Jesus: **"[14]And if you are willing to accept it, John himself is Elijah who was to come" (Matthew 11:14).** But later, Jesus tells the disciples that Elijah is still yet to come: **"[11]And He answered and said, "Elijah is coming and will restore all things" (Matthew 17:11).** As we have seen, there are times when Scripture speaks metaphorically. But we need to read carefully to see when this is the case and not assume everything in Scripture that is difficult to understand is metaphor or symbolism.

Returning to the subject of the thousand-year reign of Jesus here on the earth, a literal interpretation of this portion of Scripture may cause a seismic change in much of Christian thinking. By this, I mean that most of Christendom looks forward to being with Jesus *in heaven*, and in fact assumes that Jesus' time on earth was limited to his human lifetime before the cross, but it appears that Jesus will be with us *here on earth.* Jesus does take us initially to heaven for the marriage supper of the Lamb, but then He brings us with Him back to earth after a brief time.

When we read Revelation 19:7, it informs us that we are blessed to be invited to the marriage supper of the Lamb, and we are given "fine linen robes, bright and clean" (Revelation 19:8). A few verses later, we see that Jesus is going to wage war, and His armies in heaven, "*clothed in fine linen, white and clean*" (Revelation 19:14), are with Him. This informs us that these armies are the saints, whom He is bringing with Him back to earth. Jesus then destroys the beast and the false prophet, casting them into the lake of fire. Satan is bound and thrown into the abyss for the millennial period and is released at the end to deceive the nations on the earth. Satan gathered mortals from "the four corners of the earth" to wage war and surround the camp of the saints and the beloved city. To grasp the full picture, we will read from Revelation 19:7 to Revelation 20:10. We see in these passages that the saints will return from the marriage supper of the Lamb in heaven to earth with Jesus as His armies. He then defeats the antichrist and casts him and the false prophet into the lake of fire. Next, Jesus sets up His reign over all the earth from Jerusalem and the saints reign with Him.

Moreover, after a thousand years, when Satan is released from his prison for a short season to deceive the nations on the earth and gather them to war against the Lord and His saints, he is then for all eternity cast into the lake of fire where the beast and the false prophet have already been thrown. Consider these events carefully and *what happens next* as we return to those same verses once more in Revelation 20: "[7]**Now when the thousand years have expired, Satan will be released from**

his prison [8]and will go out to deceive the nations which are in the four corners of the earth, Gog and Magog, to gather them together to battle, whose number is as the sand of the sea. [9]They went up on the breadth of the earth and surrounded the camp of the saints and the beloved city." It seems clear that the saints are on the earth reigning with Jesus here. **"And fire came down from God out of heaven and devoured them. [10]The devil, who deceived them, was cast into the lake of fire and brimstone where the beast and the false prophet are. And they will be tormented day and night forever and ever" (Revelation 20:7–10, NKJV).** This last verse shows us the final end of Satan.

What Scripture Reveals About the Millennial Reign

Now let me pose a question: When Satan is released to deceive the nations for a brief time, *who exactly is it who is being deceived*? Would it be some of the saints whom God brought back to life from the dead? Scripture informs us concerning the saints "that the second death could not harm them." However, these who are deceived *are destroyed* by fire from heaven. If not saints, then who? I submit that those who are deceived *are the unsaved* who survived the tribulation and the wrath of God. Therefore, during the millennial reign, there are two groups, the saints, who are clothed with immortality at the rapture, and those remaining mortals whom God allowed to survive His wrath. I will go into more detail in chapter 9 regarding this period of time.

It appears that the lifespans of those who are mortal are greatly extended during this time after the tribulation. Moreover, I believe that during this thousand-year period, people are still being born and still dying. Consider this Scripture: "[20]**No longer will there be in it an infant who**

lives but a few days, Or an old man who does not live out his days; For the youth will die at the age of one hundred *and the one who does not reach the age of one hundred will be thought accursed"* […]"'[25] *The wolf and the lamb will graze together*, and the lion will eat straw like the ox; and dust will be the serpent's food. They will do no evil or harm in all My holy mountain,' says the LORD." (Isaiah 65:20,25, emphasis mine).

This passage in Isaiah describes a time when once again, much like the time on earth before the flood, people will live extraordinarily long lives. These are the unbelieving mortals who lived through the wrath of God, for the saints are immortal. Consider that *during the first millennia* (from the creation of Adam to the time of Noah) men lived to be almost a thousand years old. It appears that there is to be yet another time in which men will live exceptionally long lives, during this thousand-year reign of Jesus on the earth. Yet, at the end of the final thousand years in which Christ Jesus reigns on the earth, many will still be deceived and follow Satan. Their fate is to be destroyed by fire from heaven. (While Jesus is reigning here on earth, God the Father is still in heaven on His throne, in the kingdom of heaven.) I do not believe that any of those who belong to the Lord will be deceived to follow Satan and be destroyed by fire. We noted that it says of the saints in Revelation 20 verse 6 that the second death has no power over them

There is a helpful section toward the end of the book of Ezekiel that contains such specific physical descriptions of what exists during the thousand-year reign of the Lord that it would be hard to read these things as metaphorical. It describes a river that flows from the new temple in Jerusalem which starts as a trickle and ends up as a torrent.

The culmination of the passage about the river reads as follows: "[12]**By the river on its bank, on one side and on the other, will grow all kinds of trees for food. Their leaves will not wither and their fruit will not fail. They will bear every month because their water flows from the sanctuary, and their fruit will be for food and their leaves for healing" (Ezekiel 47:12).**

Also, this section of Ezekiel contains detailed descriptions of the division of the land of Israel to the various tribes of Israel, and to the Lord, and to the prince. You will see later that King David is the prince. It declares that the prince may give a portion of his land to his descendants: "[7]**The prince shall have land on either side of the holy allotment and the property of the city, adjacent to the holy allotment and the property of the city, on the west side toward the west and on the east side toward the east, and in length comparable to one of the portions, from the west border to the east border" (Ezekiel 45:7).** Further on we read: **"[16] Thus says the Lord God, 'If the prince gives a gift out of his inheritance to any of his sons, it shall belong to his sons; it is their possession by inheritance. [17]But if he gives a gift from his inheritance to one of his servants, it shall be his until the year of liberty; then it shall return to the prince. His inheritance shall be only his sons'; it shall belong to them" (Ezekiel 46:16–17). And a couple of chapters later: "[21]The remainder shall be for the prince, on the one side and on the other of the holy allotment and of the property of the city; in front of the 25,000 cubits of the allotment toward the east border and westward in front of the 25,000 toward the west border, alongside the portions, it shall be for the prince. And the holy allotment and the sanctuary of the house shall be in the middle of it" (Ezekiel 48:21).**

These passages are but a few of many that provide explicit details concerning land, duties, inheritance, the new temple, and so forth. These have yet to be fulfilled, and the details are so specific that they rule out any interpretation as just a symbol or as a metaphor. They clearly point to a time that could only be the period during which the Lord Jesus is reigning here on the earth.

Remember, however, that even with the Lord Jesus Himself present on earth for a thousand years and reigning in wisdom, glory, and power, Satan, during his brief release at the end of the millennium, will still deceive many. Satan will bring about their eternal destruction along with his own at the end of this period.

After Satan's destruction, God destroys the current heavens and earth with intense heat and creates a new heaven and a new earth: **"1Now I saw a new heaven and a new earth, for the first heaven and the first earth had passed away. Also there was no more sea. 2Then I, John, saw the holy city, New Jerusalem, coming down out of heaven from God, prepared as a bride adorned for her husband. 3And I heard a loud voice from heaven saying, 'Behold, the tabernacle of God is with men, and He will dwell with them, and they shall be His people. God Himself will be with them and be their God'" [...]Revelation 21:1–3) (NKJV) "23The city had no need of the sun or of the moon to shine in it, for the glory of God illuminated it. The Lamb is its light" (Revelation 21:1-3, 23, NKJV).** I have taken these excerpts from Revelation, but there is much more detail contained in the final two chapters of the last book of the Bible on this subject. I encourage you to read and meditate on what is contained there. I believe all of this is to be understood just as it is written not as a symbol of something else.

The "First Resurrection"

Let us consider some implications contained in the Scriptures dealing with this thousand-year reign of Jesus. First, the Lord Christ Jesus is reigning *on earth.* Saints who were beheaded *are raised from the dead,* given new bodies, and we are told they reign with Him for a thousand years. Are they the only saints who are raised at this time, with the rest of the saints waiting until the end of the thousand years to be raised from the dead and given new bodies? It tells us that this is the "first resurrection": **"...And I saw the souls of those who had been beheaded because of their testimony of Jesus and because of the word of God, and those who had not worshiped the beast or his image, and had not received the mark on their forehead and on their hand; and they came to life and reigned with Christ for a thousand years. [5]The rest of the dead did not come to life until the thousand years were completed. *This is the first resurrection*" (Revelation 20:4–5, emphasis mine).** The rest of the dead are all the unsaved who arise to stand before the great white throne judgment.

Two possibilities occur to me. One possibility is that all the saints, from the beginning of time through the end of the great tribulation, are raised from the dead at this, the "first resurrection." This would include Enoch, Job, Noah, Abraham, Isaac, Jacob, Joseph, Moses, Elijah, David, Isaiah, Daniel, Peter, Paul, John, Mary (Jesus' mother), and so on. This seems the most likely scenario. The second possibility is that only saints who were killed for their testimony of Jesus during the time when the beast and the false prophet forced people to take the mark of the beast or be killed would be raised. This second possibility seems unlikely. Most of the twelve disciples were martyred for their faith in Jesus (all but

John). Would they not be raised in this first resurrection? But they were not beheaded. John the Baptist was beheaded, but not for refusing to take the mark of the beast during the great tribulation. Would he not be included? Are they not to rule with Jesus during this thousand-year period? We just read in 1 Thessalonians 4:17 "and so we shall always be with the Lord." Therefore, it is most likely that *all the saints* are reigning with Christ on earth.

What becomes clear since this is stated to be the "first resurrection" is that *there has not been a prior resurrection of the dead* (aside from Jesus); otherwise, this could not be called *the first.* And because Scripture also plainly states that those saints who are alive and remain *will not precede* those who have died in Christ at His return, there cannot have been a secret "rapture" of saints prior to the time when the great tribulation occurs. These who were martyred in the great tribulation had not died yet, so they could not be a part of a resurrection of the dead before the great tribulation. Scripture tells us *the dead in Christ rise first*: "[15]**For this we say to you by the word of the Lord, that *we who are alive and remain until the coming of the Lord, will not precede those who have fallen asleep.*** [16]**For the Lord Himself will descend from heaven with a shout, with the voice of the archangel and with the trumpet of God, and *the dead in Christ will rise first.*** [17]**Then we who are alive and remain will be caught up together with them in the clouds to meet the Lord in the air, and *so we shall always be with the Lord*" (1 Thessalonians 4:15–17, emphasis mine).** To assert that there has been a prior resurrection would be to state that Scripture just does not mean what it says here.

The "Second Resurrection"

Since the Scripture in Revelation 20:5 says "the rest of the dead do not come to life until the thousand years are completed," we must ask "who are 'the rest of the dead'?" Personally, I do not believe the Lord is likely to keep the faithful believers from the beginning of time from reigning with Jesus during this period, so I believe Scripture is informing us that the unsaved dead will arise to judgement at the end of the thousand years. This interpretation is confirmed as we continue to read the following Scriptures in Revelation 20:11-15: "[11]**Then I saw a great white throne and Him who sat on it, from whose face the earth and the heaven fled away. And there was found no place for them. [12]And I saw the dead, small and great, standing before God, and books were opened. And another book was opened, which is the Book of Life. And the dead were judged according to their works, by the things which were written in the books. [13]The sea gave up the dead who were in it, and Death and Hades delivered up the dead who were in them. And they were judged, each one according to his works. [14]Then Death and Hades were cast into the lake of fire. This is the second death. [15]And anyone not found written in the Book of Life was cast into the lake of fire." (Revelation 20:11–15, NKJV).** The saints had previously been rewarded, having already been given the righteousness of Christ by faith. This will be discussed in further detail later in this book.

Why did God not just plainly tell us in Revelation 20:4 that all his saints are included, and not single out those saints from the great tribulation who were there during the time of the beast and the false prophet? The Lord is making it plain to us that no resurrection occurs until those saints who were to die for a testimony to Him in the great tribulation have suffered and died. Again, Scripture states that when these saints who were beheaded during the great tribulation come to life, they do so in "the first resurrection." (Revelation 20:4-5)

As we continue in God's Word, we will examine thoroughly the subject of the antichrist (the beast) and clear, unmistakable signs that must occur before the Lord Jesus will return. Much of what we will look at requires us to study the prophecies in Daniel, which the archangel Michael told us were concealed and sealed up until the end time. Hopefully, I am correct that we are now in the end time, and the Lord, by his Holy Spirit dwelling in each of us His saints, will open our minds and give us understanding regarding these things that have been sealed up.

chapter FOUR
Keep On The Alert

When Does Jesus Return?

Scripture warns us to always keep on the alert, otherwise we may, among other things, have our hearts weighed down with cares of this life:

"34 But take heed to yourselves, lest your hearts be weighed down with carousing, drunkenness, and cares of this life, and *that Day* come on you unexpectedly. 35 For it will come as a snare on all those who dwell on the face of the whole earth. 36 "But keep on the alert at all times, praying that you may have strength to escape all these things that are about to take place, and to stand before the Son of Man" (Luke 21:34-36). The inference contained in this warning is that if we do remain alert for the coming of the Lord, we will not be caught off guard. Jesus warns us in this passage to watch over our hearts, and pay attention to the signs. We are put on notice that what is coming is going to be so difficult that He says we should be "praying that we may have strength *to escape all these things* that are about to take place." Some versions translate this part as "praying that you may be *worthy* to escape all these things." He is addressing our readiness for "that Day." This is the coming "day of the Lord."

Will There Come a Time When It Is Too Late?

Suppose that a rapture occurs before the great tribulation. This would mean Scriptures that say we must endure and persevere are primarily addressing a group of people who had not believed by the time the rapture occurred. These people were therefore “left behind” by the Lord when He gathered His saints to be with Him. Teachers of this theory call this new group who repent and are saved “tribulation saints.” We must look closely at Scripture to see if there is any evidence (or even a hint) of these “left behind” people repenting and coming to faith to become these theoretical tribulation saints who must endure the tribulation.

Consider this parable which Jesus told about ten virgins: “[1]**Then the kingdom of heaven will be comparable to ten virgins, who took their lamps and went out to meet the bridegroom”** They were to be invited to a wedding feast. The feast the parable points to is the “marriage supper of the Lamb.” In the parable, five virgins were wise, and they had oil in their lamps, and were prepared for the bridegroom to come and tell them, “Now is the moment, come to the feast.” The others were foolish, and neglected their lamps; they were unprepared when He came. Both groups grew drowsy and fell asleep. The foolish ones were not allowed in and were “left behind.” The wise ones went with him to the feast. Did those five virgins who were “left behind” still get to go to the wedding feast? Scripture says “Those who were ready went in with him to the wedding feast, and the door was shut” (Matthew 25:10). The foolish ones thought they could still go buy oil for their lamps, doing the preparation they should have done sooner, and then be allowed to join the bridegroom at the feast. When they came later saying, “Lord, lord, open up for us,” did they get in to the feast? Read the account of what Jesus said: “[10]**And while they were going away to make the purchase, the bridegroom came, and those who were ready went in with him to the wedding feast; *and the door was shut.* [11]Later the other virgins also came, saying, ‘Lord, lord, open up for us.’ [12]But he answered,**

'Truly I say to you, I do not know you''' (Matthew 25:1, 10-12). For those who were *left behind,* there was no second chance. The final words from the Lord after this parable were these: "[13]**Be on the alert then, for you do not know the day nor the hour" (Matthew 25:13).**

Perhaps you do not think this parable relates to Jesus' return for His saints. But when you look at the context where this is found, Jesus has been teaching about the signs of His return right before this, giving His disciples details about what to expect, and warning them to pay attention and not be caught "like a thief in the night" will catch unbelievers. One group had oil, the other did not. The clear message is that once the Lord comes, there is no second chance. This teaching alone should answer the question about the theory of a pre-tribulation rapture.

Remember, Jesus taught in parables to the crowds, later disclosing in private to His disciples what the parables meant. He explained that He did this because the crowds were not meant to know the meanings, only His disciples. If you are truly a disciple of Christ, you are set apart from the crowds, from whom things are hidden: "[10] **And the disciples came and said to Him, 'Why do You speak to them in parables?' [11] He answered and said to them, 'Because it has been given to you to know the mysteries of the kingdom of heaven, but to them it has not been given''' (Matthew 10:10-11).** This teaching should further call into question the theory that a secret rapture will occur, the idea that after gathering all the saints to enter the wedding feast, all these others will get a second chance. This notion was never taught in the church until the nineteenth century. It became popular based on the teaching of John Darby, about 1830. It was later picked up by Cyrus Scofield and included in the commentator notes in a Bible he edited and annotated in 1909. I will present clear Scriptural evidence to rebut the possibility of a secret rapture, called by some a "pre-tribulation rapture," so please don't dismiss what follows, but persevere and keep studying until you are fully informed by the Word. For people who are "left behind" at the rapture to get a "second chance," *they must repent.* The foolish virgins in the parable were sorry they got "left behind." But that did not enable them to enter the wedding feast. Likewise, we read of Esau who sold his birthright. Later, he regretted it; he was sorry. Here is what Scripture said about him: "[17]**For you know that even afterwards, when he desired to inherit the blessing, he was rejected, for he found no place for repentance, though he sought for it with tears" (Hebrews 12:17).** To be saved, one must truly repent. I expect that once the gathering of the saints occurs, there will be people who will say to themselves, "Uh oh, it must be true what all those Christians believed about the Lord coming back one day." Scripture also tells us in James 2:19, **"[19]You believe that God is one. You do well; the demons also believe, and shudder" (James 2:19).**

We will examine Revelation and see where *three times* it states that *mankind does not repent* during the period of the great tribulation or during the subsequent wrath. It is not possible to be saved without repentance. We read from Matthew that when Jesus began His ministry, He preached the necessity of repentance: "[17]**From that time Jesus began to preach and say, "Repent, for the kingdom of heaven is at hand" (Matthew 4:17).** In Luke we read where Jesus again informed of the necessity to repent. He brought up an example of a calamity that occurred to a group of people, and posed a question to His listeners: "[2]**And Jesus said to them, 'Do you suppose that these Galileans were greater sinners than all other Galileans because they suffered**

this fate? [3]I tell you, no, *but unless you repent*, you will all likewise perish. [4]Or do you suppose that those eighteen on whom the tower in Siloam fell and killed them were worse culprits than all the men who live in Jerusalem? [5]I tell you, no, *but unless you repent*, you will all likewise perish'" (Luke 13:2–5, emphasis mine). Jesus did not let just one example suffice; He went on to drive His point home by giving His listeners another and repeated His message, "you must repent, or you will also perish." However, just as was the case with Esau, there will come a time when it will be too late to repent, even though we cry out and seek for it with tears.

So we see that there are verses in Scripture that indicate that there comes a time *when it is too late to seek the Lord*, just as is the case with this parable regarding the ten virgins. Consider the message these next verses convey, From Revelation 22:11 we read: **"Let the one who does wrong, still do wrong; and the one who is filthy, still be filthy; and let the one who is righteous, still practice righteousness; and the one who is holy, still keep himself holy" (Revelation 22:11).**

To understand this remonstration, I believe it is crucial to consider these verses in context, so let us read the preceding verses: "**[6]Then he said to me, 'These words are faithful and true.' And the Lord God of the holy prophets sent His angel to show His servants the things which must shortly take place. [7]'Behold, I am coming quickly! Blessed is he who keeps the words of the prophecy of this book.' [8]Now I, John, saw and heard these things. And when I heard and saw, I fell down to worship before the feet of the angel who showed me these things. [9]Then he said to me, 'See that you do not do that. For I am your fellow servant, and of your brethren the prophets, and of those who**

keep the words of this book. Worship God.' [10]And he said to me, 'Do not seal the words of the prophecy of this book, for the time is at hand. [11]*He who is unjust, let him be unjust still; he who is filthy, let him be filthy still*; he who is righteous, let him be righteous still; he who is holy, let him be holy still." (Revelation 22:6-11, NKJV). Do we see any words that say "repent and be saved"? On the contrary, it appears that the time was reached when no one new is going to be saved. We have been told in Scripture by Jesus, "[44]**No one can come to Me unless the Father who sent Me draws him; and I will raise him up on the last day" (John 6:44).** There is a time when it becomes too late "to enter His rest." If we hear His voice, we must act while it is still called "today."

Let us add to what we've learned another Scripture, this time from Daniel 12: "[10]**Many will be purged, purified and refined, but the wicked will act wickedly; and none of the wicked will understand, but those who have insight will understand" (Daniel 12:10).** As we did with the passage from Revelation, let us now view this verse from Daniel in its full context: "[4]**'But as for you, Daniel, conceal these words and seal up the book until the end of time; many will go back and forth, and knowledge will increase.' [5]Then I, Daniel, looked and behold, two others were standing, one on this bank of the river and the other on that bank of the river. [6]And one said to the man dressed in linen, who was above the waters of the river, 'How long will it be until the end of these wonders?' [7]I heard the man dressed in linen, who was above the waters of the river, as he raised his right hand and his left toward heaven, and swore by Him who lives forever that it would be for a time, times, and half a time; and as soon as they finish shattering the power of the holy people, all these events will be**

completed. [8]As for me, I heard but could not understand; so I said, 'My lord, what will be the outcome of these events?' [9]He said, 'Go your way, Daniel, for these words are concealed and sealed up until the end time. [10]Many will be purged, purified and refined, but the wicked will act wickedly; and none of the wicked will understand, but those who have insight will understand'" (Daniel 12:4–10). We see in verse 7 in this passage that the power of the holy people will be shattered. This passage seems to indicate that those who are wicked continue to act wickedly; it does not even hint that some repent and are saved. Those who were claiming to be God's people are purged, purified, and refined. When we look at a parallel passage from the previous chapter of Daniel that uses almost identical language we gain further understanding: "[32]**By smooth words he will turn to godlessness those who act wickedly toward the covenant, but the people who know their God will display strength and take action. [33]Those who have insight among the people will give understanding to the many; yet they will fall by sword and by flame, by captivity and by plunder for many days. [34]Now when they fall they will be granted a little help, and many will join with them in hypocrisy. [35]Some of those who have insight will fall, in order to refine, purge and make them pure until the end time; because it is still to come at the appointed time. [36]Then the king will do as he pleases, and he will exalt and magnify himself above every god and will speak monstrous things against the God of gods; and he will prosper until the indignation is finished, for that which is decreed will be done" (Daniel 11:32–36).** Similar to the previous passage, this passage also gives the sense that God's people, those who have insight, are being attacked; they fall by sword and by flame, by captivity and by plunder for many days. Do some join them, claiming to be members of the kingdom of God? Verse 34 says, "when they fall, they will be granted a little help, and many will join them in hypocrisy." But the sense is that there are no true new believers, people who truly repent and are saved. It is clear these verses are found in passages of Scripture dealing with the last days. These verses are describing the time of the great tribulation.

There are other Scriptures which inform us that after being called, there comes a time when it is too late to repent. From Proverbs 1 we read: "[24]**Because I called and you refused, I stretched out my hand and no one paid attention; [25]And you neglected all my counsel And did not want my reproof; [26]I will also laugh at your calamity; I will mock when your dread comes, [27]When your dread comes like a storm And your calamity comes like a whirlwind, When distress and anguish come upon you. [28]"Then *they will call on me, but I will not answer*; *They will seek me diligently but they will not find me*, [29]Because they hated knowledge And did not choose the fear of the Lord. [30]"They would not accept my counsel, They spurned all my reproof. [31]So they shall eat of the fruit of their own way And be satiated with their own devices. [32]For the waywardness of the naive will kill them, And the complacency of fools will destroy them" (Proverbs 1:24–32, emphasis mine).** Verse 28 from this passage in Proverbs succinctly states the truth the five unwise virgins discovered too late. There will come a time when it is too late, even if one reconsiders and has a change of heart. It says, "They will call on me, but I will not answer; they will seek me diligently, but they will not find me." For those who were "left behind" in the teaching of the parable of the ten virgins, it truly was too late; the door was shut, not to be opened again.

In Hebrews we are given an understanding that *for a time*, a promise remains of entering His rest. This passage conveys a clear understanding that this time will not last forever: "[1]**Therefore, let us fear if, *while a promise remains of entering His rest*, any one of you may seem to have come short of it. [3]*For we who have believed enter that rest*, just as He has said, 'As I swore in My wrath, They shall not enter My rest,' although His works were finished from the foundation of the world.** Finally, in Hebrews 4:7, we have the truth about those who are left behind after the rapture: "[7] **He again fixes a certain day, "Today," saying through David after so long a time just as has been said before, "Today if you hear His voice, Do not harden your hearts" (Hebrews 4:1,3,7; emphasis mine).**

It is noteworthy that verse 9 of Hebrews 4 contains a reference to a "Sabbath rest" for the people of God, indicating it "remains." We are warned in verse 1 "let us fear if, while a promise remains of entering His rest, any one of you may seem to have come short of it." Turning to the New King James Version, from Leviticus 23 we read the following from the chapter in which the Lord spoke through Moses and declared the annual feasts the Israelites were commanded to keep annually: **"[24]Speak to the children of Israel, saying: 'In the seventh month, on the first day of the month, you shall have a *sabbath-rest*, a memorial of *blowing of trumpets*, a holy convocation'" (Leviticus 23:24, NKJV, emphasis mine).** This Scripture refers to the establishment of the *Feast of Trumpets*, in the seventh month of the Jewish calendar, on the first day of the month. Later on, we will examine how the Lord is fulfilling each of these feasts, which were a foreshadowing of events yet to come. For example, He fulfilled the Feast of Passover with the sacrifice of the Lamb of God, Jesus, when He was crucified on Passover. We will see that there is a connection to the “sabbath rest” of the Lord, promised to believers, and the Feast of Trumpets called a “sabbath rest,” and the day of the Lord.

All of these foregoing passages, the ones from Revelation 22, Daniel 11 and 12, Proverbs 1, and Hebrews 4 contain a message similar to the parable of the ten virgins. The message is that while there is still time, believe and repent; do not harden your heart, for there will come a day when time has run out. My concern is two-fold. First, that many of my fellow saints are being misled and taught that they will be raptured before the tribulation, and consequently they will not seriously pray and prepare their hearts to persevere and endure to the end. Second, many are being misled and taught that after the rapture, there will still be time to repent and be saved. Once the first gathering of the saints occurs, Jesus takes us to heaven for the marriage supper, His wedding feast. Then, as in the teaching of the ten virgins, the door is shut, and no one else is allowed to enter. Let’s look at selected passages in Revelation that speak directly to this second issue.

In Revelation chapter 6, Jesus begins to open the seven seals. Look at what happens when the fourth seal is opened, **“[8]I looked, and behold, an ashen horse; and he who sat on it had the name Death; and Hades was following with him. Authority was given to them over a fourth of the earth, to kill with sword and with famine and with pestilence and by the wild beasts of the earth (Revelation 6:8).”** Almost eight billion people live on earth presently, so this passage informs us that one fourth, or two billion people will perish from the sword (wars), famine, pestilence, and by the wild beasts of the earth. But in chapter 9 of Revelation, we discover God is not finished, and three more plagues are released on the earth that result in massive deaths. Six billion people remain after one fourth of mankind perished from these previous causes.

The passage here in chapter 9 begins by telling us that an additional third of mankind was killed by plagues: "[18]**A third of mankind was killed by these three plagues, by the fire and the smoke and the brimstone which proceeded out of their mouths" (Revelation 9:18).** Thus, of the six billion souls still remaining on earth, two billion more will die of these prophesied plagues, leaving only four billion still alive out of eight billion currently on the earth at present in 2023. How do those still alive respond? **"[20] But *the rest of mankind*, who were not killed by these plagues, *did not repent* of the works of their hands, that they should not worship demons, and idols of gold, silver, brass, stone, and wood, which can neither see nor hear nor walk. [21] And *they did not repent* of their murders or their sorceries or their sexual immorality or their thefts" (Revelation 9: 20-21).** After this, Scripture continues to confirm that men did not repent. **"And men were scorched with great heat, and they blasphemed the name of God who has power over these plagues; *and they did not repent* and give Him glory."** [...]**"They blasphemed the God of heaven because of their pains and their sores, *and did not repent of their deeds*" (Revelation 16:9,11, emphasis mine).** These statements in Scripture are clear that men, *the rest of mankind*, refused to repent.

Does a Time Come When No One Else Is Saved?

During the opening of the seals, but before any of the trumpets are sounded, it appears that what God allows are more of the same things He has allowed throughout the ages: He allows war, the removal of peace from the earth, famine resulting in great shortages and exceedingly high prices for just enough food to keep one alive. Also, suddenly, death is brought upon mankind in massive proportions. These conditions have all existed before, but during this period while the seals are being opened, the intensity of each one is greatly increased: "[18]**A *third of mankind was killed* by these three plagues, by the fire and the smoke and the brimstone which proceeded out of their mouths" (Revelation 9:18).**

Aside from God's people, how does the rest of mankind respond to these things? Do many repent and become children of God at the time of the end? Unfortunately, no, as we just read they continue in lawlessness. These declarations tell us that despite the plagues that He brings on the earth that kill billions of people, the rest of mankind refuses to repent. When the seventh angel sounds, the Lord comes to gather his saints and take them to be with Him in heaven. At this time God has begun to pour out His wrath on those who dwell on the earth. Does mankind repent now in the midst of the wrath of God? Do they cry out to Him for mercy? Job gave us the answer thousands of years ago: "[13]**But the godless in heart lay up anger; They do not cry for help when He binds them" (Job 36:13).** Once again, man does not repent or cry to Him for help. They do rather the reverse, as we see in Revelation chapter 16: "**Men were scorched with fierce heat; and *they blasphemed the name of God* who has the power over these plagues, and *they did not repent* so as to give Him glory. [10] Then the fifth angel poured out his bowl on the throne of the beast, and his kingdom became darkened; and they gnawed their tongues because of pain, [11] and they blasphemed the God of heaven because of their pains and their sores; *and they did not repent* of their deeds" (Revelation 16:9, 11).** Remember that by now the saints have been gathered off the earth, for the seventh trumpet has sounded. At this point people who dwell on the earth are experiencing the wrath of God. We are told they blaspheme God and do not repent. During both the great tribulation and afterward when the wrath of God comes, we find no one who repents and is saved. Instead, we are told specifically that mankind does not repent. To state the obvious, if no one repents and is saved, then where did those saints who were there in the great tribulation come from? The saints could not have been raptured beforehand because we find no one repenting and becoming new saints. These verses from Revelation 16:9 and 11 describe the period when the bowls of God's wrath are being poured out on mankind after the seventh trumpet, the last trumpet when Jesus comes with His angels and gathers His saints. Therefore, no one who has the Holy Spirit in them is now on the earth during this period. After all the saints have been taken from the earth, it should not be a surprise that no one who is left repents and is saved. If the theory was sound that there are people who were left behind, "people who repented and were saved after the rapture, becoming tribulation saints," then surely somewhere in Scripture it would tell us of these who were saved, giving glory to God. Instead, it tells us repeatedly that the rest of mankind does not repent.

When men everywhere in the stubbornness of their own hearts refuse to repent, Scripture declares the consequences: **"So I gave them over to the stubbornness of their heart, To walk in their own devices" (Psalm 81:12).** And in the New Testament we read that **"In the generations gone by He permitted all the nations to go their own ways" (Acts 14:16)**, but we are also told that there will be a judgment day: **"[12]For the LORD of hosts will have a day of reckoning Against everyone who is proud and lofty And against everyone who is lifted up, That he may be abased" (Isaiah 2:12).** We are now discussing the point at which the day of reckoning has arrived for those still dwelling on the earth after the seventh trumpet blast.

God's desire is only good for all mankind, but He has set a day that marks the end of his patience. What is to be done? While there is still time, we must repent: **"'For I have no pleasure in the death of anyone who dies,' declares the Lord God. 'Therefore, *repent* and live'" (Ezekiel 18:32). [30] "Therefore having overlooked the times of ignorance,"** We are also told that **"God is now declaring to men that *all people everywhere should repent*, [31] because He *has fixed a day* in which He will judge the world in righteousness through a Man whom He has appointed, having furnished proof to all men by raising Him from the dead" (Acts 17:30-31).**

Up until the point of the seventh trumpet, the saints have been given over to the antichrist-beast, who will overcome them. He will kill, plunder, and take into captivity the saints because God in His wisdom and sovereignty has decreed it, and it will be for God's glory. The Scripture says, "the one who endures to the end will be saved," which is the perseverance and the faith of the saints. Why am I so determined to convince my readers that their endurance will be necessary? I am convinced that if you do not reconcile yourself to this beforehand, you are in danger of not enduring, of abandoning your faith. You may face death and think, "But I was taught that the saints were not appointed unto wrath. Why am I not being raptured?" You must steel your heart to have faith and persevere. Dying for the testimony of our faith in Christ Jesus is not God's wrath on us. It is an honor and a blessing if that is what God has determined for us. We then enjoy the victory forever in Christ Jesus and will accompany Him when he returns to rule on the earth. We are warned our time here on earth will not be easy: **"You will be hated by all because of My name, but it is the one who has endured to the end who will be saved" (Matthew 10:22). We are thus exhorted to hold fast to our faith in Christ, who "was faithful as a Son over His house—whose house we are, *if we hold fast our confidence and the boast of our hope firm until the end.* [...] [14] For we have become partakers of Christ, *if we hold fast the beginning of our assurance firm until the end*" (Hebrews 3:6,14).** It is crucial that we prepare our hearts in advance to persevere and hold fast to our faith to the end.

Some teach that a rapture will occur before the tribulation which will remove all the saints from the earth before the events described in Revelation up to chapter 9. They also teach that "a multitude so great that no one could count came out of the great tribulation" (Revelation 7:9) is comprised of people who repent and are saved. If this is what you believe because you have been taught it, I urge you to search for some mention of *this great repentance* of people in Revelation. You will not find one. But we do have statements that the rest of mankind *refused to repent.* That begs the question, "well, since it is clear there are saints present during the great tribulation, but there is no evidence anyone repented and was saved, then how did these saints get there?" We know there is a great apostasy, a falling away of those who abandon their faith. We are repeatedly told by Jesus, "It is he who endures to the end that will be saved." The entire theory of a pre-tribulation rapture rests on the premise that these many saints who are in the great tribulation are ones who repent and are saved, after the bridegroom has come, and has taken His invited guests to His wedding feast and shut the door behind them.

In order to accept the above premises that a rapture will occur before the great tribulation, and subsequently that millions upon millions will repent and be saved to then also be raptured in a second coming of Jesus, one must ignore much straightforward teaching from Scripture. Instead, one must assert that some Scriptures do not mean what they say, forcing the Scripture to bend to a particular ideology, rather than forming an ideology based on the teaching of Scripture. One must ignore Scripture that informs us that Jesus cannot come until the man of lawlessness, the son of perdition is revealed. One must ignore Scriptures that tell us that "the rest of mankind refused to repent." You will discover as you continue to read further, there are other straightforward declarations from Scripture that you must also ignore to accept the teaching that a rapture occurs before the great tribulation.

In the beginning of this chapter, we read the passage of Scripture from 2 Thessalonians 2 which informed us that two specific things are declared in Scripture to be required to happen before the Lord's return. One of those is a great falling away of the faith, called "the apostasy." The other is the revealing of "the man of sin, the son of perdition," who makes himself out to be god. He will rule the world and require all to worship him, and people are going to be forced to take his mark. Many refer to him as the antichrist, and we have noted that Scripture in Revelation and in Daniel call him "the beast." The passage in 2 Thessalonians 2 informs us that he is presently being restrained: **"6 And now you know what is restraining, that he may be revealed in his own time. 7 For the mystery of lawlessness is already at work; only *he who now restrains will do so until he is taken out of the way*" (2 Thessalonians 2:6-7, emphasis mine).** At the time appointed by God, that which is restraining the antichrist will be removed, and he will be revealed. The saints who are alert and are watching will recognize him. We will study this individual who is to rule the world and demand worship from all in chapter seven of this book.

Some believe it is the Holy Spirit that is restraining the antichrist from presently appearing, and that is not an unreasonable assumption. There may be another reasonable possibility regarding the identity of the restrainer as well. However, if the restrainer is the Holy Spirit, and He is "taken away" by a rapture before the great tribulation, and all who are indwelt with His presence are removed from the earth, that could present a problem for proponents of a pre-tribulation rapture. Without the influence of the Holy Spirit, there would be no one left on earth who would be able to become a new saint. It is the work of the Holy Spirit in us that changes us, as we are informed in Titus: "[5]**He saved us, not on the basis of deeds which we have done in righteousness, but according to His mercy, by the washing of regeneration *and renewing by the Holy Spirit*, (Titus 3:5, emphasis mine).** Further, we read in 1 Corinthians 2 that without the Holy Spirit, man in his natural state (the natural man) cannot understand the things of God: "[12]**Now we have received, not the spirit of the world, but *the Spirit who is from God*, so that we may know the things freely given to us by God, [13]which things we also speak, not in words taught by human wisdom, but in those taught by the Spirit, combining spiritual thoughts with spiritual words. [14]But *a natural man does not accept the things of the Spirit of God, for they are foolishness to him; and he cannot understand them*, because they are spiritually appraised (1 Corinthians 2:12–14, emphasis mine).** In chapter 7 of this book I suggest an alternative that God is using an angel to restrain the antichrist, and cover this in more detail.

Is Tribulation Different From Wrath?

Some teachers proclaim the events associated with the opening of the seals and the sounding of the trumpets in Revelation to be "seal judgements" and "trumpet judgements." With such proclamations, it is easy to make the leap to also label these events as "God's wrath." However, we should examine the Scripture to determine if these things are declared by the Word to be "God's wrath."

You may have been taught that the Lord comes to rapture the saints before the great tribulation to save them from God's wrath. Subsequent references in both Revelation and Daniel to saints during this period of the great tribulation who must endure exceedingly difficult trials are explained by these teachers who theorize that these saints found in the great tribulation are people who were "left behind" (at the pre-tribulation rapture) and then became believers during the tribulation. As stated before, some books call these people who were left behind and became believers "tribulation saints." We have already seen how the five unwise virgins who were left behind when the bridegroom came for his invited guests fared after the first group of wise virgins were taken in with him to the wedding feast. The door was shut, and they were denied entrance when they called out "Lord, lord, open up for us" (Matthew 25:10-11).

We have also seen that Jesus clearly taught that unless we repent, we will perish. We just read in multiple Scriptures indications that *no one repents* during this tribulation period, or afterward, when Scripture announces the wrath of God does come on those who dwell on the earth. Scripture informs us of this three separate times. Make no mistake, God promised to rescue us who are His children from the wrath to come, and He absolutely will do that. He said we are not appointed unto wrath.

But trials and tribulation are not the same as wrath. There is no mention in Revelation after the warnings to the churches in chapters 2 and 3 of anyone repenting and being saved during the great tribulation or afterward when the wrath comes. However, we are faced with multiple references to saints and "of those who keep the testimony of Jesus" still being on earth during the great tribulation. Because *we are informed that no one repents*, and furthermore *we have no mention of anyone repenting*, there is no explanation for how these saints come to be there if we hold on to the idea that the Lord returns before the great tribulation and raptures all the saints from the earth. Of even greater concern, with regard to your loved ones, and even yourself if you are unsure of your salvation, Scripture tells us three times in Revelation that mankind does not repent after a certain time.

Consider the following verses: "[13]**But he who endures to the end shall be saved. [14]This gospel of the kingdom shall be preached in the whole world as a testimony to all the nations, and *then the end will come*" (Matthew 24:13-14, emphasis mine).** 2 Timothy provides further insight into this same idea: "**If we endure, we shall also reign with Him" (2 Timothy 2:12).** It certainly appears that Scripture warns us that we must endure something extremely hard.

The Completion of the Wrath of God

In contrast to having to endure suffering and tribulation for the testimony of Jesus and the Word of God, now we examine what the actual wrath of God will entail. The seven bowls of wrath that are to be poured out on those dwelling on earth start to be poured out right after the believers are taken off the earth at the 7th trumpet. Revelation 11:15 announces that the seventh angel sounded (meaning the seventh trumpet). This passage records that loud voices in heaven announced the beginning of the wrath of God. The Word then tells us: [18]**"And the nations were enraged, and *Your wrath came*, and the time came for the dead to be judged, and the time to reward Your bond-servants the prophets and the saints and those who fear Your name, the small and the great, and to destroy those who destroy the earth." (Revelation 11:18)** The Scripture gives the details of the outpouring of God's wrath beginning in Revelation 16, but it began at the sounding of the last trumpet. So this reveals that at the last trumpet, Jesus returns to rapture His saints and take them to heaven and simultaneously God begins to pour out His wrath on the unbelievers on earth.

When Jesus returns from heaven with His armies, the saints, He wages war against the beast and the false prophet and their armies. His defeat of these forces and the destruction of the beast and the false prophet are the culmination of the wrath of God for this period. [15]**From His mouth comes a sharp sword, so that with it He may strike down the nations, and He will rule them with a rod of iron; and *He treads the wine press of the fierce wrath of God*, the Almighty. (Revelation 19:15)** We read in the last portion of this verse, "He treads the wine press of the fierce wrath of God, the Almighty." Here is where Jesus finishes the wrath of God which began to be poured out on mankind when the seventh angel sounded. Until the final great white throne judgement at the end of the millennium I find no other mention in Scripture of the wrath of God.

After the thousand-year reign of Christ on earth, Satan is released for a short time and gathers the nations for one final rebellion against the Lord. The rest of the dead, we learned in Revelation 20:5, do not come to life again until the end of the thousand-year reign of Jesus, when they are raised to stand before His great white throne judgement. We read: Revelation 20: [11]**Then I saw a great white throne and Him who sat on it, from whose face the earth and the heaven fled away. And there was found no place for them.** [12]**And I saw the dead, small and great, standing before God, and books were opened. And another book was opened, which is the Book of Life. And the dead were judged according to their works, by the things which were written in the books.** [13]**The sea gave up the dead who were in it, and Death and Hades delivered up the dead who were in them. And they were judged, each one according to his works.** [14]**Then Death and Hades were cast into the lake of fire. This is the second death.** [15]**And anyone not found written in the Book of Life was cast into the lake of fire. (Revelation 20:11–15) (NKJV)** Thus, for those whose name was not found written in the book of life, they experience God's wrath for eternity in the lake of fire.

Does Your Current View Produce Fruit or Complacency?

For many, but perhaps not all, the fruit of teaching a pre-tribulation rapture tends to produce two things that Scripture warns against. First, this view breeds complacency; rather than preparing yourself to give up your life rather than denying Christ, you are led to think you will not be faced with that possibility, and that all that awaits you is the glorious return of Christ whisking you out of your current difficulties or sufferings. Second, this view tends to make people ignore the warnings from Jesus to be on the alert and watch for His return. It teaches that the Lord can come any moment, rather than as Scripture says, only after certain events happen first.

Suppose we think we are going to be spared the trials of the great tribulation and discover we must face these exceedingly difficult trials after all? We could be mentally, emotionally, but most important, spiritually unprepared for what we must face. We do not want to risk that, based on warnings from the Word. How hard will it be? Scripture says: "[25] **And there will be signs in the sun, in the moon, and in the stars; and on the earth distress of nations, with perplexity, the sea and the waves roaring;** [26] ***men's hearts failing them from fear*** **and the expectation of those things which are coming on the earth, for the powers of the heavens will be shaken.** [27] ***Then they will see the Son of Man coming*** **in a cloud with power and great glory.** [28] **Now** ***when these things begin to happen, look up and lift up your heads, because your redemption draws near*****" (Luke 21:25-28, emphasis mine).** Clearly, the believers are still on the earth, as the things described in the verses above unfold. Scripture is telling believers who see these things unfolding that their redemption draws near. Jesus says in the above verses "Then…," meaning after these things that make men's hearts fail from fear, and "when these things begin to happen, look up because your redemption draws near." Jesus tells us to pray we may be strong enough to escape, but warns us not to deny Him, and that we must endure to the end.

If we deny Him, He also will deny us: **"But whoever denies Me before men, him I will also deny before My Father who is in heaven" (Matthew 10:33).** To think that Christians (particularly American Christians) in this day will not have to suffer, not have to endure great trials, is completely contrary to 2000 years of the experience of the church, from the time of Jesus until now. Even today, there are Christians dying by beheading, torture, being burned alive, etc. in Syria and Iraq by ISIS. The same is true today for Christians in China, India, Sudan,

Nigeria, and many other places as well.

Some argue that "if we are once saved, then we are always saved." I do not fault this argument. However, it will not be known who is truly saved until the Lord comes to rapture His saints. He has told us there are many who will say on that day, "Lord, Lord, didn't I do…" but He will say to them, "depart from me you who practice lawlessness, I never knew you" (Matthew 7:22-23). Consider this passage from Revelation:
9Then another angel, a third one, followed them, saying with a loud voice, "If anyone worships the beast and his image, and receives a mark on his forehead or on his hand, 10he also will drink of the wine of the wrath of God, which is mixed in full strength in the cup of His anger; and he will be tormented with fire and brimstone in the presence of the holy angels and in the presence of the Lamb. 11"And the smoke of their torment goes up forever and ever; they have no rest day and night, those who worship the beast and his image, and whoever receives the mark of his name." 12Here is the perseverance of the saints who keep the commandments of God and their faith in Jesus. Just as many saints have had to give up their lives for their testimony of Jesus and the Word of God, many of us may also have to do likewise. If this is what the Lord has appointed for us, look at what the last verse in this passage tells us: **13And I heard a voice from heaven, saying, "Write, 'Blessed are the dead who die in the Lord from now on!' " "Yes," says the Spirit, "so that they may rest from their labors, for their deeds follow with them" (Revelation 14:9–13).** Clearly, we can see from the above passage, that those who take the mark of the beast were not ever truly saints, for the smoke of their torment from fire and brimstone goes up forever and ever (verses 10-11).

One Rapture or Two?

Scripture indicates that Jesus comes after the tribulation we have been discussing: "[24] **But in those days, *after that tribulation*, the sun will be darkened, and the moon will not give its light; [25] the stars of heaven will fall, and the powers in the heavens will be shaken. [26] Then they will see the Son of Man coming in the clouds with great power and glory. [27] And *then He will send His angels, and gather together His elect from the four winds, from the farthest part of earth to the farthest part of heaven*" (Mark 13:24-27, emphasis mine).** Matthew 24 tells us the same thing: "For *then there will be great tribulation,* such as has not been since the beginning of the world until this time, no, nor ever shall be. [22] **And unless those days were shortened, no flesh would be saved; *but for the elect's sake those days will be shortened.* [27] For as the lightning comes from the east and flashes to the west, so also will the coming of the Son of Man be. [29] "*Immediately after the tribulation of those days* the sun will be darkened, and the moon will not give its light; the stars will fall from heaven, and the powers of the heavens will be shaken. [30] Then the sign of the Son of Man will appear in heaven, and then all the tribes of the earth will mourn, and *they will see the Son of Man coming on the clouds* of heaven with power and great glory. [31] *And He will send His angels with a great sound of a trumpet, and they will gather together His elect from the four winds, from one end of heaven to the other"* (Matthew 24: 21-22, 27,29-31, emphasis mine).** *Immediately after the tribulation of those days,* He will send His angels with the sound of a great trumpet, and they will gather the elect.

My purpose is to urge you to examine the Scriptures more closely to clearly see the answers regarding suffering through the tribulation so you will not be unprepared. We have examined Scripture regarding repenting and being saved after the rapture for the eternal sake of your loved ones, and yourself as well if you are not certain of your salvation. I have gathered many of the relevant Scriptures in one place, laying them out for you to consider. I urge you not to be complacent and turn away, "**For the turning away of the simple will slay them, and the complacency of fools will destroy them" (Proverbs 1:32).** For Christians who have lived in the last two hundred years, the time in which this error in teaching has been spread, this error has not cost them their faith because they died without having to endure the great tribulation. But many things indicate the time of the great tribulation and Jesus' return is near. These are things that have never been the case before in the last two thousand years. Chief among them is Israel being regathered in her land, the land God gave to Abraham. More significantly, as of 1967, the Jews now have control over Jerusalem for the first time in over two and a half millennia, over 2,500 years. I remind you that in Luke 21:24 in the last half of the verse, Jesus said something that is often overlooked: **"And Jerusalem will be trampled under foot by Gentiles until the times of the Gentiles are fulfilled."** It is likely that the return of Jerusalem to Jewish control after a period of over 2,500 years marks the end of the period called "the times of the Gentiles." If so, what would Scripture call the next period? Again, I suggest the next period, our period, would be called "The End Time," or "the time of the end." As I stated, I believe this period began in 1967 when the Jews regained control over Jerusalem. (This does not mean they are not still being assaulted on every side by enemies.) I remind you that Jesus also said shortly afterward in this section of Scripture: **"Assuredly, I say to**

you, ***this generation will by no means pass away till all things take place*****" (Luke 21:32, emphasis mine).** Also, I have already indicated, I believe He meant *the generation alive when Jerusalem is no longer "trampled under foot" (controlled) by the Gentiles.* Taken together with the fact that we will be at the beginning of the seventh "day" of a thousand years when we get to 2030-2035, the imminence of Jesus' return seems more likely than ever before.

As said in chapter 1, if Jesus is to return in the early 2030's, we may be extremely near the time of the great tribulation, since that must precede Jesus' return for His elect. The final seven years could start as soon as late summer of 2024. As previously noted, because we are almost at the completion of six thousand years according to the Bible (six one-thousand-year "days"), it is not unreasonable that we may be remarkably close to His return. As we get closer, there are still things that must happen that we as Christians must learn to recognize. If we do not see the revealing of the antichrist-beast, then we know the Lord is waiting longer, for that must happen first, among other things. When He does come, those who have died in Christ and those still alive who remain faithful and endure to the end will be caught up to meet Him in the air at His second coming, and thus spared the wrath of God. After Jesus's return for the saints, then the wrath of God is poured out on the earth, on those still there. Chapter 9 in this book will provide much more detail about the wrath of God.

The One Who Would Save His Life Will Lose It

We need to purpose beforehand to be steadfast in our faith so we may endure to the end. Consider again these words of the Lord Jesus: **"[20]The one on whom seed was sown on the rocky places, this is the man who**

hears the word and immediately receives it with joy; yet he has no root in himself, but endures only for a while. *For when tribulation or persecution arises because of the word, immediately he stumbles"* (Matthew 13:20-21, emphasis mine). When Jesus was asked by His disciples, "what will be the signs of the end of the age and of your return?" He gave them a number of signs to watch for: "[6]**You will be hearing of wars and rumors of wars. *See that you are not frightened,* for those things must take place, but that is not yet the end. [7]For nation will rise against nation, and kingdom against kingdom, and in various places there will be famines and earthquakes" (Matthew 24:6-7, emphasis mine).** Jesus tells us, "See that you are not frightened." His next words are "Then" they will deliver you to tribulation. This is at the hands of men; *it is not the wrath of God.* Mark informs us during this time that family members betray one another, resulting in the death of the one betrayed: "[12]**Brother will betray brother to death, and a father his child; and children will rise up against parents and have them put to death" (Mark 13:12).** Jesus told us what our attitude must be: "[33]**Whoever seeks to keep his life will lose it, and whoever loses his life will preserve it" (Luke 17:33).** This is why I stress to you we must prepare our minds to give up our lives rather than deny Him.

We have seen that when we suffer for His name's sake, our reward in heaven is great. We saw that our suffering trials and persecution are proof that we are worthy of the kingdom of God, and they show that God is just when He deals out wrath and retribution to those who afflict His people: **"[9]*Then they will deliver you to tribulation, and will kill you,* and you will be hated by all nations because of My name. [10]At that time many will fall away and will betray one another and hate one another" [...]"Immediately *after the tribulation,*" He sends His**

angels to gather His elect from all over the earth." (Matthew 24:9-10, 29-31, emphasis mine).

We have already briefly examined the question: Do the Scriptures teach the idea of a pre-tribulation "rapture" of the saints? In chapter 5 entitled "Differing Views of the Lord's Return," I will let the Scriptures show conclusively when the Lord does return.

A word of caution: don't assume you have all the time in the world to consider these things. I certainly don't know when Jesus will return. There have been numerous people over the past centuries who predicted His return at a specific date only to be proven wrong. I have asserted that if He is coming in the time period of 2030-2035 then a three-and-a-half-year period right before He returns will be unlike any other from the time of creation and will never be again. I think it is very realistic to look for Jesus to return in this time frame, and if He does, what lies ahead for believers will require preparing your heart and mind to persevere and endure to the end, so you will not lose your reward. The Word of God tells us that some will say, "Things continue as they were from the beginning of creation," meaning "Let's not get carried away, it has been two thousand years and He hasn't come, it isn't likely He will anytime soon. Don't get worked up." We read in 2 Peter that we must be mindful " **of the words which were spoken before by the holy prophets, and of the commandment of us, the apostles of the Lord and Savior, 3 knowing this first: that scoffers will come in the last days, walking according to their own lusts, 4 and saying, "Where is the promise of His coming? For since the fathers fell asleep, all things continue as they were from the beginning of creation" (2 Peter 3:2-4).** Don't be a scoffer. The purpose of what follows next is to hopefully convince you that it is in your own best interest to begin to study Bible prophecies, especially those dealing with the end of time so that you may become one of those “who have insight.”

chapter FIVE
Differing Views of the Lord's Return
Three Primary Schools of Thought

Does the Bible support the return of our Lord Jesus Christ before, during, or after the great tribulation? Scripture describes **"a great tribulation, such as has not occurred since the beginning of the world until now, nor ever will. [22]Unless those days had been cut short, no life would have been saved; but for the sake of the elect those days will be cut short" (Matthew 24:21–22).**

There are three primary schools of thought on when the Lord comes to gather His saints to himself:

1) The pre-tribulation view theorizes that Jesus comes back to gather the saints secretly before the great tribulation begins and that He also comes again a second time after the great tribulation to gather new "tribulation saints" from the earth. Those who hold this view base their argument for believing this primarily on the following observations from Scripture:

   First, they note correctly that Scripture informs us that God has not destined us for wrath. They reason therefore that He must take us from the earth before the occurrence of the terrible things promised in Revelation when the seals are opened, the trumpets are sounded, and the bowls of wrath are poured out. These events include, but are not limited to the following: one-fourth of mankind, two billion people, will be killed by plagues, war, famine, and wild beasts (Revelation 6:8); mankind will be tortured by demonic locusts (Revelation 9:3-5); And a third of the earth is burned up, all of the green grass on earth is burned up, and a third of the trees are burned up (Revelation 8:7). Among other verses, proponents of this view cite **1 Thessalonians 5:9,** which tells us: **"God has not destined us for wrath, but for obtaining salvation through our Lord Jesus Christ,"** and **Revelation 3:10**, a statement from Jesus to the church in Philadelphia: **"Because you have kept the word of My perseverance, I will keep you from the hour of testing which is about to come on the whole world."**

Second, because the word "church" does not appear in Revelation after the third chapter, they believe this must indicate that the Lord has taken the church from the earth before the events beginning in Revelation chapter four begin.

Third, because the 24 elders are observed being in heaven beginning in Revelation 4:4 and afterward, they assert that this must mean all the saints are present in heaven as well.

Fourth, because in **Revelation 4:1** John the Apostle is told, **"Come up here and I will show you what must take place after these things,"** they believe this must be applicable to all believers and all are taken up to heaven at this point.

Fifth, they reason that God loves His children, the bride of His son Jesus, and therefore they ask in general terms, "Why would God want His children, the bride of Christ His son, to suffer through the great tribulation?"

Sixth, they point to 2 Thessalonians 2:1-2 and observe that the believers in Thessalonica were expecting Jesus to come any moment. They call this the doctrine of "imminence," meaning that Jesus could be expected to come unexpectedly at any moment:**"[1] Now we request you, brethren, with regard to the coming of our Lord Jesus Christ and our gathering together to Him, [2] that you not be quickly shaken from your composure or be disturbed either by a spirit or a message or a letter as if from us, to the effect that the day of the Lord has come" (2 Thessalonians 2:1–2).** Additionally, they cite **1 Thessalonians 5:2: "[2] For you yourselves know full well that the day of the Lord will come just like a thief in the night."** They assert this also indicates that Jesus can come unexpectedly at any moment.

Seventh, they point to the verses about the "Restrainer" in 2 Thessalonians: The Apostle Paul speaks of a restrainer holding back the revelation of the "man of lawlessness" (Antichrist) until the appointed time (2 Thessalonians 2:6-7). They suggest the "restrainer" refers to the Holy Spirit working through the Church and that the removal of the Church, through the rapture, will allow the Antichrist to be revealed.

Taken together, all these points make for a persuasive case in favor of a pretribulation gathering of the saints. As noted previously, we are told in **1 Thessalonians 5:21 "to examine everything carefully and hold fast to that which is good."** We will shortly do this not only with this view of the Lord's return and His gathering of His saints, but also of the other views as well. This is not an exhaustive list of the points that teachers of this view use to support it, but it does represent a good sampling of the primary arguments.

2) The mid-tribulation view, sometimes called a "pre-wrath" view holds that Jesus comes sometime in the middle of the events described as the end times in Revelation. Those who subscribe to this view most often take the position that He comes at the opening of the sixth seal. This view seems to be a minor variation of the pre-tribulation view. Primary arguments cited by proponents of a mid-tribulation gathering of the saints are as follows:

First, similar to those who hold the pre-tribulation view, proponents of this view likewise argue that the saints will escape God's wrath and cite Scriptures such as 1 Thessalonians 5:9 above (God has not destined us for wrath) and 1 Thessalonians 1:10 which tells us: "Jesus rescues us from the wrath to come." They point to Revelation 6:16-17 in which men cry out **"to the mountains and to the rocks, 'Fall on us and hide us from the presence of Him who sits on the throne, and from the wrath of the Lamb; 17 for the great day of their wrath has come, and who is able to stand?'" (Revelation 6:16–17).** They reason that this must be the point where Jesus comes to gather the saints to save them from the wrath of God. Advocates of the mid-tribulation view contend that the Church will be spared from the full outpouring of God's wrath, which they believe is primarily reserved for the latter part of the tribulation period.

Second, similar to the pre-tribulation proponents, they also point to the "Restrainer" in 2 Thessalonians: Refer to the last point of the previous section for a review of this argument. They argue that the removal of the Church, through the rapture, will allow the Antichrist to be revealed, aligning with the midpoint timing.

Third, they point to the pattern of biblical typology: Some mid-tribulation proponents draw parallels between the tribulation period and the biblical account of the Israelites' deliverance from Egypt. They argue that, just as the Israelites experienced the initial plagues but were then protected during the later more severe plagues, so too will the Church endure the early tribulation events but be raptured before the full wrath of God is unleashed.

Again, this list is not comprehensive, but it does list the primary reasons given for these viewpoints. Now let us examine the post-tribulation view of the return of Jesus.

3) The post-tribulation view holds that Jesus comes after the great tribulation to gather His saints. Those who support this position also note that according to Scripture the saints are not appointed to wrath. They believe that even though exceedingly difficult trials are in store, Scripture makes a distinction between tribulation and wrath, and that the Lord does not pour out His wrath on His people. Therefore, speaking from a strictly biblical perspective, it would be accurate to also call this a pre-wrath view. Following are the primary arguments given for holding to a post-tribulation view.

First, they note that Scripture indicates exactly when the Lord gathers His saints and subsequently when loud voices in heaven declare that His wrath has come, citing Revelation 11:15-18. They also note that this passage informs us that "this is when the wrath of God came" as announced from heaven, not by the declaration of man on the earth as was the case in Revelation 6:15-17. Therefore, they assert that indeed, Jesus does rescue His saints from the wrath to come.

Second, they point out that this passage of Scripture informs us that "now is the time for the dead to be judged, and your bond servants the prophets and the saints and those who fear the Lord to be rewarded." The rewards referred to here are related to Jesus' teaching in the parable of the minas in Luke. **[16]"The first appeared, saying, 'Master, your mina has made ten minas more.' [17]"And he said to him, 'Well done, good slave, because you have been faithful in a very little thing, you are to be in authority over ten cities' (Luke 19:16–17).** We are saved based on our faith, and credited with His righteousness. But when the saints return to earth from heaven with Jesus to reign with Him, our rewards will be according to our deeds, whether good or bad. **[10]For we must all appear before the judgment seat of Christ, so that each one may be recompensed for his deeds in the body, according to what he has done, whether good or bad (2 Corinthians 5:10).**

Third, they point out that this passage also informs us that this is "the exact time when the kingdoms of this world become the kingdoms of our God and of His Christ."

Fourth, they base their belief on the Scripture in 2 Thessalonians 2:1-4 that states the Lord cannot return until both the apostasy occurs and the man of lawlessness is revealed.

Fifth, they note the multiple Scriptures that state the Lord's coming is accompanied by a trumpet blast (Matthew 24:31, 1 Corinthians 15:52, 1 Thessalonians 4:16, Revelation 11:15).

Sixth, they point out Jesus' words in Matthew 24:29-31 stating that "immediately after the tribulation He sends His angels to gather His elect."

Seventh, they point to the teaching of Jesus in Matthew 25:1-13 that there is one group that will be taken into the marriage feast by the bridegroom, after which the door is shut and is not reopened. They point out the assertion by pre-tribulation teachers that the possibility of a second chance for a left behind group to repent after the saints are taken from the earth actually contradicts the teaching of Jesus we just looked at. They also note that in order to be saved, one must repent, and Revelation informs us repeatedly that mankind refused to repent, even after a third of all mankind was killed by plagues (Revelation 9:15,18,20-21 and 16:9,11).

Eighth, they note that Jesus told us His return would be expected based on the signs that precede it (Matthew 24:32-33). Also, they note the use of the Scripture saying Jesus comes as a thief in the night is taken out of context when used to support a pre-tribulation view; they assert that it must be read together with the verses immediately following it as they inform us that He only comes unexpectedly as a thief in the night on the world of unbelievers but that those who walk in the light will not be caught unaware (1 Thessalonians 5:2-6).

Ninth, they point to the statement in Revelation 20:4-6 that those killed in the great tribulation for the testimony of Jesus will come to life and reign with Him, and they do so in the first resurrection, meaning there could not be a resurrection before the great tribulation. Because Scripture clearly teaches that those who are alive and remain will not precede those who have died in Christ, no gathering of saints before the great tribulation is possible (1 Thessalonians 4:15).

Tenth, they point out that Scripture informs us that God has multiple purposes for having His children endure suffering, affliction, and persecution. They cite 2 Thessalonians 2:4-10 to support this point. This is not an exhaustive list of the points that teachers of this view use to support it, but are a good sampling of the major arguments. Let's examine the three positions.

Pre-Tribulation

Things to consider that must be answered for a pre-tribulation rapture to be true:

1. There are clear references to saints and those who keep the testimony of Jesus being still on earth during the great tribulation in the later chapters of Revelation (Revelation 20:6) as well as in the book of Daniel (Daniel 7:25). These are just two of many such references to the saints being there on the earth and being persecuted and killed by the antichrist-beast. Since the pre-tribulation view generally holds that a secret rapture occurs shortly after chapter 3 of Revelation, an explanation must be given for those saints who are in evidence after that. The answer given by those who hold this view is that these people who are referred to in later chapters of Revelation are believers who repented of their sins after the rapture and came to faith in Christ Jesus and are referred to as "tribulation saints," but we have already seen the Scriptures disprove the notion of tribulation saints
2. There are references pointing to the fact that when Jesus returns, He will be accompanied *by a great trumpet sound* (Matthew 24:31, 1 Corinthians 15:52, Revelation 11:15). There needs to be an explanation for how a rapture can occur secretly or quietly when there is no Scriptural support for it.

   Numerous Scriptures tell us the saints must endure to the end, and that perseverance is required of us. An explanation must be offered as to why an elite group of saints would be exempt from this requirement. We acknowledge that in the letters to the churches from Jesus in Revelation 3:10, the Lord tells the saints in the church of Philadelphia that they will be spared "the hour of testing": "[10] **'Because you have kept the word of My perseverance, I also will keep you from the hour of testing, that hour which is about to come upon the whole world, to test those who dwell on the earth'" (Revelation 3:10).** No other churches are given this assurance. He does not say how he will keep them from the hour of testing. It does not have to be protection by rapture (gathering them from off the earth). They could die. He could give them a place to flee to safety. He could simply not allow the plagues that will afflict the rest of mankind to afflict His chosen ones. Since only one church out of seven is given this promise, should most believers today assume they will be in the one-seventh that receives this promise or the other six-sevenths which do not get kept "from the hour of testing?"

As we examine the possibilities, for argument's sake, let's assume for a moment that the Lord comes and raptures all the believers on earth and takes them to heaven before the great tribulation begins. It is clear from Scripture that "saints" are still on the earth when the antichrist is there, during the great tribulation. (We see this in Daniel and Revelation. Perhaps the clearest statement to this effect is here in Daniel: **"He shall speak pompous words against the Most High, *Shall persecute the saints of the Most High*, And shall intend to change times and law. Then the saints shall be given into his hand For a time and times and half a time" (Daniel 7:25).** Likewise, we read in Revelation, **"[5] And he was given a mouth speaking great things and blasphemies,**

and *he was given authority to continue for forty-two months.*" (Three and a half years.) **"[6] Then he opened his mouth in blasphemy against God, to blaspheme His name, His tabernacle, and those who dwell in heaven. [7] *It was granted to him to make war with the saints and to overcome them*" (Revelation 13:5-7).** Clearly, some saints are still on earth, being persecuted by the antichrist during the last three and a half years before the Lord comes to destroy him. (We know this time of the saints being in great tribulation is the last half of this seven-year period because Jesus told us that "immediately after the tribulation of those days He sends His angels to gather the elect." Matthew 24:29-31) Therefore, one question that must be answered is "*where* do the saints who are on the earth during the great tribulation *come from*?" The explanation given by those who teach a pre-tribulation view is that these saints who are there during the great tribulation are people who repent of their sins after the rapture and come to faith in the Lord Jesus Christ. So, they were not believers when Jesus came for the Church and were therefore "left behind." Is this assumption a sound one?

Note, only two possibilities exist:

1. One possibility is that these are new believers in Jesus Christ as their Lord and Savior, and they repented and believed after the rapture.
2. The other possibility is that these saints who are there in the great tribulation were there because the rapture had not occurred yet to take them away.

Is There Biblical Support for a Huge Revival After a Rapture?

We have verified *that we see saints were there during the great tribulation.* We then need to determine *where they came from.* In addition to Daniel 7:25 above, we find this in Revelation: **"[9] After these things I looked, and behold, a great multitude which no one could number, of all nations, tribes, peoples, and tongues, *standing before the throne and before the Lamb*, clothed with white robes, with palm branches in their hands, [13] Then one of the elders answered, saying to me, 'Who are these arrayed in white robes, and where did they come from?' [14] And I said to him, 'Sir, you know.' So he said to me, '*These are the ones who come out of the great tribulation.*'"** These saints "came out of," meaning they were in, the great tribulation. It does not say "they came from before the great tribulation." The Greek word found here is **ἐκ**, which is translated "out of, from, or out from." Then these same saints **"washed their robes and made them white in the blood of the Lamb" (Revelation 7:9, 13-14, emphasis mine).** So, we can be certain these saints were there during the great tribulation but are now in heaven because we just read that a great multitude that no one could count came *out of* the great tribulation. Scripture here does not describe this group as coming out *before* the great tribulation. We can reason that these who make up this great multitude which no one could count got to heaven by being killed for their faith. We know this because the Lord told the saints under the altar at the opening of the fifth seal that they should rest a little while longer, **"until the number of their fellow servants *who were to be killed as they were* was complete."** Just as these souls under the altar got to heaven by having *been slain for the word of God and for the testimony which they held*, so also can we reason that this great multitude from out of the great tribulation gets to heaven by being killed for their testimony of the Word of God, and of the gospel of Christ Jesus.

Moreover, you would think that if a great multitude of saints *which no one could count* repented and came to faith after the rapture and were there on earth after the great tribulation began, we would be told that somewhere in the Scripture. This would be one of the greatest revivals of all time. Yet there is not even a hint found in Revelation that any such revival takes place. Furthermore, we are informed by Scripture that rather than a great revival occurring in the last days, instead there is a great apostasy, a great *falling away* from the faith. We will shortly examine Scripture that informs us that rather than repenting, mankind refused to repent.

Contrast the absence of any mention anywhere in Revelation that men repented, believed, and were saved during this time period with the abundant mentions in Scripture of when people *do* come to faith in the Lord. When many were saved on the day of Pentecost, Scripture told us about that: **"Then those who gladly received his word were baptized; and that day about three thousand souls were added to them" (Acts 2:41).** In Acts 10, when Cornelius and his household believed, we are told, and in Acts 16:22-34 we are told when the Philippian jailer and his entire household were saved. *Can there be a great widespread revival* Does it make sense then that there would be a widespread revival leading to repentance and saving faith going on during the great tribulation if we are not told of it? Instead, the Word tells us that "because of lawlessness, the love of most will grow cold (Matthew 24:12)." We know in addition that the antichrist-beast cannot be revealed until *there* *is a great apostasy,* so rather than many people coming to faith in a great revival, most are doing the opposite; they are abandoning the faith in a great apostasy. We discover in Daniel 11:33-35 that during this time when the saints are given into the hand of the antichrist, they are given a little help, and "some join them in hypocrisy." This is the only reference regarding this time period that indicates anyone joins the saints, and it is said of these that *they join in hypocrisy.* Further, it reveals the purpose here was to purify and purge the people who know their God.

In Revelation, not only is Scripture silent with regard to men repenting and being saved, *it states that they refused to repent.* Revelation mentions three times that mankind refused to repent. After learning that three plagues had *caused the death of one third of mankind,* one would expect that this result would grab the attention of the survivors. The current world population is in excess of 7.5 billion people. When these plagues are released, it will result in the death of 2.5 billion people. It is telling that the next response from Scripture begins with the Greek conjunction **καί,** which the New King James Version renders "but", as in "you would think, but…" read what Scripture next says: **"[20] But *the rest of mankind,* who were not killed by these plagues, *did not repent* of the works of their hands, that they should not worship demons, and idols of gold, silver, brass, stone, and wood, which can neither see nor hear nor walk. [21] And *they did not repent* of their murders or their sorceries or their sexual immorality or their thefts" (Revelation 9:20-21, NKJV).** This statement about repentance is all-inclusive, for it says, "the rest of mankind did not repent." It does not say that most did not repent, or that many refused to repent. This statement is made before the sounding of the seventh trumpet, the last trumpet which the Word tells us is when the Lord will come to gather

His saints. This event is before the wrath of God comes on the earth. We find in 1 Corinthians the Scripture that confirms that the Lord comes for His saints at the last trumpet. "[51]**Behold, I tell you a mystery; we will not all sleep,"** meaning we will not all die, **"but we will all be changed, [52]in a moment, in the twinkling of an eye, *at the last trumpet*; for the trumpet will sound, and the dead will be raised imperishable, and we will be changed" (1 Corinthians 15:52).** Those who hold a pre-tribulation view of the rapture, thinking that the Lord will come in two different raptures to gather His saints, will assert that this verse from 1 Corinthians 15 must surely be the place where the "second rapture" occurs. The problem with this theory of two raptures is that it rests on the concept that a massive revival must occur among the unsaved who repent and believe to replenish the earth with true believers, a revival for which we find no biblical evidence. Otherwise, they have no explanation for who all the saints are that Scripture shows to be present during the great tribulation.

Furthermore, after the gathering of the saints which happens when the seventh angel sounds his trumpet in Revelation 11:15, we read that the wrath of God comes. We touched on this in chapter one, but now we connect the beginning of God's wrath with the moment that the saints are gathered: *"[15]Then the seventh angel sounded*; **and there were loud voices in heaven, saying, '*The kingdom of the world has become the kingdom of our Lord and of His Christ*; and he will reign forever and ever.'""** Here we have loud voices in heaven telling us the kingdom of the world has become the kingdom of our Lord and of His Christ. **"[16]And the twenty-four elders, who sit on their thrones before God, fell on their faces and worshiped God, [17]saying, 'We give You thanks, O Lord God, the Almighty, who are and who were,**

because *You have taken Your great power and have begun to reign.*'" Jesus now has begun to reign over the kingdom of the world. **"[18]And the nations were enraged, *and Your wrath came,*"** --this is a declaration from heaven, with loud voices, telling us "Your wrath came"--" **and *the time came for the dead to be judged, and the time to reward Your bond-servants the prophets and the saints* and those who fear Your name, the small and the great, and to destroy those who destroy the earth" (Revelation 11:15,18, emphasis mine**). God's wrath comes on the earth here, when the seventh angel sounds. This is the beginning of the day of the Lord. The saints are raised, to rewards, along with the prophets, and gathered to be taken to heaven. But this also marks the beginning of what Isaiah spoke of: "**[9]Behold, *the day of the LORD is coming*, Cruel, with fury and burning anger, To make the land a desolation; And He will exterminate its sinners from it" (Isaiah 13:9).** The day of the Lord arrives here. This begins the wrath of God.

In verse 18 above, we see the resurrection of the saints. It tells us, **"This is the time *to reward the saints* and His bond servants, the prophets, and those who fear His name."** The dead in Christ are raised, and they are judged for rewards. As saints, we have already been judged righteous, having been credited with righteousness through faith in Christ, just as righteousness was credited to Abraham because he believed God.) (Words in parentheses are mine.) **"[22]Therefore it was also credited to him** (Abraham) **as righteousness. [23]Now not for his sake only was it written that it was credited to him, [24]but for our sake also, to whom it will be credited, as those who believe in Him who raised Jesus our Lord from the dead," (Romans 4:22–24).**

We learn from Revelation 20:4-5 that included in this resurrection are those who were martyred during the great tribulation for not worshiping the beast or taking his mark. It tells us that *they are raised in the first resurrection.* It also tells us the rest of the dead are not raised until the end of Jesus's thousand-year earthly reign with His saints. The rest of the dead *are those who are unsaved,* and they stand before Christ's judgment seat at the great white throne and are judged according to their deeds: **"[4]And I saw thrones, and they sat on them, and judgment was committed to them. Then I saw the souls of those who had been beheaded for their witness to Jesus and for the word of God, who had not worshiped the beast or his image, and had not received his mark on their foreheads or on their hands. And they lived and reigned with Christ for a thousand years. [5]But the rest of the dead did not live again until the thousand years were finished. *This is the first resurrection*" (Revelation 20:4–5, NKJV, emphasis mine**).

We read in Revelation 11:18 confirmation *from heaven* that *this is when God's wrath comes,* along with telling us that now the Lord begins to reign over the kingdom of the world. The saints are raptured at this point, and just as God promised, *He rescues us from the wrath to come.* He waits to bring His wrath on the earth until He takes us to heaven for the marriage supper of the Lamb. After this, Scripture continues to confirm that men do not repent: "**And men were scorched with great heat, and they blasphemed the name of God who has power over these plagues; *and they did not repent* and give Him glory [...](Revelation 16:9)** Two verses later we read: "**They blasphemed the God of heaven because of their pains and their sores, *and did not repent of their deeds.*" (Revelation 16:9,11, emphasis mine).** These Scriptures are clear that men, *the rest of mankind,* refuse to repent. Because no one repents, it is not possible that a great multitude, so great no one could count, come to faith after the rapture. The only explanation we are left with for why we see saints still on earth during the great tribulation *is that the rapture has not yet occurred.*

Let's examine more evidence that saints are there during the great tribulation. The Bible calls the antichrist "the beast." It says repeatedly that the antichrist (beast) will make war with the saints and prevail against them. We find this antichrist-beast first described in Revelation 11, right after the two witnesses have given their testimony: **"[7] Now when they have finished their testimony, the beast that comes up from the Abyss will attack them, and overpower and kill them" (Revelation 11:7).** We get more detail on the antichrist (the beast) two chapters later in Revelation 13: **"[1] Then I stood on the sand of the sea. And I saw a beast rising up out of the sea, having seven heads and ten horns,"** (heads and horns are both kings) **"and on his horns ten crowns, and on his heads a blasphemous name. [2] Now the beast which I saw was like a leopard, his feet were like the feet of a bear, and his mouth like the mouth of a lion. The dragon"** (Satan) **"gave him his power, his throne, and great authority. [3] And I saw one of his heads as if it had been mortally wounded, and his deadly wound was healed."** This event appears to be a counterfeit copy—a mockery-- of the death and resurrection of Christ. We are told in 2 Thessalonians 2: 9 that he comes with power and signs and false wonders **"And all the world marveled and followed the beast. [4] So they worshiped the dragon who gave authority to the beast; and they worshiped the beast, saying, 'Who is like the beast? Who is able to make war with him?' [5] And he was given a mouth speaking great things and blasphemies, and *he was given authority to continue for forty-two months.* [6] Then he opened his mouth in blasphemy against God, to blaspheme His**

name, His tabernacle, and those who dwell in heaven. [7] ***It was granted to him to make war with the saints and to overcome them."*** (Clearly, the saints are present; they have not been raptured yet.) **"And authority was given him over every tribe, tongue, and nation.** [8] **All who dwell on the earth will worship him, whose names have not been written in the Book of Life of the Lamb slain from the foundation of the world" (Revelation 13:1-8, NKJV, emphasis mine)** This passage clearly states that the beast or antichrist *will make war with the saints* and overcome them, and it gives a specific time frame.

Summarizing what we have examined in this section, there should be no question that there will be saints on the earth during the great tribulation, during the time the antichrist is on earth. Also, the *Scripture is silent about anyone at all repenting and being saved during the great tribulation*, but instead states that *the rest of mankind did not repent.* This is consistent with the rest of Scripture which tells us that in the last days, the love of most will grow cold, and there will be a great falling away of the faith. All of these observations are supported by Jesus' teaching from the parable of the ten virgins. After the bridegroom came, His invited guests entered the wedding feast, and the door was shut, not to be reopened again. Those *left behind* cried out "Lord, lord," but he said, "I do not know you." Jesus' teaching in this parable was unmistakably dealing with His coming, as the bridegroom, for His saints. Once the Lord comes to gather His saints, there is no second chance for those left behind.

One argument used by pre-tribulation teachers to support their theory of the church being raptured before the great tribulation is the absence of the word "church" in the later chapters of Revelation. They claim this must indicate that Jesus removed the church from the earth by the rapture. They call this reasoning "an argument from silence." However, this argument fails to adequately account for the saints, of which the church is comprised, still present and mentioned throughout Revelation. To explain the presence of the saints, they theorize that a great revival must occur in which multitudes repent, believe, and are saved, despite a distinct lack of biblical evidence for any such revival.

The argument from silence regarding the absence of the word "church" is not sufficient evidence to support a pre-tribulation rapture. In fact, the argument from silence applies much more aptly to the absence of any evidence or prophecies about anyone repenting and being saved in the later chapters of Revelation. Instead, as we noted, despite the difficult events, including the plagues and the tribulation, we have declarations that mankind refused to repent, which we must assume indicates that no one is saved during the period in question.

There is a type of reasoning that can be characterized by the following example: A group of people assert, "The sky is blue." They insist, "Go, look for yourself and see." As a result, you may feel compelled to examine everything with the expectation of finding what you've been told to look for. However, a rational and objective approach would be to begin the examination process with an open mind and allow the conclusion to be revealed through an impartial and truthful search. Keep this in mind as you reflect on both what we have already examined objectively and what we examine next.

Along these lines of reasoning, some who hold the theory of a pre-tribulation gathering of the saints point to Revelation 4:1, where John is told to "come up here." They suggest this is the point where all the saints are raptured. However, this is not what this passage or its context suggests: "[1]**After these things I looked, and behold, a door standing open in heaven, and the first voice which I had heard, like the sound of a trumpet speaking with me, said, '*Come up here*, and I will show *you* what must take place after these things.' [2]Immediately *I was in the Spirit*; and behold, a throne was standing in heaven, and One sitting on the throne" (Revelation 4:1-2, emphasis mine).** The original language addresses "you" in the singular, referring to John. It is clear that John is in the spirit, and has not himself been changed and "put on immortality" as is indicated will be the case at the rapture for all saints in 1 Corinthians 15: **"[51]Behold, I tell you a mystery; we will not all sleep, but we will all be changed, [52]in a moment, in the twinkling of an eye, at the last trumpet; for the trumpet will sound, and the dead will be raised imperishable, and we will be changed. [53]For this perishable must put on the imperishable, and *this mortal must put on immortality"* (1 Corinthians 15:51–53, emphasis mine).** Further, our passage from Revelation 4 tells us that as John receives this revelation from the angel, he is at that moment being caught up "in the spirit" before the throne in heaven, experiencing it in the present. This was John's present when he wrote it.

In the next verse of this chapter, we see the twenty-four elders: "[4]**Around the throne were twenty-four thrones; and upon the thrones *I saw twenty-four elders* sitting, clothed in white garments, and golden crowns on their heads" (Revelation 4:4, emphasis mine).** First, who are the twenty-four elders? Jesus told His disciples they would sit on twelve thrones, judging the twelve tribes of Israel (Matthew 19:18). The identity of the remaining twelve elders is not specified in Scripture. Perhaps the others are notable saints from among the Gentiles who God has appointed to this office. Some argue that the presence of the twenty-four elders suggests the presence of the saints also. But once again, this is reading something into this passage that is not there. That the elders are there is not in question; Scripture confirms this. How they got there is not revealed. The Lord may have decided to bring them into His presence in heaven, perhaps so that like the angels, they may watch what He is doing with mankind. A passage from 2 Timothy may shed some light on the presence of the elders here: **"[6]The hard-working farmer ought to be *the first to receive his share of the crops.* [7]Consider what I say, for the Lord will give you understanding in everything" (2 Timothy 2:6–7, emphasis mine).** The context of this verse from 2 Timothy is about running the race to win and about being a soldier who seeks to please the one who enlisted him by not being concerned with the affairs of everyday life; it is about enduring hardship. It is therefore not about farming in the sense of actually planting crops, and harvest, and so forth. It is not even about ministers of the gospel deriving their income from the gospel. It is not unreasonable for us to "understand" or deduce that these twenty-four elders, who were "hard working" for the Lord in caring for His people, are "the first to receive their share." Thus, we see no other saints present with them yet, for they are the first. Even though we find the twenty-four elders in heaven at this moment, we must be careful not to build a complete doctrinal belief based on what *we wish to be the case*, but rather let Scripture reveal truth to us as we study all of the passages dealing with a subject. If we have been told the sky is blue, we are looking to find that is the case. If we have been told here is where the saints are raptured before the tribulation, we are looking to find evidence of that. But that assertion is not supported in this passage, just as other pre-tribulation arguments are not supported by the proof texts that are offered.

Test All Things, Hold Fast What Is Good

Some proponents of the pre-tribulation theory accuse those who reject their teaching of stealing their "blessed hope." This is a reference to the following Scripture from Titus: "[13]**looking for the blessed hope and the appearing of the glory of our great God and Savior, Christ Jesus," (Titus 2:13).** A closer examination of the context surrounding this verse reveals that these exhortations by Paul are simply meant to encourage his audience of believers to put their hope in their eternal reward and the ultimate life they will have with Christ Jesus because of their faith; those who use it to support the idea of a pre-tribulation rapture are taking it out of context to further their own views. Furthermore, the assertion that someone is "stealing their blessed hope" is a personal attack and an indictment of the character of the individual who disagrees with the pre-tribulation theory. Rather than attacking someone personally, we should openly examine the Scriptures with one another to discover the truth for the sake of the unity of the church.

You recall that Scripture commends the Bereans as noble-minded for their willingness to "examine the Scriptures." Paul and Silas had been falsely accused in Thessalonica and had to flee the city because of the danger they faced: "[10]**The brethren immediately sent Paul and Silas away by night to Berea, and when they arrived, they went into the synagogue of the Jews. [11]Now these were more noble-minded than those in Thessalonica, for they received the word with great eagerness, examining the Scriptures daily to see whether these things were so" (Acts 17:10–11).** In fact, the Bible encourages us to "[21]**Test all things; hold fast what is good" (1 Thessalonians 5:21,**

NKJV) .Therefore, it is important to approach these discussions with an attitude of humility and a willingness to learn from one another.

It is important to note that the concept of a pre-tribulation rapture was not widely taught or accepted in Christian theology until the 19th century, and it is not found in the early Christian writings or the historical creeds of the church. It is a relatively recent interpretation of Scripture that has gained popularity in some circles.

However, some scholars have argued that certain passages in the early Christian writings might be interpreted as supporting a pre-tribulation rapture. For example, in his letter to the Corinthians, Clement of Rome (1 Clement), who lived in the late first century, speaks of the "sudden coming of the Lord." (1 Clement 23:1) and the catching up of the believers (1 Clement 50:5-7). Similarly, in his book *The Shepherd of Hermas*, which was written in the early second century, Hermas describes a vision in which the faithful are taken up into the air to meet the Lord (The Shepherd of Hermas, Vision 2:4).

These passages from the first and second century are not specifically referring to a pre-tribulation rapture; they simply reinforce and parallel the Scriptures which inform us regarding the coming of the Lord, which indicate that we will be "caught up to meet the Lord in the air." Read 1 Thessalonians: "[17]**Then we who are alive and remain will be caught up together with them in the clouds to meet the Lord in the air, and so we shall always be with the Lord" (1 Thessalonians 4:17).** Scripture also informs us that "we will be changed in a moment, in the twinkling of an eye" **(1 Corinthians 15:52).** Additionally, these extra-biblical writings are not considered authoritative Scripture by most Christian denominations, and their interpretation is subject to debate.

The scant "evidence" for a pre-tribulation belief by early church fathers in addition to the absence of such a doctrine until the nineteenth century further invalidate this interpretation as sound teaching.

We still have one more lengthy portion of Scripture to examine in relation to the theory of a pre-tribulation rapture. We will begin in Revelation 19:11 and will continue into Revelation 20, in which the saints come to life and reign with Jesus on earth for a thousand years:

"11 And I saw heaven opened, and behold, a white horse, and He who sat on it is called Faithful and True, and in righteousness He judges and wages war. 12 His eyes are a flame of fire, and on His head are many diadems; and He has a name written on Him which no one knows except Himself. 13 He is clothed with a robe dipped in blood, and His name is called The Word of God. 14 And *the armies which are in heaven, clothed in fine linen, white and clean*, were *following Him on white horses*." The armies, clothed in fine linen are the saints. We are with Him, having just been with Him at the marriage supper of the Lamb in heaven. We see this in the verses just preceding this passage, in Revelation 19:7-8 **"15 From His mouth comes a sharp sword, so that with it He may strike down the nations, and *He will rule them with a rod of iron;* and He treads the wine press of the fierce wrath of God, the Almighty."** Jesus will not use a rod of iron on His saints, for He will not need it. But this indicates that during His upcoming reign which will last a thousand years, He has allowed the nations who are still mortal to continue on the earth. **"16 And on His robe and on His thigh He has a name written, 'KING OF KINGS, AND LORD OF LORDS.' 17 Then I saw an angel standing in the sun, and he cried out with a loud voice, saying to all the birds which**

fly in midheaven, "Come, assemble for the great supper of God, [18] so that you may eat the flesh of kings and the flesh of commanders and the flesh of mighty men and the flesh of horses and of those who sit on them and the flesh of all men, both free men and slaves, and small and great." [19] And I saw the beast and the kings of the earth and their armies assembled to make war against Him who sat on the horse and against His army." Again, the saints are His army. "[20] **And *the beast was seized, and with him the false prophet* who performed the signs in his presence, by which he deceived those who had received the mark of the beast and those who worshiped his image; *these two were thrown alive into the lake of fire which burns with brimstone.* [21] And the rest were killed with the sword which came from the mouth of Him who sat on the horse, and all the birds were filled with their flesh" (Revelation 19:11-21, emphasis mine** "The rest" here refers to those who are to be killed. But not all are killed, otherwise there would be none left at the end of Jesus's thousand-year reign that are deceived when Satan is released for a short season and who go to war against the Lord and His saints at that time. Satan, through the antichrist, brings war against the saints before the millennium begins. Jesus ends it when He returns from heaven with the saints and casts the antichrist into the lake of fire. This is the second and final war at the conclusion of the millennium. So, in this passage, right before the Lord Jesus returns, there is *a beast* (a world ruler, in this case, the antichrist-beast) *and a false prophet* on the earth. Many are deceived and receive the mark of the beast and worship his image. Now Jesus is on earth and has destroyed the beast and his empire. We are with Him.

Let us continue reading to see what takes place next: "[1]**Then I saw an angel coming down from heaven, having the key to the bottomless**

pit and a great chain in his hand. [2]He laid hold of the dragon, that serpent of old, who is the Devil and Satan, and bound him for a thousand years; [3]and he cast him into the bottomless pit, and shut him up, and set a seal on him, so that he should deceive the nations no more till the thousand years were finished. But after these things he must be released for a little while. [4]And I saw thrones, and they sat on them, and judgment was committed to them. Then I saw the souls of those who had been beheaded for their witness to Jesus and for the word of God, who had not worshiped the beast or his image, and had not received his mark on their foreheads or on their hands. And they lived and reigned with Christ for a thousand years. [5]But the rest of the dead did not live again until the thousand years were finished. This is the first resurrection." The rest of the dead are the unbelievers. They are raised to face judgement at the second resurrection. " **[6]Blessed and holy is he who has part in the first resurrection. Over such the second death has no power, but they shall be priests of God and of Christ, and shall reign with Him a thousand years" (Revelation 20:1–6, NKJV, emphasis mine). (NKJV)**

Here we see that the saints must resist taking the mark of the beast, and many are killed because they refuse to take the mark. At the seventh trumpet, Jesus rescues the saints, *after which* wrath is poured out, and the beast and false prophet are still there. When Jesus comes back to reign, with His saints following behind Him, they (the beast and the false prophet) are cast alive into the lake of fire by Christ himself. Many others are killed, and all the birds are filled with their flesh. Note, the heavens and the earth have not yet been burned up with intense heat. This does not occur until after Jesus has reigned on the earth for a thousand years, and after Satan is released for a short season to gather the nations to war against the Lord and His saints. But all that we are examining, from the gathering of the saints at the sounding of the seventh trumpet, to the release of Satan after Jesus has reigned for a thousand years on earth, all occur "on the day of the Lord." This day is a thousand years long, and it is at the end of this day that God burns up the earth and the heavens with intense heat and then creates a new heaven and a new earth. To help give clarity to this, think of the day of the Lord as twenty-four hours long. The day begins at 12:00:00 am. It ends at 11:59:59 pm twenty-four hours later (almost). In this scenario, Jesus comes for His saints at the beginning of the day, at 12:00:00 am. At 12:01 am, with the saints safely in heaven, beginning to celebrate the marriage supper of the Lamb, the angels begin pouring out the wrath of God on those who dwell on the earth. Just a little while later, perhaps at 12:05 am, Jesus brings us with Himself back to earth to destroy the beast and the false prophet and begin His reign on the earth. At the end of the day, perhaps about 11:45 pm, Satan is released and gathers men from all over the earth to wage war against the Lord and His saints at Jerusalem. God rains down fire and brimstone on these rebels, destroying them, except for Satan, whom Jesus throws into the lake of fire where the beast and the false prophet are. Then at 11:59:59 pm, at the end of the day, God burns up the heavens and the earth and creates a new heaven and a new earth. The difference between this scenario and what will occur is that the day of the Lord is actually a thousand years long. So, Jesus comes at the very beginning, and Satan is let loose at the end, perhaps in year 999, and then the Father burns up the heavens and earth right after Satan and the rebels are destroyed, right at the end, in year 1000.

Now let us return briefly to Revelation 20 which we know follows the defeat of the antichrist-beast and his armies:"[1]**Then I saw an angel**

coming down from heaven, having the key to the bottomless pit and a great chain in his hand. [2]He laid hold of the dragon, that serpent of old, who is the Devil and Satan, and bound him for a thousand years; [3]and he cast him into the bottomless pit, and shut him up, and set a seal on him, so that he should deceive the nations no more till the thousand years were finished. But after these things he must be released for a little while" (Revelation 20:1-3). So, Satan is captured by an angel, bound for a thousand years, and cast into the bottomless pit. Satan will be released for a brief time after a thousand years. "[4]**And I saw thrones, and they sat on them, and judgment was committed to them. Then I saw the souls of those who had been beheaded for their witness to Jesus and for the word of God, who had not worshiped the beast or his image, and had not received his mark on their foreheads or on their hands. And they lived and reigned with Christ for a thousand years."** These martyrs, who were present during the great tribulation, and did not take the mark of the beast or worship him, rose from the dead and lived to reign with Christ, and *we are next told this is the first resurrection.* The Lord waited to come for His people, for anyone to rise from the dead, until the total number who were to die for their faith was complete, just as He told the souls under the altar when the fifth seal was broken. Otherwise, we would not be told this is *the first resurrection.* "[5] **But the rest of the dead"** --*the unsaved*, who rise after the thousand years to face the great White Throne Judgment-- **"did not live again until the thousand years were finished. *This is the first resurrection*"** This refers to those had been beheaded and who came to life and reign with Jesus. "[6] **Blessed and holy *is* he who has part in *the first resurrection.* Over such the second death has no power"** --these are the Lord's saints, who are now immortal, because they "put on immortality" when they rose from the dead-- **"but they shall be priests of God and of Christ, and shall reign with Him a thousand years" (Revelation 20:4-6, NKJV).**

Again, let's review what just happened. After Jesus defeats the beast and the false prophet and casts them into the lake of fire, an angel binds Satan, throwing him into the bottomless pit until the thousand years are finished. Satan will not be able to deceive the people living on the earth for this time. During this time, the Lord Jesus is reigning on earth and His saints reign with Him.

Some teach that the rapture occurs before the seven-year period, and these saints who were martyrs were saved after the saints were caught up to heaven, still adhering to a pre-tribulation theory of when Christ comes to rescue His saints. But unfortunately, that is not possible. Notice in verses 5 and 6 Scripture plainly states, "this is the first resurrection." Because we know "that those who are alive and remain will not precede those who have died in Christ" when the Lord comes to gather His saints, no rapture prior to this could have occurred (1 Thessalonians 4:15-17), secretly or otherwise, since the one these martyrs arose in is declared clearly to be the *first* resurrection. Frankly, I would like to believe in a pre-tribulation rapture scenario. What we just read about the martyrs who were beheaded during the great tribulation means no one who God intended to save got "left behind" after the rapture, and later repented and believed. We just read that many saints during the great tribulation were killed for their faith, and then arose from the dead, to reign with Jesus.

To better understand why it is not possible that a rapture could have occurred until these people died in the great tribulation, and they arose from the dead, consider the following story which may help bring clarity.

To set the stage, suppose I said I am going to throw a party and invite you. For the sake of the story, let's say you and I are part of a group we call "Believers". But to even have the party (the resurrection and rapture), I explain that our friends, whose names are "Asleep" and "Martyr," must get there before you can come. Until both "Asleep" and "Martyr" arrive, the party cannot begin. (This is because we know those who are alive and remain will not precede those who have died in Christ.) If either "Asleep" or "Martyr" delays his arrival, we must postpone the party. You are a Believer, and your friends named "Asleep", and "Martyr" must come to the party (the party is the rapture) or we postpone the party. In this case, "Martyr" represents those who were killed for their faith by the beast during the great tribulation. "Asleep" stands for all those who have died in Christ up to the great tribulation. "Believer" represents those who are believers and are alive when Jesus comes to gather all His saints. Scripture makes it very plain, as noted before in 1 Thessalonians 4:16-17, that the dead in Christ rise first; they must come before those who are alive and remain at His coming. So, until there is a resurrection of the dead in Christ, *it is not possible for any saints still alive on the earth to be raptured.* The dead must rise first. Until the dead rise, we must postpone the "party" (the rapture) for everyone. The rapture does not occur until all who were appointed by God to die for their faith is complete. This includes those saints who were to be killed during the great tribulation, those who were beheaded for not taking the mark of the beast. Hence, Scripture tells us that these saints who were beheaded for not taking the mark of the beast and were raised from the dead rose in the *first* resurrection. To assert otherwise means you must try to make Scripture mean something other than what it is saying. You either accept that this is the first resurrection and there has been no resurrection of the dead prior to this time, or you must assert that this is really not the first resurrection.

Some teachers of a pre-tribulation view point to 2 Thessalonians 2:1-2 and assert that the early believers must have believed that Jesus could come back at any moment to gather His saints: **"[1]Now we request you, brethren, with regard to the coming of our Lord Jesus Christ and our gathering together to Him, [2]that you not be quickly shaken from your composure or be disturbed either by a spirit or a message or a letter as if from us, to the effect that the day of the Lord has come" (2 Thessalonians 2:1–2).** It is apparent that Paul was in fact addressing this belief because it was in error. We find other examples in Scripture in which Paul addresses error in doctrine. We find Paul doing just this in Galatians 3:1:**"[1]You foolish Galatians, who has bewitched you, before whose eyes Jesus Christ was publicly portrayed as crucified?" (Galatians 3:1).** Here he goes on to remind them they are saved by faith, not by works. His correction for the saints at Thessalonica is to explain that no, Jesus cannot come unexpectedly, that there are two requirements that must take place preceding the Lord's return: **"for it will not come unless the apostasy comes first, and the man of lawlessness is revealed, the son of destruction, [4]who opposes and exalts himself above every so-called god or object of worship, so that he takes his seat in the temple of God, displaying himself as being God. [5]Do you not remember that while I was still with you, I was telling you these things?" (2 Thessalonians 2:3–5).** So rather than supporting the concept of a "doctrine of imminence" this portion of Scripture directly refutes such a teaching. Clearly, the message of Scripture here and elsewhere is that Jesus's return will not be unexpected by those who walk in the light, His saints, for we will have signs that give us warning.

A pre-tribulation rapture theory is a relatively modern idea and was not a view held by the church from the time of the early church fathers until it was popularized in the West by inclusion in the notes of the Scofield Reference Bible at the beginning of the 20th century. The Scofield Reference Bible is a widely circulated study Bible edited and annotated by the American Bible student Cyrus I. Scofield; it popularized dispensationalism at the beginning of the 20th century. Published by Oxford University Press and containing the entire text of the traditional, Protestant King James Version, it first appeared in 1909 and was revised by the author in 1917.

I find no clear Scripture that directly supports the theory of a pre-tribulation rapture. All the supposed "proof texts" its' proponents use are suppositions that are not indicated by their use of Scripture, and are in many cases not only without basis, but are contradicted by the direct teaching of other Scripture on the subject. We just read the direct teaching of Scripture informing us that the first resurrection did not occur until the martyrs from the great tribulation arose and came to life.

Mid-Tribulation

Is there support in Scripture for a "**mid-tribulation" rapture?** Some people theorize that the Lord comes back "mid-tribulation," which they sometimes call "pre-wrath." The most commonly held premise for this is the assertion that since Scripture tells us that "He rescues us from the wrath to come," and the declaration regarding the wrath of the Lamb is seen at the opening of the sixth seal, it is reasoned this must be the point when the Lord comes for His people.

Again, some who advocate for this as the moment of the rapture call it "pre-wrath" rather than "mid-tribulation." Let me state emphatically, I agree, *the Lord does rescue His saints from the wrath to come.* We have observed that the Lord showed us where His wrath actually does begin, and it is right after the saints are gathered. We reviewed this in the previous section and note Revelation 11:15-18 makes this clear. Therefore, *we must be discerning about the difference between what is "enduring suffering, trials, tribulation, and persecution," and what is wrath.* We have already examined the point where it is declared in heaven that God's wrath came as opposed to *the cry of man that His wrath had come.* I find the argument that the Lord returns when the sixth seal is opened unconvincing for several reasons. Firstly, aside from observing humanity's reaction to frighteningly challenging events, proponents of this viewpoint often focus on the events that occur during the sounding of the trumpets as evidence for the timing of the saints' rapture. They believe these events would be so intolerable that they conclude they must signify God's wrath. However, they mistakenly *assume* that the opening of the sixth seal *is accompanied* by *an announcement confirming* the arrival of God's wrath.

Because of the numerous places in Scripture where we are told that we are not appointed to wrath such as this one in 1 Thessalonians 5 **9For God has not destined us for wrath, but for obtaining salvation through our Lord Jesus Christ, (1 Thessalonians 5:9)** we expect God to rapture us before the wrath. We have seen this is exactly what He does. We previously noted when the seventh angel sounded the last trumpet, (Revelation 11:15) the Lord at this moment rescues His saints, taking them from the earth. Then we have the announcement from heaven "Your wrath came." (Revelation 11:18) *But the cry of man prior to this, at the sixth seal opening, does not signify the beginning of God's* *wrath.* No doubt they were terrified, but it had not yet begun. As you continue to examine the events that occur from the opening of the sixth seal to the sounding of the seventh trumpet, you will see that God does perform His Word. He does protect us from His wrath. Then we find that when loud voices in heaven announce the beginning of His wrath, He has gathered all the saints from the earth, rescuing them from the wrath to come.

Also, consider what happened right before the opening of the sixth seal, when the fifth seal was opened: **9 When He opened the fifth seal, I saw under the altar the souls of those who had been slain for the word of God and for the testimony which they held. 10 And they cried with a loud voice, saying, "How long, O Lord, holy and true, *until You judge and avenge[1] our blood on those who dwell on the earth?"* 11 Then a white robe was given to each of them; and *it was said to them that they should rest a little while longer*, until *both the number of their fellow servants and their brethren, who would be killed***

1 In Deuteronomy 32:43, in the last verse of the Song of Moses, we read: "Rejoice, O nations, with His people; For He will *avenge the blood of His servants, And will render vengeance* on His adversaries, And will atone for His land and His people." Scripture is referring in this passage before the nation of Israel had even crossed over the Jordan river to take possession of the land of the time of vengeance when the Lord will avenge the blood of His servants. This does not take place until all those who were to be killed as their fellow servants had been killed is complete. Those who insist that the time of vengeance began with the beginning of the seven-year period or even at the mid-point with the great tribulation miss this vital truth. God does not begin avenging and pouring out His vengeance until the number of martyrs to be killed is fulfilled.

as they were, was completed. **(Revelation 6:9-11)** They are told to rest a little while longer, *until the number of their fellow servants and brethren, who would be killed as they were, was completed.* It makes no sense to contend that immediately at the opening of the next seal this is completed and that the saints are taken to heaven. *Nothing has changed since God told them to rest a little while longer.* The Lord just informed them that He has more to accomplish before he judges and avenges (judging and avenging is the outpouring of His wrath). We must read further to see how these "fellow servants of those who have been killed *will themselves also be killed.* This is key to understanding when the work of God is *finished*, when Jesus rescues the saints, and God pours out His wrath. Otherwise, the answer to the souls under the altar would have been, "right now I am judging and avenging your blood." So, it is clear that judgment and wrath on the unbelieving world does not start yet.

Should you desire to examine the signs described at the opening of the sixth seal, "the sun became black as sackcloth made of hair, and the whole moon became like blood," I have included a lengthy discussion on this topic in Appendix 4 at the end of this book. Because a full examination is lengthy and involved, I decided to cover it for those interested, but not to include it in this section.

Does God Protect His Saints From His Wrath?

We will continue shortly to examine Scripture to receive assurance that we are not subjected to God's wrath. Jesus comes for us and rescues us before God's wrath is poured out. Before going further into detail to see exactly how we are kept from His wrath, let's step back and get a perspective of how and when things occur. We saw previously that "the day of the Lord" begins when Jesus comes to gather His saints. (1 Thessalonians 4:16-5:2)

Please let me encourage you to approach your examination of end time Scriptures with a fresh set of eyes. I found I had to put away my former notions and wrestle with all of the Scriptures to better understand what they are saying. In 2 Peter 3, we read that the present heavens and earth are being reserved for fire, kept for the day of judgment and *destruction of ungodly men.* In this passage, we can clearly see that, just as God destroyed the world before with the flood, this will be a complete destruction of the world and all mortal men living in it. We read from 2 Peter: [5]**For when they maintain this, it escapes their notice that by the word of God the heavens existed long ago and the earth was formed out of water and by water, [6]through which *the world at that time was destroyed, being flooded with water.* [7]But by His word *the present heavens and earth are being reserved for fire*, kept for the day of judgment *and destruction of ungodly men.* (2 Peter 3:5-7)** Just a few verses later it goes on to say [10]**But the day of the Lord will come like a thief, in which the heavens will pass away with a roar and the elements will be destroyed with intense heat, and the earth and its works will be burned up. (2 Peter 3:10)** How can it be that on "the day of the Lord" all men will be destroyed, along with the earth, but some men escape? It is possible because as we have previously seen, the "day of the Lord" is one-thousand years long. The earth is completely destroyed with intense heat on the day of the Lord, but this event happens at the end of the "day." In a moment, we will see from Scripture that after the beast and the false prophet were cast into the lake of fire, *some mortals are allowed to survive the first outpouring of the wrath of God and enter the millennium.* At the end of the millennium, they are deceived by Satan and that is when they are destroyed, and when the earth and all its works are burned up. Therefore, just as Scripture said, on the "day of the Lord" the heavens pass away with a roar and the elements will be destroyed with intense heat, and the earth and its works will be burned up. All this takes place at the end of the day, but as Scripture indicates, still on the day. I must say, trying to understand and reconcile what appear to be contradictions in descriptions of "the day of the Lord" is difficult. Comprehending challenging passages requires keeping in mind other relevant teachings of the Word of God pertaining to the topic I am grappling with.

We know He saves us from the wrath to come. We also read that "your wrath came" when the seventh angel sounded his trumpet. We know from Revelation 19 Jesus comes back to wage war, to destroy the beast and the false prophet, and his armies. Jesus has His armies with Him, clothed in fine linen, white and clean. We the saints are His armies. After He completes the destruction of the beast and the false prophet, ending the dominion of the antichrist-beast, we find that some mortals were allowed an extension of life. We learn this from Daniel 7: [11]**"Then I kept looking because of the sound of the boastful words which the horn was speaking; I kept looking until the beast was slain, and its body was destroyed and given to the burning fire.** [12]**"As for the rest of the beasts,** ***their dominion was taken away, but an extension of life was granted to them for an appointed period of time.*** **(Daniel 7:11–12)** This informs us that the final world ruler, the antichrist-beast, and his dominion was destroyed, having been cast into the lake of fire. However, Scripture reveals to us here that there are those to whom an extension of life was granted, so there are survivors. The passage from Daniel uses the word "beasts," but we have been told by Scripture in Daniel that beasts are kings, and their dominions are their empires. These are mortal men who remain alive after the wrath of God was poured out and the subsequent war which Jesus together with His saints waged on earth. The Lord and His saints reign over these mortals. We know the saints are now immortal. This period of Jesus's reign lasts for one thousand years and is known as the millennium. Then Satan is released from the abyss where he had been bound to deceive the nations and gather them for one last battle against the Lord and His saints. God destroys these rebels with fire from heaven. Then the "day of the Lord," having been a thousand years in duration, comes to a close with the final event being *the destruction of the present heavens and the earth by fire*, in which the earth and all living mortal men are burned up with intense heat.

The Second Resurrection and the Judgment of the Unsaved

Next comes the resurrection of all "the rest of the dead." These stand before the great white throne judgment, and all who did not have their names in the book of life were thrown into the lake of fire. **5The rest of the dead did not come to life until the thousand years were completed. *This is the first resurrection.*** (The "first resurrection" refers back to the reference in verse four that those who were beheaded in the great tribulation for their testimony of God came to life and reigned with Christ for a thousand years). **4And I saw thrones, and they sat on them, and judgment was committed to them. Then I saw the souls of those who had been beheaded for their witness to Jesus and for the word of God, who had not worshiped the beast or his image, and had not received his mark on their foreheads or on their hands. And they lived and reigned with Christ for a thousand years. (NKJV) 11Then I saw a great white throne and Him who sat on it, from whose face the earth and the heaven fled away. And there was found no place for them. 12And I saw the dead, small and great, standing before God,**

and books were opened. And another book was opened, which is the Book of Life. And the dead were judged according to their works, by the things which were written in the books. (NKJV) Revelation 20:15 (NKJV) [15]**And anyone not found written in the Book of Life was cast into the lake of fire. (Revelation 20:5, 4, 11-12, 15) (NKJV)** (Words in parentheses are mine.)

How Does God Protect His Saints

How does God protect His saints from these terrifying events as the seals are opened, and the trumpets are sounded? It certainly is the case that for some men, the events that unfold from the opening of the sixth seal and through the seven trumpets will be terrifying. Before we come to any conclusions, let's see what Scripture reveals about how the saints might come safely through this time, yet still be waiting for the Lord to gather us to Himself.

Continuing our examination of how we are protected, an example of this protection in the interim by God is clear as we examine what follows immediately after the sixth seal was opened. We find ourselves in Revelation 7; this is where 144,000 of the tribes of Israel *are sealed.* We learn in Revelation 9:4 that this serves *to protect them* from the demonic locusts: [4] **They were commanded not to harm the grass of the earth, or any green thing, or any tree, but only those men who *do not* have *the seal of God* on their foreheads. (Revelation 9:4)** *Only those men without the seal of God will be harmed.* The *seal of God* protects those whom He chose to have sealed. The saints *chosen* of God in Christ Jesus *have already been sealed.* This sealing will protect us as well, just as God's seal will protect those of the tribes of Israel. We read in Ephesians: [4]***just as He chose us in Him before the foundation***

***of the world,* that we would be holy and blameless before Him. In love [5]He predestined us to adoption as sons through Jesus Christ to Himself, according to the kind intention of His will, [6]to the praise of the glory of His grace, which He freely bestowed on us in the Beloved. (Ephesians 1:4–6) [13] And you also were included in Christ when you heard the message of truth, the gospel of your salvation. When you believed, *you were marked in him with a seal, the promised Holy Spirit,* [14] who is a deposit guaranteeing our inheritance until the redemption of those who are God's possession—to the praise of his glory. (Ephesians 1:13-14) (NIV)** Again, in another version: **[13] In Him you also trusted, after you heard the word of truth, the gospel of your salvation; in whom also, having believed, *you were sealed* with the Holy Spirit of promise, [14] who is the guarantee of our inheritance until the redemption of the purchased possession, to the praise of His glory. (NKJV)** In addition to protecting us, this seal is a guarantee of our inheritance, until Jesus comes, and we are redeemed. This guarantee is spoken of also in 2 Corinthians where we again read of our being sealed: **[21] Now He who establishes us with you in Christ and has anointed us is God, [22] *who also has sealed us* and given us the Spirit in our hearts *as a guarantee.* (2 Corinthians 1:21-22) (NKJV)** In the New International Version we read: **[21] Now it is God who makes both us and you stand firm in Christ. He anointed us, [22] *set his seal of ownership on us*, and put his Spirit in our hearts as a deposit, *guaranteeing what is to come.* (NIV)**

We have observed when *loud voices in heaven announced the coming of God's wrath.* This happened right after we were gathered by the angels ("raptured" in current jargon) and taken to heaven. Let us now see if it is possible for the Lord to rescue us from unbelievably terrifying events that *some call* the coming wrath of God, and to do it without coming to rapture the saints before the great tribulation. While we just observed that He does rescue us just before the wrath of God is poured out on the earth, He does not spare us from trials and suffering in the great tribulation, and we examined why He does this.

It helps to examine some history of how He has dealt with His people, and you will find this to be very reassuring. Consider what the people of Israel had to endure when they were enslaved in Egypt. After much suffering, God sent Moses to rescue them. But they still had to be in the land and endure while the plagues were going on around them that God brought through Moses on the Egyptians. But they were themselves not harmed by the plagues. So, we see precedent for God protecting His saints amid plagues. God told us in Exodus what His purpose was when He hardened the heart of Pharoah, so he continued to refuse to let the people go. I believe just as God protected Israel from the plagues in Egypt in ancient times, He will protect his saints in the end time. To better understand this, study for a moment the table that follows below. The table compares events that occur during the time the seven trumpets are blown in Revelation to the Plagues in Egypt as recorded in Exodus.

Trumpet Events in Revelation Compared to Plagues on Egypt[2]

---

2 (Source: The table above is from the "Book of Revelation Study Guide," by Mike Bickle, page 40.)

Trumpet events			**Plagues on Egypt**
1st: hail with fire	Rev. 8:7	7th: hail with fire	Ex. 9:22-26
3rd: rivers turn bitter	Rev. 8:8-11	1st: Nile turns to blood	Ex. 7: 19-25
4th: darkness	Rev. 8:12	9th: darkness	Ex. 10:21-23
5th: demonic locusts	Rev. 9:1-12	8th: natural locusts	Ex. 10:12-20
6th: widespread death	Rev. 9:13-21	10th: widespread death	Ex. 12:29-30

You see there are direct parallels in the events during the seven trumpet blasts, leading up to the Lord's return at the seventh trumpet, and the plagues on Egypt, leading up to the deliverance of Israel by God through Moses. I present this because it is not a coincidence. God caused the parallels to exist for a reason, so we see His protection for His people then and trust Him to protect His saints during this period. I point out that God protected and preserved all the children of Israel during the plagues in Egypt, and so it will be that He will protect His saints from these events described in Revelation. With the sounding of the first trumpet, there is hail. When the Lord sent hail on all the land of Egypt, read how he protected the sons of Israel: **"Only in the land of Goshen, where the sons of Israel were, there was no hail." (Exodus 9:26)** When the fourth angel sounded his trumpet, the Lord sent darkness. When the Lord sent darkness so great that it could be felt over all the land of Egypt, read how he protected Israel: **"They did not see one another, nor did anyone rise from his place for three days, *but all the sons of Israel had light in their dwellings.*" (Exodus 10:23)** The point is, *He does not have to gather us off the earth before this time for us to be safe*. We will still be on the earth and be safe. Some teachers call these events the wrath of God. However, just because they declare something to be His wrath does not make it so. They go on to say this must be proof of a rapture before these events, even though there is no evidence of one. We have seen when Scripture told us the wrath came, and it was immediately after the rapture at the last (seventh) trumpet. Some who argue for a mid-tribulation rapture have labeled the things that happen during the trumpet blasts "trumpet judgments" but Scripture does not proclaim these events to be judgments from God. Nonetheless, these events may still be the judgment of God. We will read shortly that Scripture says, "judgement begins with the household of God."

We have seen that numerous parallels exist between these events and the plagues of Egypt, and God's people were protected through all of those. Therefore, I believe God will protect His people during this time. It is clear that very many saints, perhaps most, will be killed for the Word of God and their testimony of Jesus. This death of His saints comes at the hand of man, not from God. We are blessed for this and rewarded. This next passage from Revelation 14 is not in chronological order with Revelation chapters 4-11. It provides a look back to a time prior to Revelation 11:15 when the saints are raptured. It warns against worshiping the beast (the antichrist) or taking his mark. It makes it clear that the consequence of refusing to take the mark of the beast may be death, and if we are appointed to be killed for our testimony we will be blessed as a result. Note especially verse 13 in the following passage.

[9]Then another angel, a third one, followed them, saying with a loud voice, "If anyone worships the beast and his image, and receives a mark on his forehead or on his hand, [10]he also will drink of the wine of the wrath of God, which is mixed in full strength in the cup of His anger; and he will be tormented with fire and brimstone in the presence of the holy angels and in the presence of the Lamb. [11]"And the smoke of their torment goes up forever and ever; they have no rest day and night, those who worship the beast and his image, and whoever receives the mark of his name." [12]Here is the perseverance of the saints who keep the commandments of God and their faith in Jesus. [13]And I heard a voice from heaven, saying, "Write, '*Blessed are the dead who die in the Lord from now on*!' " "Yes," says the Spirit, "so that they may rest from their labors, for their deeds follow with them." (Revelation 14:9–13) In chapter one we examined why God will allow His saints, His bride, to suffer and die in this time. Remember the Word in James: **"Blessed is a man who perseveres under trial; for once he has been approved, he will receive the crown of life which the Lord has promised to those who love Him." (James 1:12)**

God does not bring His wrath on the unbelieving world until the seventh angel sounds. However, *judgment, but not wrath, on the household of God* may very well begin before that. Consider what is said in 1 Peter 4: **[17] For *it is time for judgment to begin with God's household;* and if it begins with us, what will the outcome be for those who do not obey the gospel of God? [18] And, "*If it is hard for the righteous to be saved*, what will become of the ungodly and the sinner?" [19] So then, *those who suffer according to God's will* should commit themselves to their faithful Creator and continue to do good. (1 Peter 4:17-19)** Does it say Christians will not be subject to judgment? No, it says judgment *begins* *with the house of God, with us.* We are already *judged righteous with regard to sin and salvation.* We have been given Christ Jesus's righteousness through faith in His death and resurrection. But *we are judged with regard to rewards.* We just read that we are saved, *but with difficulty.* The question is asked, if it is with difficulty that we are saved, then what about the ungodly and the sinner? Does it say we will not suffer? Quite the contrary, for it says "Therefore, *those who suffer according to the will of God* shall entrust their souls to a faithful Creator in doing what is right." Given this warning, we should prepare our hearts and minds to persevere and endure to the end so as to be saved. Jesus did say to one church, the church at Philadelphia, or **"Because you have kept My command to persevere, I also will keep you from the hour of trial which shall come upon the whole world, to test those who dwell on the earth." (Revelation 3:10)** Aside from the fact that He only said this *to one church out of seven,* you read something into this Scripture if you take it to mean that He raptures you before this hour of trial. It does not say that explicitly. Be careful not to try to make Scripture say what you want it to, for you may then find yourself believing something that is contradicted by other Scripture. We may be protected from the hour of trial in any number of ways, including death.

Neither judgment nor tribulation is wrath. Persecution and trials are not wrath. We saw in chapter one, Scripture tells us that when we suffer persecutions and afflictions and we persevere and endure them, it is evidence, a plain indication of God's righteous judgment so that we will be considered worthy of the kingdom of God, for which indeed we are suffering.

Those who teach either a pre-tribulation or mid-tribulation view both accurately point out that the Scripture tells us that "we are not appointed unto wrath." But they inaccurately label these events as God's wrath, and then conclude that the Lord must rapture us to rescue us before His wrath. I agree, He does rescue us from God's wrath, and He showed us that He gathers us before the coming of His wrath. What they are failing to discern is that what they call wrath is not wrath at all.

Also, we see from the Scripture that when Jesus returns, it is with a *trumpet* sound. What does the reference to the trumpet tell us? Both in the words of Jesus and of the apostles, we see that when the Lord does return, *there is a trumpet sound associated with the event.* Ask yourself, in either the pre-tribulation or mid-tribulation view, why do teachers of these theories just ignore the many verses that inform us His return is accompanied by the sound of a trumpet? You will see that this is part of Scripture that must be fulfilled. We will see that just as Jesus fulfilled the feast of Passover, He will also fulfill the feast of Trumpets. Jesus said in Matthew 24:31: **"And He will send His angels *with a great sound of a trumpet,* and *they will gather together His elect* from the four winds, from one end of heaven to the other. (Matthew 24:31) [16]"For the Lord Himself will descend from heaven with a shout, with the voice of the archangel and *with the trumpet of God*, and the dead in Christ will rise first." (1 Thessalonians 4:16)** So, we read that when the Lord returns, among other things it will be with a trumpet sound, the trumpet of God (verse 16). We learned this is the "last trumpet" from reading 1 Corinthians 15:51-52: [51] **"Behold, I tell you a mystery; we will not all sleep, but we will all be changed, [52] in a moment, in the twinkling of an eye, *at the last trumpet; for the trumpet will sound*, and the dead will be raised imperishable, and we will be changed." (1 Corinthians 15:51-52)** So, we know that the trumpet that sounds is called "the last trumpet." That means there are no other trumpets to sound after it because it is the last. To be last, it must be included in a series of other trumpets. When we read Revelation chapter 8 and following about the seven trumpets that are blown, we can be confident that the Lord has not returned during six of these, because none of them is the last trumpet. We know His believers are still on earth for the events that unfold as each one of these six are blown. We can also be sure that the Lord returns at the seventh trumpet because it is the last; there are no other trumpets recorded in the Bible after that one. Once again let's look more closely at what the Word says about the events that accompany the blowing of the seventh trumpet. We read in Revelation 10: [7] **"but in the days of the sounding of the seventh angel, when he is about to sound, the mystery of God would be finished, as He declared to His servants the prophets." (Revelation 10:7)** Next, we read in Revelation 11 that the seventh trumpet is blown. [15] **"Then *the seventh angel sounded*: And there were loud voices in heaven, saying, "*The kingdoms of this world have become the kingdoms of our Lord and of His Christ*, and He shall reign forever and ever!" (Revelation 11:15)** Doesn't this event signal the very thing that all Christians are waiting for? Christ at this point has now become King and Lord of the kingdoms of this world! Was this not just announced at the seventh trumpet, the last trumpet? We observed previously that the next few verses announce, "and your wrath came." [18]**"And the nations were enraged, and Your wrath came, and the time came for the dead to be judged,** ***and the time to reward Your bond-servants the prophets and the saints and those who fear Your name*****, the small and the great, and to destroy those who destroy the earth." (Revelation 11:18)** In addition to the announcement of the start of His wrath, we see *this is the time to reward the saints*. The saints are at this very point raptured and gathered to the Lord in the clouds at the seventh and last trumpet *before* his wrath was poured out.

Reassurance for Christians

Let me provide you with reassurance that the Lord saves His people. The Word tells us [9]"**For *God has not destined us for wrath*, but for obtaining salvation through our Lord Jesus Christ," (1 Thessalonians 5:9)** Another is also from 1 Thessalonians where we read: [10]**and to wait for His Son from heaven, whom He raised from the dead, that is *Jesus, who rescues us from the wrath to come.* (1 Thessalonians 1:10)**

Despite these assurances, Scripture provides us with many exhortations telling us we must endure to the end, that it is the one who endures that will be saved. Jesus told us with regard to the time before His coming for us, [33]**"Whoever seeks to keep his life will lose it, and whoever loses his life will preserve it. (Luke 17:33)** The following passage is exactly the reason I have authored this book. I want my fellow brothers and sisters in Christ to prepare themselves and have a mindset to remain steadfast in their faith should they be alive when the great tribulation begins. It would be a terrible mistake to think you will escape having to endure to the end by expecting to be raptured beforehand. The Scripture just does not teach this. [34] **"But take heed to yourselves, lest your hearts be weighed down with carousing, drunkenness, *and cares of this life*, and *that Day* come on you unexpectedly. [35] For it will come as a snare on all those who dwell on the face of the whole earth. [36] "But keep on the alert at all times, *praying that you may have strength to escape all these things that are about to take place*, and to stand before the Son of Man." (Luke 21:34-36)** I frequently pray this just as Jesus has instructed here in verse 36, and urge you to do so as well.

I believe many people just *want* to believe in a pre-tribulation or mid-tribulation coming of the Lord to rescue them so they will not have to think about enduring this great tribulation that Scripture says will be unlike any ever before or ever again. But that is not what Scripture teaches. There is still more in Scripture to confirm when the Lord returns.

Post-Tribulation

We just saw that the Lord returns, and the angels gather His elect *at the sound of a great trumpet*. We saw that Christians are taken off the earth at the seventh trumpet, which is the last trumpet. The saints go to heaven with the Lord Christ Jesus, I believe for *a brief time*, before returning with Him back to the earth. All saints, both the dead who arose and those still alive at His second coming *will at this time receive immortal bodies*. (This is detailed in 1 Corinthians 15:52-53) Then a brief time later, at the conclusion of the bowls of wrath, the saints return with Jesus to earth. He wages war against the antichrist-beast and destroys him by casting him and the false prophet into the lake of fire. Then He begins His thousand-year reign on earth, and we reign with Him. Recall what we just read in Revelation 11:15, at the blowing of the seventh and last trumpet, it states: "The kingdoms of this world have become the kingdoms of our Lord and of His Christ," (NKJV) so Christ at this very point is now proclaimed to take possession of the kingdoms of this world. He will reign here, on this earth and the saints will reign with Him. Reviewing again what has been shown before, the day of the Lord *begins at the same time the saints are raptured.* While we are in heaven, during this period the wrath of God is poured out on the earth. The "day of the Lord" means *wrath for those on earth* and it means rescue to the saints who are gathered and go with Jesus to Heaven.

I acknowledge that to hold on to a view of Scripture that supports a pre-tribulation rapture is more comfortable than one which teaches that we must endure the tribulation if we are alive when it occurs. But as you will see from studying this subject intently, the comfortable view, in this case, is not supported by Scripture.

When Does the Rapture Occur?

What does *Jesus* say about *when* the elect will be gathered, before, during, or after the great tribulation? Matthew 24 gives us a clear answer. [29] ***"Immediately after the tribulation of those days*** **the sun will be darkened, and the moon will not give its light; the stars will fall from heaven, and the powers of the heavens will be shaken.** [30] **Then the sign of the Son of Man will appear in heaven, and then all the tribes of the earth will mourn, and they will see the Son of Man coming on the clouds of heaven with power and great glory.** [31] ***And He will send His angels with a great sound of a trumpet,*** **and they will gather together His elect from the four winds, from one end of heaven to the other. (Matthew 24:29-31)** To summarize what we have observed in Scripture thus far: Jesus said, "after the tribulation of those days" and at "the sound of a great trumpet." That is when the elect will be gathered. This is the *last trumpet* as described in Scripture. When the seventh angel sounds, the Scripture states plainly in the very next verse that this is when the kingdoms of this world become the kingdoms of our Lord and of His Christ. It told us also that *this is the time to reward the saints*.

Scripture has told us outright some things that must occur before Christ Jesus can return. An *apostasy must occur*, a widespread falling away from the faith. The man of lawlessness, the son of perdition (*the antichrist*) must first appear before the Lord comes to gather His saints. When the antichrist appears, we are in the final seven years before Jesus returns for His saints. You will learn more about the antichrist in chapter 7, who Scripture calls a *beast,* in the section on the antichrist in this book.

The falling away is what is referred to by Jesus in Matthew 24 as He is explaining the signs of His return to His disciples. We just read in Matthew 24 that Jesus told us it would be *immediately after the tribulation of those days when He would send His angels to gather His saints*. Now we look at what Jesus said in the verses leading up to that statement. [10] **"At that time *many will turn away from the faith* and will betray and hate each other, [11] and *many false prophets will appear and deceive many people.* [12] Because of the increase of wickedness, the *love of most will grow cold,* [13] but *the one who stands firm to the end will be saved.*" (Matthew 24:10-13) (NIV)** Jesus tells us plainly that we must endure and stand firm to the end. It is helpful to read this same warning in the New King James Version: [11] **"Then many false prophets will rise up and deceive many. [12] And because lawlessness will abound, the love of many will grow cold. [13] *But he who endures to the end shall be saved.*" (Matthew 24:11-13 NKJV)** This period will be so bad that Jesus told us even family members will betray us, resulting in our death. [12]**"Brother will betray brother to death, and a father his child; and children will rise up against parents and have them put to death. (Mark 13:12)** Not only must we endure the tribulation and persecution, but we are warned *not to be deceived by false prophets*. The false prophets of the Old Testament proclaimed a message of "peace and safety" in contrast to those who truly spoke for God who warned the people about extremely hard things to come. We must not be taken in by those who ignore God's Word and proclaim a different message. Scripture warns us, **"[3]For the time will come when they will not**

endure sound doctrine; but wanting to have their ears tickled, they will accumulate for themselves teachers in accordance to their own desires." (2 Timothy 4:3)

Jesus tells us here the one who endures to the end shall be saved. The idea that Christians get "raptured" before these trials negates the words of Jesus here. It also contradicts the teaching of Jesus in the parable of the ten virgins from Matthew 25.

A Look Back Two Thousand Years Ago

Revelation 12, 13, and 14 are a departure from the chapters that lead up to them. They are not in chronological order with the previous chapters. These chapters instead give us a view that takes us back to previous events in history and move forward from there to future events which will occur. For example, we look back to the birth of Christ and in one verse summarize His earthly time and return to heaven. **"[5]And she gave birth to a son, a male child, who is to rule all the nations with a rod of iron; and her child was caught up to God and to His throne." (Revelation 12:5)** We read in Revelation 14 that Babylon the great has fallen, and we are even at this point still being given an account of past events. **[8]And another angel, a second one, followed, saying, "Fallen, fallen is Babylon the great, she who has made all the nations drink of the wine of the passion of her immorality." (Revelation 14:8)** We know this must take place before the gathering of the saints in Revelation 11:15, because the people of God had to still be present when Babylon the Great was destroyed, otherwise we would not be been warned in Revelation 18:4 to "come out of her, My people" if God was going to take them out by the rapture. "**[4]I heard another voice from heaven, saying, "Come out of her, my people, so that you will**

not participate in her sins and receive of her plagues;" (Revelation 18:4) (You may read full details about this event in the back of this book, in appendix 5 regarding America in the end times.) We know the gathering of the saints by Jesus occurred at the seventh trumpet, which occurred in the middle of Revelation 11. These chapters serve to give us more detail about the events that lead up to the rescue of the saints when the Lord Jesus comes for us and to reinforce our need to endure to the end. Then in Revelation 15:1, Scripture resumes unfolding the wrath of God: **I saw in heaven another great and marvelous sign: seven angels with the seven last plagues—last, because with them God's wrath is completed. (Revelation 15:1)**

The good news is we are not there. God spares us from His wrath, but not from suffering or possible death for our faith in Christ. We see this plainly stated in Scripture. Jesus rescues us from the wrath of God. Again, remember this encouragement we find in 1 Thessalonians 1: [10] **and to wait for his Son from heaven, whom he raised from the dead—Jesus, *who rescues us from the coming wrath*. (1 Thessalonians 1:10)** Jesus sends his angels to gather us at the seventh trumpet, before the wrath begins, rescuing us from it. We are gathered to Him and transformed into our new bodies.

The last portion of 1 Corinthians 15 describes this transformation. [42]**So also is the resurrection of the dead. It is sown a perishable body, *it is raised an imperishable body*;** (after the resurrection, we are imperishable, immortal, we cannot die again) [43]**it is sown in dishonor, it is raised in glory; it is sown in weakness, it is raised in power; [44]it is sown a natural body, it is raised a spiritual body. If there is a natural body, there is also a spiritual body. [51]Behold, I tell you a mystery;**

we will not all sleep (we will not all die)**, but we will all be changed, [52]in a moment, in the twinkling of an eye,** ***at the last trumpet*****; for the trumpet will sound** (this is the moment when the Lord comes and gathers His saints)**,** ***and the dead will be raised imperishable, and we will be changed.*** **[53]For this perishable must put on the imperishable, and this mortal must put on immortality. (1 Corinthians 15:42–44; 51–53)** (My explanation in parentheses) All the saints, those who had previously died, and those remaining, are in a moment, in the twinkling of an eye, changed. We are together caught up to meet the Lord in the air. He then takes us to heaven for the marriage supper of the Lamb. While we are with Him in heaven, the wrath of God is poured out on the earth. This is when the Lord judges the ungodly on the earth and deals out retribution to them.

We reviewed in chapter one that Scripture explains to us why God has the saints endure persecution and even death. This applies to all saints who suffered trials and persecution during the centuries before the very end, and to those in the great tribulation as well. It is to demonstrate our perseverance and faith. It shows that we are worthy of the kingdom of God, for this is why we are suffering. Scripture informs us this demonstrates that God is just when He imposes righteous judgement on those who afflicted His people, and informs us this happens when the Lord Jesus is revealed from heaven.

What happens next? Jesus returns to earth with His armies (the saints) following behind Him. He throws the antichrist-beast and the false prophet into the lake of fire. He subdues those who were not killed during the period when the wrath of God was poured out on all who dwell on the earth. He is coming to reign over all the nations, over all the peoples of the earth. He will rule them with a rod of iron. He will reign for a thousand years, and we, His saints reign with Him.

Will a Special Group of Saints Reign with Jesus on Earth?

In the following we read in Revelation 19:11-21 more specifics about the return of the Lord to reign and what He does upon His return: (my words are in parentheses.) A question often arises when considering the Scripture that we examined in Revelation 20:4-5 dealing with the statement that "those who had been beheaded… rose and reigned with Jesus for a thousand years." The question is "do only an elite group of 'unique saints,' just those who were beheaded in the great tribulation and did not take the mark of the beast, rise to reign with Jesus at this time?" The answer is no. All saints, both Old and New Testament saints, rise in this first resurrection. Would it be likely that the Lord would exclude the apostles who were martyred because they do not fit the description of being beheaded and not taking the mark of the beast? Is it likely He would exclude John the Baptist, who was beheaded, but did not live in the great tribulation period in the end to not take the mark of the beast? In Matthew 19: Peter is asking what reward will they, His disciples have. (We know this from the context.) [27] **Then Peter answered and said to Him, "See, we have left all and followed You. Therefore what shall we have?"** [28] **So Jesus said to them, "Assuredly I say to you, that in the regeneration, when the Son of Man sits on the throne of His glory, you who have followed Me will also sit on twelve thrones, judging the twelve tribes of Israel. (Matthew 19:27-28)** The answer is all twelve will reign with Him on thrones, including John who was not appointed to martyrdom. So, it is with all believers. All rise in the first resurrection when the seventh angel sounds, not just those who were martyred by beheading. This includes Noah, Abraham, and Job. And Moses, Elijah, Daniel, Samuel, and King David. Would the Lord exclude all the saints who were burned at the stake for their faith, but because they were not beheaded, they don't qualify? No, all the saints are with Him in His millennial reign on the earth.

Why does the Word inform us specifically that those beheaded for not taking the mark of the beast rise from the dead and reign with Christ? When Scripture states in Revelation 20:4-5 that *this is the first resurrection* and gives the specifics telling us that *those who died by beheading when the beast (the antichrist) was on the earth* arose in this first resurrection to reign with Christ for the thousand years, it was for a purpose. It eliminates any possibility that a prior resurrection and rapture has occurred. Otherwise, it could not be said "this is the first resurrection."

So, there has been no rapture, no catching up in the air of saints who were alive until this event. That means all the saints still alive when the great tribulation begins must endure through the time the beast is on the earth forcing the entire world to worship him and his image. No one will be able to buy or sell without the mark of the beast. Most will be killed for refusing the mark. It is crucial to understand correctly what Scripture teaches regarding the Lord's return and the gathering of the saints. While we have touched on this previously, it is worth revisiting here. In Revelation 14:9, we are warned about taking the mark of the beast. [9] **"Then a third angel followed them, saying with a loud voice, "If anyone worships the beast and his image, and receives his mark on his forehead or on his hand, [10] he himself shall also drink of the wine of the wrath of God, which is poured out full strength into the cup of His indignation. He shall be tormented with fire and**

brimstone in the presence of the holy angels and in the presence of the Lamb. [11] And the smoke of their torment ascends forever and ever; and they have no rest day or night, who worship the beast and his image, and whoever receives the mark of his name." ***[12]Here is the perseverance of the saints who keep the commandments of God and their faith in Jesus.*** **[13] Then I heard a voice from heaven saying to me, "Write: '*Blessed are the dead who die in the Lord from now on.*'" "Yes," says the Spirit, "that they may rest from their labors, and their works follow them." (Revelation 14:9-13)** No one who takes the mark of the beast can be saved.

By now, we should be clearly of the mind that we must not deny Christ. We must be prepared to give up our lives for our faith in Him.

chapter SIX Unfulfilled Prophecies

Can Jesus Return at Any Moment?

The Bible provides quite a bit of detail regarding what things will occur in the "time of the end" right before the Lord Christ Jesus returns to gather His saints to Himself when we "meet Him in the air." It can be difficult to put all the passages together and arrive at a point of clarity, however. So let me begin by stating plainly what I hope to show from the Scriptures about what we can expect to unfold.

Unfulfilled Prophecies that Must Be Fulfilled Before Jesus Comes Back

I believe the Lord has given believers some events that must happen, or "dominoes that must fall," to watch for as the end of time and the return of our Lord Christ Jesus draws near. Some are obvious because He has told us outright what they are. An apostasy must occur, a falling away from the faith. The apostasy must occur before Christ Jesus returns for His saints. This is referred to by Jesus in Matthew as He is explaining the signs of His return to His disciples: **11 "Then many false prophets will rise up and deceive many.** (False prophets lie, and their message is contrary to what God really has in store. They say, "peace and safety, don't be concerned." However, in the final seven-year period before the Lord returns, we know there will be a false prophet who causes people to worship the beast, the antichrist.) **12 And because lawlessness will**

abound, ***the love of many will grow cold.*** (He is referring to the apostasy, the great falling away from the faith.) **13 But he who endures to the end shall be saved." (Matthew 24:11-13 NKJV)** (Words in parentheses are mine.) It should be noted that both the NIV and the NASB verse 12 above reads "the love of *most* will grow cold." Jesus tells us here the one who endures to the end shall be saved. The idea that Christians get "raptured" before these trials negates the words of Jesus here. Ask yourself, why would he say "the one who endures to the end shall be saved" if the saints are not going to be there to have to endure? There will be wars, earthquakes, famines, and pestilence in various places. But the end is not yet. **4 "And Jesus answered and said to them: "Take heed that no one deceives you.** 5 **For many will come in My name, saying, 'I am the Christ,' and will deceive many.** 6 **And you will hear of wars and rumors of wars. See that you are not troubled; for all these things must come to pass,** ***but the end is not yet.*** 7 **For nation will rise against nation, and kingdom against kingdom. And there will be famines, pestilences, and earthquakes in various places.** 8 **All these** ***are*** **the beginning of sorrows." (Matthew 24: 4-8)** Therefore, we are to be on guard against false Christs. People will claim to be the Lord, and many will be taken in. But these events are "birth pangs," the beginning of sorrows. More will have to happen. We also know the antichrist-beast must be revealed. Scripture refers to him in different ways, also calling him "the man of lawlessness, the son of perdition." **3 "Let no one deceive you by any means; for** ***that Day will not come unless the falling away comes first, and the man of sin is revealed, the son of perdition, 4 who opposes and exalts himself above all that is called God or that is worshiped,*** **so that he sits as God in the temple of God, showing himself that he is God." (2 Thessalonians 2:3-4)**

We also know from Scripture that in addition to multiple false prophets, there is a unique false prophet who arises in the time of the antichrist. He performs great signs and can call down fire from heaven in the presence of men and causes people to worship the antichrist. He causes men to make an image of the antichrist and has power to give breath to the image so that it can speak. Anyone who will not worship the image of the antichrist he can cause to be killed. We read of this individual in Revelation 13: [11]**Then I saw another beast coming up out of the earth; and he had two horns like a lamb and he spoke as a dragon.** [12]**He exercises all the authority of the first beast in his presence. And he makes the earth and those who dwell in it to worship the first beast, whose fatal wound was healed.** [13]**He performs great signs, so that he even makes fire come down out of heaven to the earth in the presence of men.** [14]**And he deceives those who dwell on the earth because of the signs which it was given him to perform in the presence of the beast, telling those who dwell on the earth to make an image to the beast who had the wound of the sword and has come to life.** [15]**And it was given to him to give breath to the image of the beast, so that the image of the beast would even speak and cause as many as do not worship the image of the beast to be killed. (Revelation 13:11–15)** True disciples of Jesus will know that we must only worship God or His son, Jesus. For this reason, it seems highly likely most believers will be killed during this time for their testimony of God and of His son Jesus.

Before Christ returns, there are some other events that also must occur first. These are last days events involving the fates of nations and are contained in prophecy. Clues to these are contained in Daniel chapters 7, 8 and 11 and Revelation chapter 17.

Dual Fulfillment of Prophecy

Before we look at these prophecies, especially the ones from Daniel, I want to explain the occurrence of what may be referred to as "dual fulfillment" of some of the prophecies in Scripture. An example of this concept of "dual fulfillment" is found in Acts. On the day of Pentecost, when the Holy Spirit that Jesus had promised was given, Peter speaks to those assembled and quotes from the Prophet Joel to explain what was occurring. He quotes from Joel 2:28-31, and we find his words in Acts 2:17-21: **17 'And it shall be in the last days,' God says, 'That *I will pour forth of My Spirit on all mankind*; And your sons and your daughters shall prophesy, And your young men shall see visions, And your old men shall dream dreams; 18 Even on My bondslaves, both men and women, I will in those days pour forth of My Spirit And they shall prophesy. 19 'And I will grant wonders in the sky above And signs on the earth below, Blood, and fire, and vapor of smoke. 20 '*The sun will be turned into darkness And the moon into blood*, Before the great and glorious day of the Lord shall come. 21 'And it shall be that everyone who calls on the name of the Lord will be saved.' (Acts 2:17–21)** We see that the Holy Spirit promised in Joel was in fact given on the day of Pentecost as recorded in Acts chapter two. But the later portion of that prophecy, referring to "the sun will be turned into darkness and the moon into blood" recorded both in Joel and Acts has yet to be fulfilled. So, we look for "dual fulfillment" of this prophecy when the remaining portion will be brought about by God.

Another example of this "dual fulfillment" is found when Jesus said in Matthew 17:11-12 regarding Elijah: [11] **"And He answered and said, "*Elijah is coming and will restore all things*; [12]*but I say to you that***

***Elijah already came*, and they did not recognize him, but did to him whatever they wished. So also the Son of Man is going to suffer at their hands." (Matthew 17:11–12)** Jesus had said previously that John is Elijah. [14]**"And if you are willing to accept it, *John himself is Elijah who was to come*." (Matthew 11:14)** Jesus was declaring that Scripture prophesying the return of Elijah had already been fulfilled in John the Baptist and that it also would be fulfilled again, as He said, "Elijah is coming and will restore all things."

Events Dealing with Iran (Persia)

So, bearing these examples in mind, as we study prophecy given over five-hundred years before Christ in Daniel chapter eight, I suggest that portions of it have already been fulfilled (with the overthrow of Persia by Alexander the Great and Greece) and yet, the angel Gabriel clearly told Daniel that this prophecy pertained to the time of the end. Therefore, I believe this prophecy will, as Gabriel indicated, have an end-time fulfillment also. Based on the Scripture, here is a summary of what I believe will yet unfold. After the summary, I will provide Scriptural support in detail. Based on Scripture, I believe events are likely to play out as follows:

Event 1: Iran (Persia) is called the Ram and will be center stage and will engage in military activity to enlarge their control over their region in the Middle East. Iran will militarily move and expand their control in three directions of the compass: west, north, and south, but not east. (Yes, Scripture is this specific.) They will take over Iraq, perhaps Syria, and countries to the north of their nation, possibly some or all of Turkmenistan, Azerbaijan, Armenia, possibly Uzbekistan and possibly part of eastern Turkey. They will likely take over some or all of Kuwait, Saudi Arabia,

Qatar, Bahrain, U.A.E., Oman, and Yemen. As this prophecy does not indicate that the Ram butts east, it will not increase its' control in the region in the direction of Pakistan, Afghanistan, or India. In contrast, the ancient Persian empire extended far eastward of present-day Iran, encompassing most of what is now Afghanistan and Pakistan.

Event 2: After Iran moves against its neighbors to the west, north, and south, it will in some way anger a power from the west (called the Goat) so greatly that it will respond militarily and defeat Iran. In the original language, this Goat is referred to as *Javan*, and is first encountered in the Bible in Genesis 10, where we also find Gomer, Tubal, Meshach, and Magog. We will explore this in detail. This could perhaps be America, or it could perhaps be England or Germany in alliance with France, Italy, and other European Union nations. It does not appear to be Israel.

Event 3: The fall of this leader. The head of this western power will be very powerful and grow more so and will be globally recognized, but when his power is at its height, then he will fall from power and the result will be a fracturing of his power leading to four separate less powerful nations or groups of nations who are no longer allied together.

Event 4: The rise of the antichrist, which Scripture calls a beast. From one of those nations (or alliance of nations), a new leader will emerge by intrigue and subtlety and will then go on to ultimately become the global ruler, the antichrist. (Questions often are asked regarding the United States in the Scriptures in end times. In Appendix 5 at the back of this book, we will examine Scripture that I believe pertains to America.) This new global leader who is none other than the antichrist will put together an alliance involving ten different nations. This new alliance under the influence of the antichrist will ultimately attack an influential, wealthy nation, one that is a primary market for the rest of the world's goods and devastate a number of its' largest cities. This nation is described as one which influences the rest of the world to engage in immorality. I believe as these events begin to unfold, the direction of things as foretold in Scripture will become increasingly clear to God's children, the saints who trust in our Lord Jesus for salvation. Scripture has instructions for us regarding what we are to do. These things will all happen *before the Lord Jesus returns to gather His saints*. Therefore, it is crucial to know what the Word instructs us to do, both from the standpoint of our attitude of persevering in faith and trust and about the action that we are advised we must take.

Words Concealed and Sealed Up until the Time of the End

To begin to understand these biblical prophecies, we will start with a study of passages in the book of Daniel. The Bible tells us these things have been *concealed until the time of the end.* But Scripture also tells us at that time that *the wise will understand.* [4]**"But as for you, Daniel, *conceal these words and seal up the book until the end of time*; many will go back and forth, and knowledge will increase." (Daniel 12:4)** [9]**He said, "Go your way, Daniel, for *these words are concealed and sealed up until the end time.*" (Daniel 12:9)** But we are told in Daniel 12:10 "the wise will understand." **"Many shall be purified, and made white, and tried; but the wicked shall do wickedly: and none of the wicked shall understand*; but the wise shall understand.*" (Daniel 12:10)**

Daniel chapter eight provides the basis for the first domino that must fall, the aggression of Persia (Iran) at the time of the end as a military power. Note that fifty years ago, Iran had nowhere near the power that it is demonstrating today. Today they are enriching uranium for building nuclear warheads and are thought to be close to accomplishing that goal. They have a massive standing army, the largest in the region, which as of fall of 2021 was estimated to number in excess of 500,000 men.

Often commentators state that the events in Daniel 8 have already been fulfilled. But is it reasonable to conclude that all the prophecy contained in Daniel chapter eight has been fulfilled already, given the clear declarations from the angel Gabriel? In Daniel chapter eight, I want to first point out several verses. Look at verses 17 and 19. Verse 17 ends with the statement: **"Son of man, understand that *the vision pertains to the time of the end.*" (Daniel 8:17)** Verse 19 reads: **He said, "Behold, I am going to let you know what will occur at the final period of the indignation, for *it pertains to the appointed time of the end.*" (Daniel 8:19)** In the NIV, this reads "later in the time of wrath, because *the vision concerns the appointed time of the end.*" Further on, Daniel is commanded by the angel: **"But keep the vision secret, *for it pertains to many days in the future.*" (Daniel 12:26)** As already noted, further on in Daniel, in Chapter 12, verse 4, again Daniel is instructed: **"But as for you, Daniel, *conceal these words and seal up the book until the end of time*; *many will go back and forth, and knowledge will increase.*" (Daniel 12:4)** (Note that travel, "many going back and forth," has exploded like never before in human history with the advent of air travel, automobiles, etc. Also, "knowledge" has exponentially exploded worldwide through the sharing of information via the internet.) The Lord saw fit to tell us once again, just a few verses later, stating: **"Go your way, Daniel, for *these words are concealed and sealed up until the end time.*" "Many will be purged, purified and refined, but the wicked will act wickedly; and none of the wicked will understand,**

but *those who have insight will understand.*" (Daniel 12:9-10)

From the previous paragraph, let me call attention to two things. First, Daniel is told that the vision (in Chapter eight, of the ram and the goat) is about *the end of time*. It is called the *time of wrath* or *the final period of indignation*. It is called *the appointed time of the end.* However, Bible commentators have for many years opined that this prophecy was fulfilled when Alexander the Great defeated Persia and then died suddenly in his early 30s to be succeeded by four of his generals who took over his empire. This took place about 335 B.C. Now, let me ask you to consider this: would something that occurred before the time of Christ qualify as happening "at the end of time"? Was God pouring out His final indignation and wrath on the world before our Lord came the first time? The answer seems obvious that He was not, and this was not the end of time. Was it perhaps a special outpouring of wrath and indignation on Israel? No. Was it the end of time for Israel? Again, the answer is no on both counts. Therefore, I believe this is a prophecy that will, like others, be one of "dual fulfillment."

After our Lord's first appearance, the Romans overran Jerusalem and destroyed the second temple, slaughtering most of the Jewish inhabitants of the city around 70 AD. Some observers have called the Nazi Holocaust the "time of Jacob's Trouble." But since then, the Jews have regained their homeland, and begun returning there in large numbers. In light of these considerations, I find it impossible to interpret events that occurred before the time of Christ as a final fulfillment of the vision of the ram and the goat given to us in Daniel eight. Moreover, this very Scripture says of itself that it is sealed up and concealed until the end of time. Therefore, attempts to interpret it to fit events that occurred nearly two thousand three hundred years ago must be viewed through the proper lens of Scripture. If we are not yet in the time of the end, then even our current musings on the interpretation of these Scriptures will be futile, as they are still concealed and sealed up until that time arrives.

Why am I focusing so much on the issue of an interpretation of the vision of the ram and the goat being fulfilled before the time of Christ? I do so for two reasons. First, because the notes from commentators in many Bibles today dogmatically inform the reader that the fulfillment of this vision occurred when Alexander the Great and Greece overthrew the Persian Empire, about three hundred years before Christ, and most ignore the declarations that this vision pertains to the time of the end. That interpretation, I believe, does Christians a great disservice, because they are no longer looking to a future fulfillment of these Scriptures "at the time of the end" as God's messenger, the angel Gabriel, stated would be the case. Second, I believe examining these Scriptures with a fresh set of eyes is imperative because when those alive see the fulfilment of these passages, they will signal to believers here in America and in other parts of the world when the "time of the end" is upon us all.

Now, if we are to be granted understanding of these Scriptures which are sealed up and concealed until the time of the end, then we must be in the time of the end. What evidence do we have from Scripture that this may be the case? We have observed that travel is increased, and knowledge is increased. But those are not conclusive indications. They serve to eliminate the time before Christ, but not to confirm ours. But neither do they rule out our time.

Imagine for a moment that rather than living in the twenty-first century, we were alive during the civil war period in the middle of the nineteenth century. Suppose we read in Scripture that God was going to regather His people into the land He swore to give to Abraham and his descendants. We might be tempted to think He had already done that when He brought them back from Babylon after seventy years of captivity. This happened about five hundred years before Christ. Historical estimates are that there were only about 5,000 Jews living in the land of Israel at the beginning of the nineteenth century, and by 1850, their numbers were still estimated to be only 12,000 to 15,000. We would probably consider it very puzzling to think that God would bring them physically back to their land again, a second time.

Is Who Controls Jerusalem an End Time Sign?

I point you to Luke 21:7 and following. Jesus is asked by His disciples what will be the signs of His return. He tells them there will be wars and rumors of wars, but the end does not follow immediately. He says that nation will rise against nation, and kingdom against kingdom, and there will be great earthquakes, and in various places plagues and famines, and there will be terrors and great signs from heaven. Remember, Jesus said in this same passage, "Jerusalem will be trampled under foot of the Gentiles until the time of the Gentiles be fulfilled." We have touched on the significance of this statement already.

It helps to have an exceptionally long view of history as a perspective as we consider this. Before 1948, the Jews did not dwell in Israel in any significant way. According to historical estimates, only about 450,000 Jews lived in the land of Israel in 1940. In the years following 1940, their numbers increased significantly due to their persecution in Europe during World War II. In 1948, Israel was allowed to become a nation again on their land. They began being gathered from the nations where

God had scattered them, back into the land He gave to Abraham, in fulfillment of prophecy, setting the stage for the return of Jerusalem to Jewish control. Today, there are approximately sixteen million Jews worldwide, about half of whom live in Israel and most of the remainder live in America.

It will be also helpful for you to understand a little detail regarding the history of Israel. Israel was originally ruled over by a single king, Saul. Then David became king, and he eventually ruled over all the tribes of Israel. Likewise, his son Solomon ruled over all twelve tribes of Israel as one nation. However, in the time of Rehoboam, Solomon's son, the kingdom split, and the ten northern tribes set up their own monarchy and choose their own king. For hundreds of years, God's people were split into two kingdoms, the northern one still called Israel and the southern one called Judah. The ten northern tribes, called Israel were taken captive by the king of Assyria about 700 B.C. He took them away from their land and dispersed them through the lands of his kingdom. They were never allowed to return to the land of Israel. A century later, the two remaining southern tribes, now called Judah, were taken captive by king Nebuchadnezzar of Babylon, and removed from the land of Israel to the land of Babylon. However, they were allowed to return to the land of Israel as prophesied by Jeremiah, after seventy years of captivity. God declared in Scripture that He would gather all of His people from all the lands where they had been scattered, back to dwell in the land He had promised to Abraham. Here are several verses to reflect on: [37]**"Behold, I will gather them *out of all the lands*** (not just the land of Babylon) **to which I have driven them in My anger, in My wrath and in great indignation; and I will bring them back to this place *and make them dwell in safety*. (Jeremiah 32:37)** (Words in parentheses are mine.) (Do the people of Israel dwell in safety? Not yet.) [11]**Then it will happen on that day that the Lord will again recover *the second time* with His hand *The remnant of His people*, who will remain, from Assyria, Egypt, Pathros, Cush, Elam, Shinar, Hamath, And from the islands of the sea. (Isaiah 11:11)** Was the Lord only going to gather the captives that were taken to Babylon? No, He had a plan all along, to reunite all of Israel, so they would no longer be two nations. We note in verse 11 above that Scripture informs us the Lord will recover *the second time* with His hand the remnant of His people. The first time was when those in captivity in Babylon returned to Jerusalem and the land. The second time is yet to be completed but has been underway since 1948. Scripture informs us they will dwell in safety when this is completed. More is made clear when you read the next passage from Ezekiel: [16]**"And you, son of man, take for yourself *one stick* and write on it, '*For Judah and for the sons of Israel*, his companions'; *then take another stick* and write on it, '*For Joseph, the stick of Ephraim and all the house of Israel*, his companions.' [17]"*Then join them* for yourself one to another *into one stick*, that they may become one in your hand. [18]"When the sons of your people speak to you saying, 'Will you not declare to us what you mean by these?' [19]say to them, 'Thus says the Lord GOD, "Behold, I will take the *stick of Joseph*, which is in the hand of *Ephraim*, and the tribes of Israel, his companions; and I will put them with it, *with the stick of Judah*, and make them one stick, and *they will be one in My hand*." ' [20]"The sticks on which you write will be in your hand before their eyes. [21]"Say to them, 'Thus says the Lord GOD, "Behold, I will take the sons of Israel from among the nations where they have gone, and *I will gather them from every side and bring them into their own land;* [22]*and I will make them one nation***

***in the land, on the mountains of Israel*; and *one king will be king for all of them*; and *they will no longer be two nations and no longer be divided into two kingdoms*. (Ezekiel 37:16–22)** God has begun to fulfill this part of His Word, and He will bring it to completion. But in 1850, if you had read this, you may have thought it was a metaphor for something else. If you had been alive in the nineteenth century, and thought, "Jesus can return at any moment," obviously that did not prove to be the case. There was, among other prophecies, a prophecy that said God was going to regather His people into the land of Israel. People probably had all kinds of speculation about whether this prophecy about the regathering of His people was literal or metaphorical in nature. To have taken a literal view at that time would have been quite unusual. Yet in quite a miraculous way, God has been regathering His people. We have the ability to see that God did intend to fulfill this literally. He is not yet through gathering His people, for the ten lost tribes (referred to in Ezekiel as Ephraim) have not been identified. They remain hidden from view.

I again call attention to verse 24 of this chapter, where he says, "*and Jerusalem will be trampled under-foot by the Gentiles until the times of the Gentiles are fulfilled.*" Now considering this statement, Jerusalem was taken captive by a Gentile king (Nebuchadnezzar of Babylon) in the time of Daniel, about 600 years before Christ. Jerusalem, the city that God calls "the habitation of His Holy Name," had been under Gentile domination for over two and a half millennia, over two thousand five hundred years. But it passed back into Jewish control after the "six days war" in 1967. From a Biblical perspective, one can argue Jerusalem is no longer "trampled under foot by the Gentiles." Is this a sign of the time of the end? Given that God let two thousand five hundred years go by before this event occurred, it would seem important.

How Long is a Generation?

Before we leave this portion of Scripture where Jesus was talking about the signs of His return and His statement about Jerusalem, He also said: **"Truly I say to you, this generation will not pass away until all things take place." (Luke 21:32)** All the disciples and those who heard our Lord make these statements *surely did pass away* and have returned to dust. So, *what generation was the Lord referring to* when He stated it would not pass away until these things all take place? I suggest it is *our generation, the generation living at the time that "Jerusalem is no longer trampled under foot by the Gentiles."* Because the Jews now control Jerusalem, we have now in our lifetimes, something that fulfills Scripture that was not the case for any generation of Christians from the time of Christ until now. The question this begs is "how long is a generation?" In Genesis 15:13,16 we get a clue about how long a generation may be. We read **Genesis 15:13,16**: **God said to Abram, "Know for certain that your descendants will be strangers in a land that is not theirs, where they will be enslaved and oppressed four hundred years. 16: "Then *in the fourth generation* they will return here..."** How long were the children of Israel in Egypt? [41]***And at the end of four hundred and thirty years, to the very day*, all the hosts of the Lord went out from the land of Egypt. (Exodus 12:41)** They came out of the land in the fourth generation, exactly four hundred and thirty years to the day later. Therefore, it would appear that *a generation could be a little over a hundred years*, as you will see *perhaps even 120 years*. It could be shorter, however. In **Psalm 90:10** we read: **"*As for the days of our life, they contain seventy years*, or if due to strength,**

eighty years..." Before the flood, man lived to be almost one thousand years old. After the flood, the Lord told man: **[3]Then the LORD said, "My Spirit shall not strive with man forever, because he also is flesh; nevertheless *his days shall be one hundred and twenty years.*" (Genesis 6:3)**

If a generation is 70 years, we add 70 to 1967 then perhaps the Lord may come back by 2037. If it is 120 years, then we add 120, and He might wait until 2087. (This does not mean the Lord must wait that long, just that He may.) We must not forget; the Lord told us in Mark 13 when describing those days: **[20]"Unless the Lord *had shortened those days,* no life would have been saved; *but for the sake of the elect, whom He chose, He shortened the days.* [32]"But of that day or hour no one knows, not even the angels in heaven, nor the Son, but the Father alone. (Mark 13:20, 32)** Returning once more to Luke 21: 29-31, we read: **"Then he told them a parable: "Behold the fig tree and all the trees; as soon as they put forth leaves, you see it and know for yourselves that summer is now near. So you also, when you see these things happening, recognize that the kingdom of God is near." (Luke 21:29-31)**

We are instructed that no man knows the day or the hour, but here the Scripture indicates that we can and will recognize the season of His return. We who are His followers will know when His return is close.

The time may be much sooner than you think. Let me also remind you that we are at the point in Biblical history that we will reach the completion of six thousand years sometime between 2030 and 2035. We recall that Scripture tells us that "with the Lord, one day is like a thousand years, and a thousand years is as a day." The nearing completion of six-thousand years represents six days with the Lord. We are on the threshold of the seventh day, His Sabbath rest, perhaps as soon as 2030. We saw in chapter one that the "day of the Lord" is a thousand years, and it represents the "seventh day." For these combined reasons, it seems very possible that the Lord may return as soon as 2030 to 2035. As we grow closer to these dates, *if He is going to return*, He told us we will know "the season is near." We will have confirmation if the antichrist is revealed, and the great tribulation begins. You will read the details about the antichrist in chapter 7 of this book. You will see that as a Christian if you let Scripture guide you, then you have much to help you recognize the antichrist. Then we know Jesus' coming is but a short time away. If for example, the Lord is to return in 2031, then seven years prior begins the seventieth week of the prophecy found in Daniel 9:25-27. Therefore, the beginning of this seven-year period could conceivably begin in 2024, for reasons we will examine later, sometime in the fall of 2024.

The Final "Seven" of Daniel 9:27

Jesus fulfilled the end of the first 69 sevens or "weeks" when He was crucified, which I believe took place in 31 AD. (I may be incorrect. Scholars disagree on the precise date.) The final "week" or seven is described as follows: **[27]He will confirm a covenant with many for one 'seven.' In the middle of the 'seven' he will put an end to sacrifice and offering. And on a wing of the temple he will set up *an abomination that causes desolation*, until the end that is decreed is poured out on him." (Daniel 9:27 NIV84)** It does not appear that this final "seven" of this prophecy has been fulfilled, at least not in its entirety. Jesus spoke about the abomination of desolation over five hundred years later, saying, [14]**"But when you see the** **ABOMINATION OF DESOLATION** **standing where it should not be (let the reader understand), then those who are in Judea must flee to the mountains." (Mark 13:14)** Obviously, the prophecy had not been fulfilled when Jesus said this, because He was instructing us to watch for this event in the future.

We read in Daniel 12: [11]**"From the time that the daily sacrifice is abolished and the abomination that causes desolation is set up, there will be 1,290 days.** [12]**Blessed is the one who waits for and reaches the end of the 1,335 days. (Daniel 12:11–12 NIV84)** The New American Standard 1995 translation gives us this for the same verses: [11]**"From the time that the regular sacrifice is abolished and the abomination of desolation is set up, there will be 1,290 days.** [12]**"How blessed is he who keeps waiting and *attains to* the 1,335 days! (Daniel 12:11–12)** In Daniel 12:12, the word that is translated as "attains" in English is the Hebrew word יַחֲזִיק (yachaziq). This word comes from the root חָזַק (chazaq), which means "to be strong, powerful, firm, or steadfast." In this context, it is often translated as "endures" or "perseveres." Therefore, a possible translation of Daniel 12:12 could be: "Blessed is the one who waits and reaches (or endures to) the end of the 1,335 days." Simple math informs us that 1,290 days is just over three and a half years. 1,290 divided by 365 equals 3.534. In Daniel's time, when this was written, the Jews kept a lunar calendar which had twelve months of thirty days each. Periodically, they would add a thirteenth month of thirty days to keep the annual calendar in sync with the solar calendar. The extra month is called Adar Sheni, and would be added approximately seventeen times in a one-hundred-year cycle or slightly less than once in six years to accomplish this. We know from Scripture that the antichrist-beast is given authority to act for forty-two months, or 1,260 days. Another reference to this time frame is found in Daniel 7, where we read: **[25]"He will speak out against the Most High and *wear down the saints of the Highest One*, and he will intend to make alterations in times and in law; and *they will be given into his hand* for a time, times, and half a time. (Daniel 7:25)** This description of the saints being given into his hand for "a time, times, and half a time" is thought to be a Hebrew idiom that means "a time, and two times, and a half a time" or three and a half times, meaning three and a half years. Speculating as to an explanation for the additional 45 days to reach the 1,335 days, I conjecture the following: Jesus is likely to fulfill the Feast of Trumpets when He comes, which is the first day of the seventh month, Tishrei. Leaving out some specifics, the first month of the Jewish calendar is Nisan, and is usually in March or April. Seven months later, in the fall in mid-September, give or take, (I am being approximate) begins the month of Tishrei. Ten days after the Feast of Trumpets is the day of Atonement, and five days after that begins the Feast of Tabernacles. So, fifteen days after coming for the saints could be the date when the marriage supper of the Lamb would begin. The normal period for celebrating this feast is seven days, with another day added on to make eight days total. Still speculating, and with no grounds for assuming this may be the proper interpretation, perhaps the Lord waits thirty days total from the beginning of the celebration of marriage supper of the Lamb, the feast for His wedding to His bride, to return to earth and begin His millennial reign. This would total 45 days from the time He came to gather His saints and take them to heaven (the rapture). You will find another and perhaps better explanation for the numbers 1,290 and 1,335 from Daniel 12:12 in Appendix 3.

We are told in Daniel 8 of some other events that occur *in the time of the*

end: [16]**And I heard a man's voice between the banks of the Ulai, who called, and said, "Gabriel, make this man understand the vision."**
[17]**So he came near where I stood, and when he came I was afraid and fell on my face; but he said to me, "Understand, son of man, that the vision refers to the time of the end."** [18]**Now, as he was speaking with me, I was in a deep sleep with my face to the ground; but he touched me, and stood me upright.** [19]**And he said, "Look, I am making known to you what shall happen in the latter time of the indignation; for at the appointed time the end shall be. (Daniel 8:16–19) (NKJV)** Quite plainly, the angel told Daniel twice, first in verse 17 and again in verse 19 that the vision pertains to the time of the end. Yet commentators have for many years treated this portion of Daniel as though it has already been fulfilled, let's move on, end of story. However, I believe this chapter in Daniel is an example of dual fulfillment of prophecy. Much of what is said has been fulfilled already when Alexander the Great and Greece overthrew the Persians. Subsequently, Alexander died in his early thirties, and four of his generals divided up his kingdom. But the prophecy was not completely fulfilled, just as is the case with the prophecy that Peter quoted on the day of Pentecost in Acts from Joel 2 that was only partially fulfilled.

Who is Javan?

To better understand how Daniel chapter eight is about the time of the end, we need to look at the original language in which it was written. Turning to an exhaustive Hebrew concordance of the Old Testament in the New American Standard Bible, **Daniel 8:21** reads: **"The shaggy (h8163a) goat (h5795) represents the kingdom (h4428) of Greece (h3120),"** Interpreters have chosen to take the last word, (h3120) which in Hebrew is *Yavan* and in English becomes *Javan*, and interpret it to mean Greece in this passage. That decision was influenced no doubt by looking back at the events that had transpired and how they fit Scripture. This has resulted in Christendom accepting that Alexander the Great, the ruler of Greece, was the fulfillment of this passage and that the vision was about a time 300 years before Christ. But *Yavan* (*Javan* in English) is the original Hebrew word here, not *Greece*. And we have Scripture to tell us who *Javan* is. Since the rest of the passage clearly tells us the vision is about the time of the end, we need to look again for insight into who Javan, the shaggy goat, is at the end of time, for the goat runs on the ram and tramples him in great rage. To learn more about Javan, I find it necessary to go back to the first time it appears in the Bible, in Genesis, chapter 10. This chapter is sometimes referred to as the "table of the nations." It tells us of the three sons of Noah and who their sons were. Since God had this written down for us, it must be relevant, and in fact, we will shortly see that it is truly relevant to us today. In verse 2, it tells us that the sons of Japheth (one of Noah's three sons) were Gomer and Magog and Madai and *Javan* and Tubal and Meshech and Tiras. For now, we need to focus on *Javan*, because he comes up later in Daniel. Verse 4 tells us *the sons of Javan* were Elishah and Tarshish, Kittim and Dodanim (or Rodanim as in 1 Chron. 1:7). Verse 5 goes on to say, **"from these the coastlands of the nations were separated into their lands, every one according to his language, according to their families, into their nations."** A word search on Tarshish and separately on Kittim indicates that both refer to people groups that settled on the coasts of the Mediterranean Sea (see Isaiah 23:6, Isaiah 66:19, also Numbers 24:24, and Jeremiah 2:10). Likewise, in Ezekiel 27:2, Elishah is referred to as a people of the coastlands. What this says to me is that Javan's sons populated the coastal regions of the Mediterranean and the Isles of that sea, and spread inland from there forming nations. The other portions of Genesis chapter 10 tell us not about Japheth's sons, but about Shem's and Ham's sons and where they migrated (Shem migrated eastward and northward of Israel, in the Middle East, and Ham migrated to Africa.) *So, Javan's sons became Europe:* i.e., migrating to Italy, Greece, France, Spain, and eventually, England. These same sons of Javan migrated to the new world, America. But they were not Middle Eastern, Asian, Russian, or African. The other sons became those people groups.

You will see why this is important as we unpack Daniel chapter eight. Beginning in Daniel 8:1 we read: **1In the third year of the reign of King Belshazzar a vision appeared to me—to me, Daniel—after the one that appeared to me the first time. 2I saw in the vision, and it so happened while I was looking, that I was in Shushan, the citadel, which is in the province of Elam; and I saw in the vision that I was by the River Ulai. 3Then I lifted my eyes and saw, and there, standing beside the river, was a ram which had two horns, and the two horns were high; but one was higher than the other, and the higher one came up last. 4I saw the ram pushing westward, northward, and southward, so that no animal could withstand him; nor was there any that could deliver from his hand, but he did according to his will and became great. 5And as I was considering, suddenly a male goat came from the west, across the surface of the whole earth, without touching the ground; and the goat had a notable horn between his eyes. 6Then he came to the ram that had two horns, which I had seen standing beside the river, and ran at him with furious power. 7And I saw him confronting the ram; he was moved with rage against him, attacked the ram, and broke his two horns. There was no power**

**in the ram to withstand him, but he cast him down to the ground
and trampled him; and there was no one that could deliver the ram
from his hand. [8]Therefore the male goat grew very great; but when
he became strong, the large horn was broken, and in place of it four
notable ones came up toward the four winds of heaven. [9]And out of
one of them came a little horn which grew exceedingly great toward
the south, toward the east, and toward the Glorious Land. [10]And
it grew up to the host of heaven; and it cast down some of the host
and some of the stars to the ground, and trampled them. [11]He even
exalted himself as high as the Prince of the host; and by him the
daily sacrifices were taken away, and the place of His sanctuary was
cast down. [12]Because of transgression, an army was given over to
the horn to oppose the daily sacrifices; and he cast truth down to
the ground. He did all this and prospered. [13]Then I heard a holy
one speaking; and another holy one said to that certain one who
was speaking, "How long will the vision be, concerning the daily
sacrifices and the transgression of desolation, the giving of both the
sanctuary and the host to be trampled underfoot?" [14]And he said
to me, "For two thousand three hundred days; then the sanctuary
shall be cleansed." [15]Then it happened, when I, Daniel, had seen
the vision and was seeking the meaning, that suddenly there stood
before me one having the appearance of a man. [16]And I heard a
man's voice between the banks of the Ulai, who called, and said,
"Gabriel, make this man understand the vision." [17]So he came near
where I stood, and when he came I was afraid and fell on my face;
but he said to me, "Understand, son of man, that the vision refers
to the time of the end." [18]Now, as he was speaking with me, I was
in a deep sleep with my face to the ground; but he touched me, and**

stood me upright. [19]And he said, "Look, I am making known to you what shall happen in the latter time of the indignation; for at the appointed time the end shall be. [20]The ram which you saw, having the two horns—they are the kings of Media and Persia. [21]And the male goat is the kingdom of Greece. The large horn that is between its eyes is the first king. [22]As for the broken horn and the four that stood up in its place, four kingdoms shall arise out of that nation, but not with its power. [23]"And in the latter time of their kingdom, When the transgressors have reached their fullness, A king shall arise, Having fierce features, Who understands sinister schemes. [24]His power shall be mighty, but not by his own power; He shall destroy fearfully, And shall prosper and thrive; He shall destroy the mighty, and also the holy people. (This is the antichrist; he gets his power from Satan.) ***He will cause astounding devastation*** (When you read the details in Appendix 5 about America you will remember this statement.) **and will succeed in whatever he does. *He will destroy the mighty men and the holy people.*** *(He wages war against the saints, and they are given into his hand.)* **[25]"Through his cunning He shall cause deceit to prosper under his rule; And he shall exalt himself in his heart. He shall destroy many in their prosperity. He shall even rise against the Prince of princes;** (He wages war against Christ.) **But he shall be broken without human means.** (Jesus destroys him. He casts him into the lake of fire.) **[26]"And the vision of the evenings and mornings Which was told is true; Therefore seal up the vision, For it refers to many days in the future." [27]And I, Daniel, fainted and was sick for days; afterward I arose and went about the king's business. I was astonished by the vision, but no one understood it. (Daniel 8:1-27) (NKJV)** (Words in parentheses are mine.)

Here are a few observations about this portion of the Word: the ram charges toward the west, the north, and the south (but not east) in verse 4. Later, in verse 20, we are told the ram represents the kings of Media and Persia. Today, Persia is the modern-day nation of Iran. The terminology used indicates that this nation does more than just "form alliances" with the west, north, and south. It is described as "charging," and no animal *could stand against him*, and no one could rescue him from his power. This seems to convey aspects of a military campaign, with the use of force to overcome those on its western, northern, and southern borders, as opposed to Iran merely influencing its neighbors or forming alliances. Because of the order of the compass points given, it seems that first Iran will move aggressively westward, into Iraq and perhaps, beyond. (It is possible that this expansion by the Ram *could be simultaneous rather than sequential.*) Next, it would forcefully move northward, toward some of the former Soviet states, Turkmenistan, and Uzbekistan, and the other -stans, and perhaps, even towards Turkey. Then a military move to the south will follow, in the direction of the Saudi Arabian Peninsula, including the United Arab Emirates, Oman, Qatar, Saudi Arabia, and Yemen. All these countries named are predominantly Muslim (most are 75% to 90% Muslim). They are also primary producers of the world's supply of oil. As of this writing, taken together, they would represent 65 to 70% of the world's current daily oil production, and if controlled by Iran could cause enormous disruption of operations essential to life in the western world, both in the U.S. and Europe. With this consolidation of Muslim peoples, Iran would control both sides of the Straits of Hormuz, through which 65% of the world's daily oil moves on tankers toward the west and the U.S. They could potentially control the flow of shipping through Turkey and Istanbul from the Aegean Sea to the Mediterranean, cutting off the supply of oil from Russia as well.

Remember in verse 21, the word in the original Hebrew text that has in the past been interpreted as "Greece" is Javan, and we have seen that Javan is identified with people groups that became nations along the coasts of the Mediterranean. Also, when Daniel received this vision, and wrote this in about 550 BC, Greece was not a power. Greece did not arise to power for 200 more years after this was written. Now go back and re-read verses 5 through 8 above, describing the actions of the goat against the ram. First the goat acts *suddenly.* He is *enraged* with the ram and runs on him *furiously.* He *attacks* the ram, and the ram is powerless to resist, and none could rescue the ram from his power. Don't miss the fact that the goat comes from the *west* and *crosses the whole earth without touching the ground.* Now, perhaps we are not yet in the end times, and my musing is futile. But if we are in the end times, who is the likely candidate to be the goat from the west, that comes across the whole earth without touching the ground and tramples the ram (Iran-Persia) to the ground in great rage? Would you think that Iran conducting military campaigns against its neighbors in the Middle East alone would be enough to cause some power from the west *to suddenly become enraged and furiously attack* and destroy it? Or *would Iran need to strike the goat* to cause it to become enraged? A nuclear detonation in some western city would enrage a nation. Or an Electromagnetic Pulse (EMP) attack with its resulting chaos and destruction and mass deaths would enrage a nation. While we are considering, is the present-day nation of Greece which is nearly bankrupt, with only about 11 million people and with only a minor military capability a candidate for the "goat from the west" that no one could resist? Further, it is implausible to believe that Iran is only pursuing nuclear power for peaceful reasons.

Iranian leaders are often bombastic or threatening toward the West and toward Israel in particular. In U.S. government documents delivered to Congress in 2008, Iran has been characterized as perhaps the world's first "suicide nation." They do not demonstrate that they value human life so greatly that they fear a retaliatory strike and therefore, would not ever preemptively strike a powerful western nation. Verse 8 above concerns me about this western power. It tells us that at the height of its power, this power (nation) is broken (the words in the original text suggest "ruined") and its power is replaced with four other powers that arise towards the four winds of heaven. The fall of this western power, the goat, *happens at the height of its power*. (Do you think the U.S. is a candidate for the goat from the west? While this may be possible, I believe a yet-to-emerge European Union strongman is just as likely. This is because of two things. First, this prophecy includes the "little horn" arising from one of the four powers that come from this entity (verses 9 and following). The description of the little horn fits with that of the antichrist, the final world ruler. We see this in verse 11 where it tells us "It set itself up to be as great as the prince of the host." Then verse 12 tells us ***"The host of the saints were given over to it."*** This directly parallels the other descriptions we have of the antichrist in Scripture, as you will discover in the chapter about the antichrist. This statement is repeated in Revelation 13 where Scripture tells us: **"[7]It was also given to him to make war with the saints and to overcome them, and authority over every tribe and people and tongue and nation was given to him." (Revelation 13:7)** As these events begin to unfold before the time of the end, it will become clear who the 'goat' from the west is, and who the 'little horn' is.

This ruler who is the antichrist grows great in power toward the south, toward the east, and toward the beautiful land. If this power originates in Europe, then the south is toward many nations that are Islamic, as is the east. From Europe, "toward the beautiful land" is southeast, again toward Islamic and Arab nations. Later in this book we will see clearly from Scripture in Revelation 17, an alliance of ten kings will give their power to the antichrist-beast, who is this final world ruler. The antichrist is defeated by Christ when He returns.

Jesus spoke about an additional sign that must appear before He returns to gather us to Himself. Scripture tells us that Elijah must come before *the day of the Lord.* **5"Behold, I am going to send you Elijah the prophet before *the coming of the great and terrible day of the Lord.* (Malachi 4:5)** When asked about this with regard to when the dead rise, Jesus responded and confirmed that, yes, Elijah must come first. This was a discussion Jesus had with Peter, James, and John after the transfiguration, as they were coming down from the mountain after seeing His glory. He told them not to tell anyone what they had seen until He had risen from the dead. This prompted them to ask about the resurrection of the dead. **9As they were coming down from the mountain, He gave them orders not to relate to anyone what they had seen, until the Son of Man rose from the dead. 10They seized upon that statement, discussing with one another what rising from the dead meant. 11They asked Him, saying, "Why is it that the scribes say *that Elijah must come first?*" 12And He said to them, "*Elijah does first come* and restore all things. And yet how is it written of the Son of Man that He will suffer many things and be treated with contempt?** (Then Jesus said something that you must look further into other Scripture to understand. In another discussion with His disciples, He explained Himself. When He did, He revealed this prophecy is another example of one that is dual fulfilled.)

13"But I say to you that Elijah has indeed come, and they did to him whatever they wished, just as it is written of him." (Mark 9:9–13) (Words in parentheses are mine.) Jesus explained that John the Baptist was Elijah. He also confirmed *that Elijah was still to come*. Matthew in his account provides clarity to this prophecy, *confirming it is fulfilled more than once*. **[10]And His disciples asked Him, "Why then do the scribes say that *Elijah must come first*?" [11]And He answered and said, "*Elijah is coming* and will restore all things; *[12]but I say to you that Elijah already came*, and they did not recognize him, but did to him whatever they wished. So also the Son of Man is going to suffer at their hands." [13]Then the disciples understood that He had spoken to them about John the Baptist.** (We read a few chapters later the clear statement that both are true, having already said "Elijah is coming, and that Elijah already came.") **(Matthew 17:10–13)** (My words are in parentheses.) **[14]"And if you are willing to accept it, *John himself is Elijah* who was to come." (Matthew 11:14)**

Another sign Jesus spoke about involves signs in the heavens. He said, "the sun would be darkened, and the moon will not give its light" *and then He will send His angels to gather His elect.* Pay attention to the timing, for it says, "after the tribulation of those days." It is the case that the saints have just been raptured when this occurs, since He states, "immediately after the tribulation of those days," but the signs in the heavens appear first. We must pay close attention to the timing of the event, for He continues, saying "then they will see the sign of the Son of Man in the sky, and they will see Him coming on the clouds of the sky, and He will send His angel to gather together His elect." The order of these things confirms that the gathering occurs *on the day of the Lord.* **[29] "But *immediately after the tribulation of those days*** THE SUN WILL BE

DARKENED, AND THE MOON WILL NOT GIVE ITS LIGHT, AND THE STARS WILL FALL from the sky, and the powers of the heavens will be shaken. [30]"And then the sign of the Son of Man will appear in the sky, and then all the tribes of the earth will mourn, and they will see the SON OF MAN COMING ON THE CLOUDS OF THE SKY with power and great glory. [31]"And He will send forth His angels with A GREAT TRUMPET and THEY WILL GATHER TOGETHER His elect from the four winds, from one end of the sky to the other. (Matthew 24:29–31)

The popular thinking is that Jesus can come at any moment. With all these clear statements about things that must precede His coming, why do some teach otherwise? Is this what the Bible really teaches? To find the answer, let's examine more of the Word together.

We read in Matthew 24: **3 Now as He sat on the Mount of Olives, the disciples came to Him *privately*, saying, "Tell us, when will these things be? And what will be the sign of Your coming, and of the end of the age?" (Matthew 24:3)** The key to understanding this verse and the ones that follow, where Jesus tells what to look for before His return, *is to see that the disciples came to Him "privately." He revealed things to his disciples that he kept hidden from the multitudes*. To examine this more carefully, we read from Matthew 13: **2 And great multitudes were gathered together to Him, so that He got into a boat and sat; and the whole multitude stood on the shore. 3 Then *He spoke many things to them in parables*, (Matthew 13:2-3)** In another passage, in Matthew 10: **10 And the disciples came and said to Him, "*Why do You speak to them in parables*?" 11 He answered and said to them, "Because it has been given to you to know the mysteries of the kingdom of heaven, but to them it has not been given. 12 For whoever has, to him more will be**

given, and he will have abundance; but whoever does not have, even what he has will be taken away from him. 13 Therefore I speak to them in parables, because seeing they do not see, and hearing they do not hear, nor do they understand. 14 And in them the prophecy of Isaiah is fulfilled, which says: *'Hearing you will hear and shall not understand, And seeing you will see and not perceive;* 15 *For the hearts of this people have grown dull. Their ears are hard of hearing, And their eyes they have closed, Lest they should see with their eyes and hear with their ears, Lest they should understand with their hearts and turn, So that I should heal them.'* 16 But blessed *are* your eyes for they see, and your ears for they hear; 17 for assuredly, I say to you that many prophets and righteous *men* desired to see what you see, and did not see *it,* and to hear what you hear, and did not hear it. (Matthew 10:10-16)

You do not want to be one of those from whom things are hidden, even though they are in plain sight. Taking a single passage like the one that teaches Jesus comes like a thief in the night and building an entire belief structure based on it when many other verses give a clear understanding of all that must happen before he can come will lead to an incorrect understanding of these matters. As you progress through these chapters, you will see that there will come a time when Jesus can come at any moment. But that time is not yet. The Word of God tells us there are things that must happen first.

chapter SEVEN The Antichrist

The Final Beast

Scripture indicates there will be a final empire on earth that will be headed by an individual who gets his power from Satan. He will seek to force everyone on earth to worship him as god. He will be aided by the false prophet and will speak blasphemy against the one true God in heaven. A careful reading of Daniel chapters 2, 7, 8, and 11 along with Revelation chapters 13 through 17 and chapter 19, focusing on references to *the beast*, will give you a more complete picture of the final empire that will come on the earth. I will for clarity refer to this individual as the antichrist-beast. The final destruction of the ruler of that empire and of his empire by the Lord Jesus Christ when He returns to reign over the earth are also described in these chapters.

Below is a summary of characteristics that Scripture reveals about the antichrist. As you read the following pages, I encourage you to be alert for these, for you truly want to be able to recognize this individual when he comes. We are told that God will send upon the rest of the world, those who did not love the truth, a great delusion so that they will believe the lie.

- His power is from Satan, will be mighty, and will appear together with signs and false wonders.. It appears that something like coming back from the dead or surviving a mortal wound is associated with him.

- Forces from him will "desecrate the sanctuary", put an end to sacrifice and offering, and set up an abomination of desolation.
- He will demand that all people worship him.
- He will crush and trample down all opposition on earth.
- He will be deceitful and shrewd, will understand sinister schemes and will be a master of intrigue. He will have "fierce features".
- He will destroy many while they are at ease to an extraordinary degree.
- He will wage war against the saints, who will be given into his hand for forty-two months. He will intend to make "alterations in times and in law." He will overcome the saints, killing many.
- Acting in concert with ten kings, or heads of nations, he will destroy many, including Babylon the Great.
- He will utter great boasts and will be pompous enough to oppose even the Prince of princes (the Lord); He will blaspheme the God of Heaven.
- His kingdom will be a divided kingdom; the people in it will not remain united.
- He will ultimately be destroyed by Christ Jesus upon His return with His saints.

Beasts are Kings or Rulers

As you consider the Scripture in this next section, take note of the following, regardless of whether you are reading from Daniel or Revelation:

1. A beast with a mouth uttering great boasts and blasphemies against the God of gods,

2. A beast with ten horns and seven heads.

When you see a beast described in this manner, know that Scripture is describing the final world ruler.

Scripture uses a word picture of a "beast" to represent empires or nations and their rulers. Daniel 7:17 says, **"Those great *beasts*, which are four, *are four kings* which arise out of the earth."** Thus, we see from this that "beasts," as used here, are kings.

Now, let us focus on a particular beast, the fourth and last beast. All these passages speak of the time of this final world ruler, which I will call the antichrist-beast: "[7]**After this I kept looking in the night visions, and behold, *a fourth beast*, dreadful and terrifying and extremely strong; and it had large iron teeth. It devoured and crushed and trampled down the remainder with its feet; and *it was different from all the beasts that were before it,* and *it had ten horns"*** --also referring to kings. [8]**"While I was contemplating the horns, behold, another horn, a little one, came up among them, and three of the first horns were pulled out by the roots before it; and behold, this horn** (king) **possessed eyes like the eyes of a man and *a mouth uttering great boasts"* (Daniel 7:7–8, emphasis mine).**

Defining Characteristics of the Antichrist-Beast

The information in the next passage reveals *it is also telling us about the fourth ruler, the antichrist-beast,* the one who will be destroyed by Jesus when He returns with His saints. His identity will be confirmed by his setting up the abomination of desolation and the monstrous things he will speak against God, together with the action he will take against the people of God. Scripture states this happens at the end time. The Word of God tells us that “Those who have insight will understand.”

31“Forces from him will arise, desecrate the sanctuary fortress, and do away with the regular sacrifice. And they *will set up the abomination of desolation.* (Jesus refers to this in Matthew 24:15.) **32By smooth words he will turn to godlessness those who act wickedly toward the covenant, but the people who know their God will display strength and take action. 33*Those who have insight among the people will give understanding to the many*; yet they will fall by sword and by flame, by captivity and by plunder for many days. 34Now when they fall *they will be granted a little help*, and *many will join with them in hypocrisy.* 35*Some of those who have insight will fall, in order to refine, purge and make them pure until the end time*; because it is still to come at the appointed time. 36Then the king will do as he pleases, and he will exalt and magnify himself above every god and *will speak monstrous things against the God of gods*; and he will prosper until the indignation is finished, for that which is decreed will be done. 45He will pitch the tents of his royal pavilion between the seas and the beautiful Holy Mountain; *yet he will come to his end, and no one will help him.* […] 10Many will be purged, purified and refined, but the wicked will act wickedly; and *none of the wicked will understand*, but *those who have insight will understand*” (Daniel 11:31-36, 12:10, emphasis mine) .**

All these preceding verses, and the ones to follow, give us a more complete picture of the antichrist-beast, the final world ruler, how he will wage war against the saints and overcome them, and how he comes to his end. When we combine the understanding we get from reading these passages in Daniel with the information in Revelation about the same antichrist-beast, we gain a much more complete understanding of what to expect as God's people during the years immediately prior to the return of Jesus.

Some of our modern Christian fiction has popularized the use of the term *antichrist* to refer to the person Bible prophecy indicates will be the head of the final world empire which will be destroyed by the Lord Jesus Christ when He returns with His saints. However, a closer look at Scripture is in order so that our understanding of this subject is not primarily informed by fiction rather than God's Word. The term antichrist appears four times only in the Bible, three times in 1st John, and once in 2nd John: **"Dear children, this is the last hour; and as you have heard that the antichrist is coming, even now many antichrists have come. This is how we know it is the last hour. [...] Who is the liar? It is whoever denies that Jesus is the Christ. Such a person is the antichrist—denying the Father and the Son" (1 John 2:18, 22) "but every spirit that does not acknowledge Jesus is not from God. This is the spirit of the antichrist, which you have heard is coming and even now is already in the world" (1 John 4:3).** (Remember, this was written almost two thousand years ago.) **"For many deceivers have gone out into the world who do not confess Jesus Christ *as* coming in the flesh. This is a deceiver and an antichrist" (2 John 1:7)** According to the Scriptures above, the term *antichrist* refers to anyone who denies that Jesus Christ came in the flesh. We are also told that many of these people with the spirit of antichrist have already come, and more will come. However, because of the current popular understanding in our culture of the term "antichrist," I will use the words *antichrist* and *beast* together to refer to the head of the final world empire that is prophesied in many places in Scripture. The Scriptures refer to this final world ruler as a "beast."

This individual is also referred to as "the son of perdition," "the man of lawlessness," and "the man of sin." We learn the details from 2 Thessalonians 2: **"[1]Now we request you, brethren, with regard to the coming of our Lord Jesus Christ and our gathering together to Him, (2 Thessalonians 2:1)** (Verse 2 contains a warning not to be convinced that "the day of the Lord" has come. The following Scriptures *inform us of what must take place before the Lord can come.*) **[2]that you not be quickly shaken from your composure or be disturbed either by a spirit or a message or a letter as if from us, to the effect that the day of the Lord has come" (2 Thessalonians 2:1-2)** Clearly here we are being warned not to be convinced that "the day of the Lord" has come, as there are specific things that must happen: (Note what two things must happen.) " **3 Let no one deceive you by any means; for *that Day will not come unless the falling away comes first*, and *the man of sin is revealed, the son of perdition, 4 who opposes and exalts himself above all that is called God or that is worshiped, so that he sits as God in the temple of God, showing himself that he is God.* 5 Do you not remember that when I was still with you I told you these things? 6 And now you know what is restraining, that he may be revealed in his own time. 7 For the mystery of lawlessness is already at work; only *he who now restrains will do so until he is taken out of the way*" (2 Thessalonians 2:3-7).** Some teach that he who "restrains" refers to the Holy Spirit, but the restraining force could be an angel. Very shortly we will examine this possibility. "**8 And then the lawless one will be revealed, whom the Lord will consume with the breath of His mouth and destroy with the brightness of His coming. 9 The coming of the lawless one is according to the working of Satan, with**

all power, signs, and lying wonders, 10 and with all unrighteous deception among those who perish, because they did not receive the love of the truth, that they might be saved. 11 And for this reason *God will send them strong delusion*, (Those who reject God, and did not receive the love of the truth will have a strong delusion sent upon them.) **that they should believe the lie, 12 that they all may be condemned who did not believe the truth but had pleasure in unrighteousness" (2 Thessalonians 2:8-12)**

1. The first thing we see in this passage is that the Lord will not come unless the falling away comes first . A falling away from the faith, elsewhere called the apostasy, must occur first, before the Lord returns for his saints. Next we see that the man of sin will be revealed, the son of perdition. This detail also tells us that the antichrist, also called *the beast*, the son of perdition, will have appeared in the world *while the saints are still there, before the rapture.*

2. This beast, the antichrist, is described as supremely arrogant and pompous, for he will oppose and exalt himself above all that is called God or that is worshiped.

3. He will "sit as God in the temple of God, showing himself that he is God." Some say that because our body is called the temple of the Lord, this is just a figure of speech indicating that this individual will put himself on the "throne" in his own life, in his own heart. I believe Scripture indicates that he will literally sit in the temple in Jerusalem and claim to be God and will try to force the entire world to worship him as God. This is more than just refusing to acknowledge God in one's own heart. Many

believe that if this final world ruler is going to sit in the temple of God, then the temple must be built again before the Lord Jesus will return. Next we see that

4. he gets his power from Satan, also called the Dragon. The coming of the "lawless one" is according to the working of Satan, with all "power, signs, and lying wonders" which will deceive the world. Of those who are deceived, a reason is given: because they "did not receive the love of the truth, " that they might be saved, a "strong delusion" was sent to them by God. Then

5. the Lord Jesus will destroy this individual (when He returns from heaven, with His saints, after the rapture and the marriage supper of the Lamb which has just occurred) and then will begin His thousand-year reign on the earth. Details of this are in the chapter on the thousand-year reign, in which we will discuss more of Revelation 19 and 20. The Lord will consume the beast (the antichrist) and the false prophet with "the breath of His mouth and destroy them with the brightness of His coming." He will cast them both into the lake of fire. Now that we have unpacked that passage, we see that we have some very specific details we can watch out for when looking for the emergence of the antichrist-beast before our Lord returns, and we know that currently the antichrist is being restrained by some force.

Who is Presently Restraining the Antichrist?

In chapter four I acknowledged that it is a reasonable assumption that it is the Holy Spirit who presently restrains the antichrist from appearing.

We examined why the complete removal of the Holy Spirit from the earth by the rapture would present a problem for anyone yet unsaved to become a new believer in Christ. Because we can see that saints are still on the earth during the period of suffering we have discussed, and we are informed that the antichrist makes war with them, the Holy Spirit must still be present, because He is present in all believers.

Another possibility is that it is an angel, appointed by God, who is the restrainer. It is not as if an angel would not be strong enough to accomplish this; we read that an angel binds Satan with a chain and throws him into the abyss.

We are offered a glimpse of the involvement by angels in the affairs of nations from Daniel 10: "[7]**Now I, Daniel, alone saw the vision, while the men who were with me did not see the vision; nevertheless, a great dread fell on them, and they ran away to hide themselves.** [8]**So I was left alone and saw this great vision; yet no strength was left in me, for my natural color turned to a deathly pallor, and I retained no strength.** [9]**But I heard the sound of his words; and as soon as I heard the sound of his words, I fell into a deep sleep on my face, with my face to the ground.** [10]**Then behold, a hand touched me and set me trembling on my hands and knees.** [11]**He said to me, 'O Daniel, man of high esteem, understand the words that I am about to tell you and stand upright, for I have now been sent to you.' And when he had spoken this word to me, I stood up trembling.** [12]**Then he said to me, 'Do not be afraid, Daniel, for from the first day that you set your heart on understanding this and on humbling yourself before your God, your words were heard, and I have come in response to your words.** [13]**But the prince of the kingdom of Persia was withstanding**

me for twenty-one days; then behold, Michael, one of the chief princes, came to help me, for I had been left there with the kings of Persia. [14]Now I have come to give you an understanding of what will happen to your people in the latter days, for the vision pertains to the days yet future" (Daniel 10:7–14). Evidently Daniel had prayed to God for understanding, and an angel was sent to provide him with what he was seeking. However, this angel messenger was detained by one called "the prince of the kingdom of Persia" for twenty-one days. This opposing force was a fallen angel, one of great power. Only when one of the archangels, Michael, came to assist this messenger was he able to prevail in his struggle and finish the task the Lord had given him. We are also told the message was to give Daniel understanding about what would happen to his people in the latter days.

First Appearance of the Antichrist-Beast in Revelation

Do we first read of this antichrist-beast after the seals are opened or somewhere else? Have any of the seven trumpets sounded yet? We first find this beast mentioned in Revelation 11, directly after the two witnesses (also called two olive trees or two lampstands) have finished their testimony: "**Now when they have finished their testimony, the beast that comes up from the Abyss will attack them, and overpower and kill them" (Revelation 11:7).** This Scripture refers to the two witnesses, called two olive trees and two lampstands. **These are the two olive trees and the two lampstands that stand before the Lord of the earth. (Revelation 11:4)** We are not informed outright here that this beast from the abyss is the antichrist-beast. We encounter the beast again in Revelation 13:1, but this time the beast is pictured as arising from the sea. A few chapters later, we are informed of a beast that is about to arise: "[8]**The beast that you saw was, and is not, and is about to come up out of the abyss and go to destruction. And those who dwell on the earth, whose name has not been written in the book of life from the foundation of the world, will wonder when they see the beast, that he was and is not and will come" (Revelation 17:8).** Revelation 17 and 18 take place before Revelation 11, for the saints are still on the earth during Revelation 17 and 18, but are gathered to be with the Lord when the seventh angel sounds in Revelation 11:15. The additional information gleaned when we read Revelation 17 joined with the cumulative understanding we gain as we consider the descriptions of the final beast from Daniel confirm for us that indeed this beast from the abyss first found in Revelation 11:7 is the antichrist-beast. We would expect this to be the case, because Scripture in 2 Thessalonians 2:3 informs us that the day of the Lord will not come, and we will not be gathered (raptured) until the man of lawlessness is revealed. We have confirmation here in Revelation 11:7 that he has been revealed, for he kills the "two witnesses," but not until they have finished their testimony. Then in Revelation 11:15 the seventh angel sounds, and the day of the Lord begins.

Who Are the Two Witnesses in Revelation 11?

Some think these two witnesses are Elijah and Moses, or Elijah and Enoch. Perhaps one of these this is the case. But consider the description of them as "olive trees" and "lampstands." We find that the Scripture uses olive trees as a metaphor in Romans chapter 11: "**But if some of the branches were broken off, and you, *being a wild olive*, were grafted in among them and became partaker with them of the rich root of *the olive tree*" (Romans 11:17, emphasis mine).** This Scripture in Romans calls Jewish believers the rich root of the olive tree, and Gentile believers are called a wild olive, who are grafted into this olive tree. Similarly, we find that Scripture uses *lampstands* as a metaphor in Revelation chapter one to indicate churches: "**As for the mystery of the seven stars which you saw in My right hand, and *the seven golden lampstands*: the seven stars are the angels of the seven churches, and the seven *lampstands* are the seven *churches"* (Revelation 1:20, emphasis mine).** Now we look at Zechariah chapter four, and we find both olive trees and lampstands in the same passage: "**Then the angel who was speaking with me returned and roused me, as a man who is awakened from his sleep. 2 He said to me, 'What do you see?' And I said, 'I see, and behold, *a lampstand* all of gold with its bowl on the top of it, and its seven lamps on it with seven spouts belonging to each of the lamps which are on the top of it; 3 *also two olive trees* by it, one on the right side of the bowl and the other on its left side.'" [...] Then I said to him, '*What are these two olive trees* on the right of the lampstand and on its left?'" 12 And I answered the second time and said to him, "What are *the two olive branches* which are beside the two golden pipes, which empty the golden oil from themselves?" 13 So he answered me, saying, "Do you not know what these are?" And I said, "No, my lord." 14 Then he said, 'These are the *two anointed ones* who are standing by the Lord of the whole earth'" (Zechariah 4:1-3, 11-14, emphasis mine).** Zechariah's conversation with the angel reveals that olive trees and lampstands are a metaphor in prophecy for "anointed ones." Does this confirm that we are surely talking about two people? We need to examine the Word further. Where else do we find *anointed ones* in Scripture? Going back to Exodus 29:4,7 and 40:15, we find the anointing of first Aaron as a priest, then of his sons as priests:

"[4]Then you shall bring Aaron and his sons to the doorway of the tent of meeting and wash them with water. [7]"Then you shall take the anointing oil and pour it on his head and anoint him" (Exodus 29:4,7). Next, in Exodus 40: **"[15]and you shall *anoint them* even as you have anointed their father, that they may minister as priests to Me; and *their anointing will qualify them for a perpetual priesthood throughout their generations*" (Exodus 40:15, emphasis mine).**

Anointing was a procedure the Lord instated to indicate his priests initially in Exodus, and then God extended this procedure to have a broader application that is worth taking a look at; in this following passage, He is speaking *of the entire nation of Israel, not only of priests*: **"[4] 'You yourselves have seen what I did to the Egyptians, and how I bore you on eagles' wings, and brought you to Myself. [5]Now then, if you will indeed obey My voice and keep My covenant, *then you shall be My own possession among all the peoples*, for all the earth is Mine; [6]and *you shall be to Me a kingdom of priests and a holy nation*.' These are the words that you shall speak to the sons of Israel" (Exodus 19:4–6).** Under these conditions, if Israel obeyed and kept God's covenant, *all Israel* was to be a "kingdom of priests." Thus the application of anointing and the purview of priests has expanded, much like the meaning of the "temple" of God to represent his presence with his people extended to encompass each of us who host the Holy Spirit in our hearts (see 1 Corinthians 6:19).

Likewise, we find in 1 Peter 2 when speaking of the saints in Christ Jesus, **"[5]you also, as living stones, are being built up as a spiritual house for *a holy priesthood*, to offer up spiritual sacrifices acceptable to God through Jesus Christ" (1 Peter 2:5).** Again, just four verses later, also speaking of all Gentile believers in Jesus, he addresses them as: [9]**But *you are* "*A CHOSEN RACE, A royal PRIESTHOOD, A HOLY NATION*, A PEOPLE FOR God's OWN POSSESSION, so that you may proclaim the excellencies of Him who has called you out of darkness into His marvelous light;" (1 Peter 2:9).** These are the exact words God used with regard to the nation of Israel, a "royal priesthood, a Holy Nation" in Exodus 19:4-6. Since the inauguration of anointing in Exodus, we can see how its purpose expanded to include the whole nation of Israel and then later on to even Gentiles who come into the family of God.

Both obedient Israel and Gentile saints are referred to as "a royal priesthood." And we see from Scripture that priests must be anointed. Do we find evidence from Scripture that we who are Gentile saints are anointed? In fact, we do. We read in **2 Corinthians 1:21-22: "[21]Now He who establishes us with you in Christ and *anointed us* is God, [22]who also sealed us and gave us the Spirit in our hearts as a pledge."** Similarly, we read in 1 John 2: **"[20]But *you have an anointing from the Holy One*, and you all know. [27]As for you, *the anointing which you received from Him* abides in you, and you have no need for anyone to teach you; but as *His anointing teaches you about all things*, and is true and is not a lie, and just as it has taught you, you abide in Him" (1 John 2:20, 27).**

The Scripture in Revelation 11:4 tells us the two witnesses are *two olive trees* and *two lampstands*. At the beginning of Revelation, Jesus revealed that the lampstands stood for churches. It is reasonable to assume that the meaning of a word used as a metaphor at the beginning of Revelation remains the same throughout. A church is a body of believers. Zechariah is told by an angel in Zechariah 4:11 and 14 that the lampstand and the two olive trees are *His anointed ones*. We see that *all priests are anointed.* The nation of Israel was called a kingdom of priests, and *a royal priesthood,* and we who are Gentile believers are called the same, *a royal priesthood.* It may be that these two witnesses in Revelation are the *Jewish saved* and the *Gentile saved.* It is something to consider.

The witnesses may also turn out to be two individuals, such as Enoch and Elijah for example, since both were "taken" and did not die as other men. Or perhaps more likely, they may be Moses and Elijah. There are some other observations about these two witnesses that may be worth considering. Scripture describes these two witnesses in Revelation 11: "[5]**And if anyone wants to harm them, fire flows out of their mouth and devours their enemies; so if anyone wants to harm them, he must be killed in this way."** Elijah did just this when he called with "his mouth" for fire to come down from heaven and consume the captain and his fifty in 2 Kings 1:10, likewise he asked God to withhold rain for three years, and God did so in 1 Kings 17:1. We read in Exodus that Moses turned waters to blood in Egypt and brought numerous other plagues. Perhaps Scripture is telling us these two witnesses will be Moses and Elijah. They were the two who Peter, James, and John saw with Jesus when He was transfigured: "[6]**These have the power to shut up the sky, so that rain will not fall during the days of their prophesying; and they have power over the waters to turn them into blood, and to strike the earth with every plague, as often as they desire" (Revelation 11:5–6).** However, I am inclined to think this prophecy regarding the two witnesses will be fulfilled with two actual individuals. Verse 12 tells us after they are killed and "**their dead bodies will lie in the street of the great city"** for three and a half days, they will come to life and then go

"up into heaven in the cloud, and their enemies [will watch] them" (Revelation 11:8, 12).. Because this event is "seen by their enemies" and occurs prior to the seventh angel sounding his trumpet, I am led to think it is speaking of two specific individuals, not using a metaphor that includes all God's faithful. **[8]And *their dead bodies will lie in the street of the great city* which mystically is called Sodom and Egypt, *where also their Lord was crucified.* [9]Those from the peoples and tribes and tongues and nations will look at their dead bodies *for three and a half days*, and will not permit their dead bodies to be laid in a tomb. [11]But after the three and a half days, *the breath of life from God came into them, and they stood on their feet*; and great fear fell upon those who were watching them. [12]And they heard a loud voice from heaven saying to them, "Come up here." *Then they went up into heaven in the cloud, and their enemies watched them.* (Revelation 11:8-9,11-12)** I note that this may be another example of prophecy with dual fulfillment.

Going back to what Revelation tells us happens to these two witnesses: **Now *when they have finished their testimony,* the beast that comes up from the Abyss will attack them, and overpower and kill them. (Revelation 11:7)** The Scripture is telling us that when these whom have been chosen by God to be His witnesses "have finished their testimony" then the beast that comes up from the Abyss will attack them, overpower them, and kill them. Jesus told us the gospel must be preached to all nations, and then the end would come "**[14]This gospel of the kingdom shall be preached in the whole world as a testimony to all the nations, and then the end will come" (Matthew 24:14).** If testimony from His witnesses is finished (the Jews of faith and the saints, having preached to all the nations), then it seems logical to conclude there is no one else God intends to save. This sounds like the requirements for the Lord's return have been met. By now, the apostasy will have clearly occurred, and a remaining stipulation from Scripture is that the "man of lawlessness, the son of perdition" will have been revealed. The very act of this "beast" beginning to overpower and kill God's people would provide clear, unmistakable evidence to God's people that the antichrist-beast has been revealed. What else must happen before Jesus returns? As God told the souls beneath the altar at the opening of the fifth seal, "The total number of those who are to be killed just as they had been, must be complete" (My paraphrase of Revelation 6:11). How does this fit with the prophecy in Daniel which says the beast, this final world ruler, will destroy "the holy people"? In separate passages of Daniel concerning different visions, both referring to the final world ruler, we read: **"[25]He will speak out against the Most High and *wear down the saints of the Highest One*, and he will intend to make alterations in times and in law; and *they will be given into his hand* for a time, times, and half a time. (Daniel 7:25) "[24]His power will be mighty, but not by his own power, And he will destroy to an extraordinary degree And prosper and perform his will; *He will destroy* mighty men and *the holy people*" (Daniel 8:24).** In Revelation 13:7, we have a confirmation paralleling what we just read in Daniel regarding this final world ruler, the beast: **"it was given to him to make war with the saints and to overcome them" (Revelation 13:7)** When we read regarding the two witnesses: **"[7] When they have finished their testimony, the beast that comes up out of the abyss will make war with them, and overcome them and kill them" (Revelation 11:7),** we are told at this point that the two witnesses "have finished their testimony" and that the beast has come up from the abyss to "overcome them and kill them" (Revelation

11:7). Now all the seals have been opened, and six of the trumpets have been blown. The saints are still on the earth because the seventh, the last trumpet, has not sounded yet. The beast, the antichrist, has begun overpowering and killing the saints. We have been told the saints have been given into his hand "for a time, times and half a time," which we have discussed refers to forty-two months. In addition to enduring to the end, and not denying Christ, what else does Scripture say that we should take to heart? Jesus tells his disciples, **"I say to you, My friends, do not be afraid of those who kill the body and after that have no more that they can do" (Luke 12:4).** We are told "blessed is he who dies in the Lord from now on (Revelation 14:13)." We are encouraged not to be afraid of dying for our testimony of Jesus as our Lord and Savior, for we shall be raised from the dead and changed, and when we put on our immortal bodies, we will be with Him forever. When the antichrist-beast begins killing the saints, he has clearly been revealed. All that remains before Jesus returns is for the full number that are to be killed set by the Lord to be completed. Remember the Lord told the saints under the altar to rest a little while longer, **"until the number of their fellow servants and their brethren who were to be killed even as they had been, would be completed also (Revelation 6:11)."**

Reflecting back on Scriptures which we have examined that could pertain to the "two witnesses," my perspective is that we likely will not know until the fulfillment of these portions of prophecy what exactly is meant. Scripture may be indicating that both two individual witnesses will be yet to come in fulfillment of these passages, and that they also refer to the faithful Jewish believers and the saints. In the latter case, perhaps the three and a half days that "their bodies lie in the streets" is a metaphorical representation for the final forty-two months (three and a half years) of the great tribulation during which the saints are killed by the antichrist.

Previously, we read from Revelation 11:7, telling us when the witnesses had finished their testimony, the beast would kill them. Just a few verses later, in Revelation 11:15, the seventh trumpet, *the last trumpet*, is sounded by an angel: "[15]**Then *the seventh angel sounded*; and there were loud voices in heaven, saying, "The kingdom of the world *has become* the kingdom of our Lord and of His Christ; and He will reign forever and ever" (Revelation 11:15).** It should be no surprise that this is when Christ Jesus returns to take His saints to be with Himself forever, for Scripture just proclaimed in verse 11 of the same chapter that the witnesses of God had finished their testimony. Then they began to be killed by the beast, the final ruler of the world. He continues until Christ Jesus comes and gathers all His saints. Jesus sends His angels to gather both those who have died by raising them from the dead, and those still alive.

Above, we were told the beast came up from the Abyss. I believe this signals that a demonic spirit or a fallen angel that had been confined to the Abyss was released and entered into an individual on the earth who is the one that becomes the ruler of the final world empire.

Seven Heads and Ten Horns

Note as we continue to examine Revelation for even more detail about the beast, the antichrist, that this beast has ten horns. We read in Revelation 13 about the same beast which was described in Daniel, but we get a bit more information about the beast in the Revelation passage. The beast is described as "having seven heads," referring to kings, along with "ten horns," which are also kings. Next we are told the beast was "like a leopard" with the "feet of a bear" and a mouth "like the mouth of a lion," which agrees with the passage from Daniel describing a leopard, a bear, and a lion. These parallel passages indicate that this ruler will resemble past rulers or great empires depicted by these animals. After that, we see in this passage that "the dragon gave him his power, his throne, and great authority," which means this antichrist-beast derives his power from Satan.

Then I stood on the sand of the sea. And I saw a beast rising up out of the sea, *having seven heads*_(heads are kings) ***and ten horns*** (horns are also kings), **and on his horns ten crowns, and on his heads a blasphemous name.** (We learn later from Scripture that the seven heads are seven kings, and also the ten horns are ten kings.) **2 Now the beast which I saw was like a leopard, his feet were like the feet of a bear, and his mouth like the mouth of a lion.** (Compare this reference to Daniel chapter 7 which describes a leopard, a bear, and a lion. This is saying this ruler, the antichrist-beast, was "like" or resembled these past rulers of great empires) **The dragon gave him his power,** (he gets his power from Satan) **his throne, and great authority. 3 And I saw one of his heads as if it had been mortally wounded, and his deadly wound was healed.** (Perhaps this will be fulfilled when the time comes, as a counterfeit "type" of the death and resurrection of Jesus.) **And all the world marveled and followed the beast. 4 So they worshiped the dragon who gave authority to the beast; and they worshiped the beast, saying, "Who is like the beast? Who is able to make war with him?"**

The Antichrist Will War Against the Saints

5 And he was given a mouth speaking great things and blasphemies, and *he was given authority to continue for forty-two months.* (Forty-two months equals three and a half years, during which he will persecute and kill the saints.) **6 Then he opened his mouth in blasphemy against God, to blaspheme His name, His tabernacle, and those who dwell in heaven. 7 *It was granted to him to make war with the saints and to overcome them.* And authority was given him over every tribe, tongue, and nation. 8 All who dwell on the earth will worship him, whose names have not been written in the Book of Life of the Lamb slain from the foundation of the world. 9 If anyone has an ear, let him hear. 10 He who leads into captivity shall go into captivity; he who kills with the sword must be killed with the sword. *Here is the patience and the faith of the saints.* (Revelation 13:1-10 NKJV)** (In the NASB, the end of this verse reads: Here *is the perseverance and the faith of the saints.*)

The False Prophet or Helper of the Antichrist

Turning our attention back to an examination of the beast, we learn this first beast will have a "helper." He is called "another beast" and we learn later *he is the false prophet*: **"11 Then I saw *another beast* coming up out of the earth, and he had two horns like a lamb and spoke like a dragon. 12 And he exercises all the authority of the first beast in his presence, and causes the earth and those who dwell in it to worship the first beast, whose deadly wound was healed. 13 He performs great signs, so that he even makes fire come down from heaven on the earth in the sight of men. 14 And he deceives those who dwell on the earth by those signs which he was granted**

to do in the sight of the beast, telling those who dwell on the earth to make an image to the beast who was wounded by the sword and lived. [15] He was granted power to give breath to the image of the beast, that the image of the beast should both speak and *cause as many as would not worship the image of the beast to be killed.* [16] He causes all, both small and great, rich and poor, free and slave, to receive a mark on their right hand or on their foreheads, [17] and that no one may buy or sell except one who has the mark or the name of the beast, or the number of his name" (Revelation 13:11-17). This second beast is called "the false prophet" and was described as "another beast," one which comes up out of the earth, not the sea, or the abyss. He causes the world to worship the first beast, the antichrist, and all to be killed who would not worship the image of the beast.

Ultimately, this beast (ruler) and the false prophet who helps him are cast into the lake of fire by the Lord Jesus himself:" [19] **And I saw the beast and the kings of the earth and their armies assembled to make war against Him who sat on the horse and against His army. [20]And the beast was seized, and with him the false prophet who performed the signs in his presence, by which he deceived those who had received the mark of the beast and those who worshiped his image; *these two were thrown alive into the lake of fire* which burns with brimstone" (Revelation 19:19–20).** Immediately after this, Christ Jesus begins His reign on earth with His resurrected saints, as described in Revelation chapter twenty.

The Statue Dream of Nebuchadnezzar

God informed us in his Word over 2500 years ago how the world would end, and about this final world ruler, the antichrist-beast. God revealed multiple empires that would emerge down through history, ending with the one at the time of the end, ruled by the antichrist-beast. We find this in Daniel chapter two: "28 **but there is a God in heaven who reveals mysteries. He has shown King Nebuchadnezzar what will happen in days to come. Your dream and the visions that passed through your mind as you were lying in bed are these: 29 As Your Majesty was lying there, your mind turned to things to come, and the revealer of mysteries showed you what is going to happen. 30 As for me, this mystery has been revealed to me, not because I have greater wisdom than anyone else alive, but so that Your Majesty may know the interpretation and that you may understand what went through your mind. 31 Your Majesty looked, and there before you stood a large statue—an enormous, dazzling statue, awesome in appearance. 32 The head of the statue was made of pure gold, its chest and arms of silver, its belly and thighs of bronze, 33 its legs of iron, its feet partly of iron and partly of baked clay. 34 While you were watching, a rock"** (this rock is Jesus) **"was cut out, but not by human hands. It struck the statue on its feet of iron and clay and smashed them. 35 Then the iron, the clay, the bronze, the silver and the gold were all broken to pieces and became like chaff on a threshing floor in the summer. The wind swept them away without leaving a trace. But the rock that struck the statue became a huge mountain and filled the whole earth. 36 This was the dream, and now we will interpret it to the king. 37 Your Majesty, you are the king of kings. The God of heaven has given you dominion and power and might and glory; 38 in your hands he has placed all mankind and the beasts of the field and the birds in the sky. Wherever they live, he has made you ruler over them all. You are that head of gold. 39 After you,**

another kingdom will arise, inferior to yours. Next, a third kingdom, one of bronze, will rule over the whole earth. [40] Finally, *there will be a fourth kingdom*" (This is the kingdom of the antichrist), **"strong as iron—for iron breaks and smashes everything—and as iron breaks things to pieces, so it will crush and break all the others."** (This fourth kingdom is the same fourth kingdom in Daniel's other vision in Daniel 7:23) **"[41] Just as you saw that the feet and toes were partly of baked clay and partly of iron, so this will be a divided kingdom; yet it will have some of the strength of iron in it, even as you saw iron mixed with clay. [42] As the toes were partly iron and partly clay, so this kingdom will be partly strong and partly brittle. [43] And just as you saw the iron mixed with baked clay, so *the people will be a mixture and will not remain united*, any more than iron mixes with clay."** (We learn new information here, that the people in this kingdom will be a mixture and will not remain united.) **[44] *In the time of those kings, the God of heaven will set up a kingdom that will never be destroyed*,** (in the time of the fourth kingdom, God sends *Jesus, the rock*, and He casts the ruler of this fourth kingdom into the lake of fire, and begins His thousand-year reign.) **nor will it be left to another people. It will crush all those kingdoms and bring them to an end, but it will itself endure forever. [45] This is the meaning of the vision of the rock cut out of a mountain, but not by human hands—a rock that broke the iron, the bronze, the clay, the silver and the gold to pieces. The great God has shown the king what will take place in the future. The dream is true and its interpretation is trustworthy" (Daniel 2:28-45,**Words in parentheses are mine).

"In the time of those kings" from verse 44, meaning during the reign of the kings of the fourth kingdom, the final kingdom, the Lord sets up

His own kingdom which will never end (This kingdom is also described in Daniel 7:7). This prophecy was given to Daniel about 2550 years ago, around 570 B.C. The part that relates to the final world ruler (the fourth kingdom) has not been fulfilled yet; all the remaining parts have been fulfilled. Verses 40 to 45 describe the final world ruler, which is synonymous with the fourth kingdom. (The ruler of this fourth kingdom is *the antichrist-beast* we have been examining in Revelation 13, the one the false prophet in that chapter urges the world to worship with great signs and wonders.) Note that verses 44 and 45 reveal the end of that kingdom, which corresponds to the return of the Lord Jesus, who will destroy that kingdom and then begin His reign here on earth, a reign that will endure forever. The account of the destruction of this fourth kingdom, and the beast and the false prophet are found in Revelation 19:19-21. We have seen that the beast and the false prophet are thrown alive into the lake of fire, burning with brimstone.

Daniel Provides Further Information about the Antichrist

When we read Daniel 7, we learn a few more things that help to complete our understanding of the antichrist, Revelation, and the end time. We learn that we are reading yet another account of four kingdoms, and the fourth is the final kingdom that Jesus will put to an end by His coming back with His saints. The new information we learn in Daniel 7 is that even though Jesus casts the beast-antichrist and the false prophet into the lake of fire, destroying the fourth kingdom, He allows the other kingdoms (dominions) to continue to exist for a season and a time. These remaining kingdoms are ruled over by Christ Jesus and His saints but allowed to remain for a while longer. Even though these kingdoms existed thousands of years ago, some of their descendants are allowed to survive the wrath of God. They are allowed to be on the earth during the thousand-year reign of Jesus here with His saints. Eventually, when at the end of the thousand-year reign Satan is released for a short time, called a "season," to gather the nations to war against the Lord and His saints, it is these people who are deceived by Satan. Satan is finally cast into the lake of fire where the antichrist-beast and the false prophet were cast at the beginning of the thousand-year reign, and all these people who joined Satan to war against the Lord and His saints are also destroyed by fire from heaven. Then God burns up the heavens and the earth with intense heat and creates a new heaven and a new earth. We see here that we are again reading about the fourth and last earthly kingdom, and the end of the antichrist-beast: "[11] **I watched then because of the sound of the pompous words which the horn was speaking; I watched till *the beast was slain, and its body destroyed and given to the burning flame*" (Daniel 7:11, emphasis mine).** Now let's read more of the passage and include a few verses that come before verse 11.

The Antichrist and the Ten Horns

"[7]**After this I kept looking in the night visions, and behold, *a fourth beast*, dreadful and terrifying and extremely strong; and it had large iron teeth. It devoured and crushed and trampled down the remainder with its feet; and it was different from all the beasts that were before it, and *it had ten horns*."** (This fourth beast is the end time antichrist-beast. The ten horns are ten additional kings. We learn from Revelation 17:12-13 that they give their power and authority to the antichrist.) "[8]**While I was contemplating the horns, behold, another horn, a little one, came up among them, and three of the first horns were pulled out by the roots before it; and behold, this**

horn possessed eyes like the eyes of a man ***and a mouth uttering great boasts.*****"** (That the little horn is uttering great boasts informs us that this is again describing the fourth beast or antichrist-beast.) **"9 I watched till thrones were put in place, And the Ancient of Days** (God the Father) **was seated; His garment was white as snow, And the hair of His head was like pure wool. His throne was a fiery flame, Its wheels a burning fire; 10 A fiery stream issued And came forth from before Him. A thousand thousands ministered to Him; Ten thousand times ten thousand stood before Him. The court was seated, And the books were opened.**

The Antichrist is Destroyed

"11 I watched then because of the sound of the pompous words which the horn was speaking; I watched till ***the beast was slain, and its body destroyed and given to the burning flame.*****"** (Again, the horn is also the beast that was slain. This is the same beast that Jesus casts into the lake of fire in Revelation 19:20, the end time antichrist-beast.) **"12 As for the rest of the beasts, they had their dominion taken away,** ***yet their lives were prolonged for a season and a time*****" (Daniel 7:7-12).**

That the "rest of the beasts" had their dominion taken away, yet their lives prolonged, reveals to us that some people from the empires that preceded the final end time fourth empire, were allowed to survive the wrath of God. These survivors are the nations that the Lord Jesus "rules over with a rod of iron" during His millennial reign. We just read that the beast (the antichrist) was slain, and its body destroyed and given to the burning flame. This is when Jesus cast the beast into the lake of fire. Next, we read that the rest of the beasts had their dominion taken away, meaning they did not rule or exercise authority. But they are allowed to continue to live for "a season and a time." "The season" is the brief time during which Satan is released to deceive the nations and gather them for war. The "time" is the thousand-year reign of Jesus that precedes the season.

The reference to the "rest of the beasts, having their dominion taken away, yet their lives prolonged for a season and a time" refers to the unsaved survivors of the seven bowls of wrath which were poured out on the earth. These unbelievers who were allowed to survive contain elements of the previous empires, the peoples of the three beasts (ancient empires) that preceded this fourth empire which the Lord brought to an end when He returned from heaven with his saints. Over many centuries, these peoples had migrated and spread over the entire earth. Christ had taken the saints off the earth to heaven during the brief period the wrath of God was poured out on the earth. Now Jesus is returning to begin His thousand-year reign. The saints who are with Him are now immortal. That there are mortals still surviving on the earth during Christ's earthly reign of a thousand years is apparent when we consult Isaiah 65:18-25 and the final chapters of Ezekiel from chapter 40 to the end. (This is explained in more depth in chapter 9 on the thousand-year reign of Christ.)

The next portion of Daniel 7 will confirm further what we learned about the final world ruler in Revelation 17: "[13] **I was watching in the night visions, And behold, One like the Son of Man, Coming with the clouds of heaven! He came to the Ancient of Days, And they brought Him near before Him.** [14] **Then to Him** (Jesus) **was given dominion and glory and a kingdom, That all peoples, nations, and languages should serve Him. His dominion is an everlasting dominion, Which shall not pass away, And His kingdom the one Which shall not be destroyed.** [15] **I, Daniel, was grieved in my spirit within my body, and**

the visions of my head troubled me. [16] I came near to one of those who stood by, and asked him the truth of all this. So he told me and made known to me the interpretation of these things: [17] '*Those great beasts*, which are four, are *four kings* which arise out of the earth. (Again, note that beasts are used to represent kings, or rulers and their empires. The ten horns are also kings. Therefore, beasts are rulers and their empires, and horns also represent kings.) **[18] But the saints of the Most High shall receive the kingdom, and possess the kingdom forever, even forever and ever.' [19] Then I wished to know the truth about *the fourth beast, which was different from all the others, exceedingly dreadful*, with its teeth of iron and its nails of bronze, which devoured, broke in pieces, and trampled the residue with its feet; [20] and the ten horns** [ten kings, refer back to Revelation 17:7 and 17:12] **that were on its head, and the other horn which came up, before which three fell** (This description is given for the saints who will be alive when these events unfold, to aid them, some of whom we may be, to recognize the antichrist-beast when is emerges)**, namely, that horn which had eyes and a mouth which spoke pompous words,** [The fourth beast and this both refer to the end time antichrist-beast] **whose appearance was greater than his fellows. [21] I was watching; and the same horn *was making war against the saints, and prevailing against them,* [22] until the Ancient of Days came, and a judgment was made in favor of the saints of the Most High, and the time came for the saints to possess the kingdom" (Daniel 7:13-22, emphasis mine).** Verses 19-21 above describe the final world ruler and his kingdom or empire. The three horns that are broken off by the other horn which came up are three kings which are subdued by the one who is the antichrist-beast. I expect the fulfillment of this part of the prophecy will be evident to those who have insight when it happens. Again, in yet another prophecy, we are told the ruler of the final kingdom will make war against the saints and prevail against them. We have now added to what we learned from the other passages about this final world ruler that he subdues three of the ten kings and that he makes war against the saints and prevails against them.

Now, as we continue to examine more Scripture about this final ruler and his kingdom, we add to the three characteristics listed previously a fourth and fifth characteristic, namely *that the antichrist-beast subdues three of the ten kings,* and *he makes war against the saints and prevails against them.* These common markers are important to keep in mind as we read and review prophecy in either Daniel or Revelation dealing with a beast. When we observe a beast in Revelation and see one or more of these traits associated with him, we know we are reading about the antichrist-beast, the final world ruler, whom Jesus casts into the lake of fire along with the false prophet.

When we see in Scripture a description of a beast (or king) noting that he exhibits these traits, we are being told more about this final world ruler, his kingdom, and what to expect. Now when you read this next Scripture from Daniel 7, it should become immediately evident that it is referring to the antichrist-beast. This beast is the fourth and final beast and is different from all its predecessors. Not only do we find as with the previous passage that he makes war against the saints, but we also understand that this is God's plan, for it states that "the saints shall be given into his hand for a time, and times and half a time." (This is one time plus two more times plus half a time, totaling three and a half times. We come to understand this is three and a half years, which is also forty-two months. We have discussed previously that this phrasing indicates three and a half years.) But we are reassured that God brings an end to his dominion and gives "the kingdom and dominion, and the greatness of the kingdoms under the whole heaven" to the saints of the Most High: "[23] **Thus he said: 'The fourth beast shall be A fourth kingdom on earth, Which shall be different from all other kingdoms, And shall devour the whole earth, Trample it and break it into pieces. [24] The ten horns are ten kings Who shall arise from this kingdom. And another shall rise after them; He shall be different from the first ones, And shall subdue three kings. [25] He shall speak pompous words against the Most High, Shall persecute the saints of the Most High, And shall intend to change times and law. Then *the saints shall be given into his hand For a time and times and half a time.* [26] 'But the court shall be seated, And they shall take away his dominion, To consume and destroy it forever. [27] Then the kingdom and dominion, And the greatness of the kingdoms under the whole heaven, *Shall be given to the people, the saints of the Most High.* His kingdom is an everlasting kingdom, And all dominions shall serve and obey Him.'** (This begins when Jesus comes to reign with His saints for a thousand years on the earth.) **(Daniel 7:23-27)**

The antichrist-beast is the last beast, who arises after the ten kings, while they are still present. He subdues three of them. We learned in Revelation 17:13 that it is God's plan and purpose for these ten kings to give their power and authority to the antichrist-beast. Once again, we see in verse 25 that the saints are still on the earth, and because it is God's plan and purpose they are being persecuted and given into the hand of the antichrist-beast, and have not been raptured yet. We must endure the great tribulation and not deny Christ. Those who are not killed for their testimony are rescued and are taken off the earth just before the bowls of wrath are poured out, when the seventh trumpet, the last trumpet sounds. Jesus takes us all to heaven for the marriage supper of the Lamb. We return with Christ after the wrath is poured out, to war against the antichrist-beast and his armies, and then to reign with Jesus on the earth for a thousand years. Jesus casts this final ruler, the antichrist-beast into the lake of fire. What follows after the beast and false prophet are cast into the lake of fire, you will see described in Daniel 7:27, **"Then the kingdom and dominion, And the greatness of the kingdoms under the whole heaven, Shall be given to the people, the saints of the Most High."** This is when the saints rule with Jesus on earth during his thousand-year reign.

In Daniel chapter 11, we pick up additional information not seen previously in other prophecies. Previously we examined a portion of Daniel 11 where we learned that forces will arise, "desecrate the sanctuary fortress," stop sacrifices, and set up the "abomination of desolation." Jesus spoke of this in Matthew 24 in answer to His disciples' question about the end of the age and the signs of His return. He said that when the abomination of desolation spoken of by the prophet Daniel was seen standing, those in Judea should flee. (We will learn where they should flee to when we read the end of Daniel 11.) From Daniel 8 we obtain an insight that applies here: **"[25]And through his shrewdness He will cause deceit to succeed by his influence; And he will magnify himself in his heart, And he will destroy many while they are at ease. He will even oppose the Prince of princes, But he will be broken without human agency".** (Jesus does this by casting him into the lake of fire, as we read in Revelation 19:20.) **(Daniel 8:25).** The antichrist-beast is a man of intrigue, full of shrewdness and deceit. People will be caught off guard by him initially because he will not immediately be causing violence. But it tells us that "He will destroy many while they are at ease." The warning sign Jesus gives is "when you see the abomination of desolation…" then flee. Let us add to this new information a bit more detail from Daniel 11: "[36] **Then the king shall do according to his own will: he shall exalt and magnify himself above every god, shall speak blasphemies against the God of gods, and shall prosper till the wrath has been accomplished; for what has been determined shall be done.** [41] **He shall also enter the Glorious Land, and many countries shall be overthrown; but these shall escape from his hand: Edom, Moab, and the prominent people of Ammon** [modern-day Jordan]" **(Daniel 11:36,41, NKJV).** Contained in verse 41 above is a key truth, often overlooked. We are told where on the earth to flee from the antichrist-beast to be safe. This may only be relevant to those living in or near Israel when these things begin to happen. Related to this are the words of Jesus to us from Matthew 24: "[15] **So when you see standing in the holy place 'the abomination that causes desolation', spoken of through the prophet Daniel—let the reader understand—** [16] **then let those who are in Judea flee to the mountains.** [17] **Let no one on the housetop go down to take anything out of the house.** [18] **Let no one in the field go back to get their cloak.** [19] **How dreadful it will be in those days for pregnant women and nursing mothers!** [20] **Pray that your flight will not take place in winter or on the Sabbath.** [21] ***For then there will be great distress, unequaled from the beginning of the world until now—and never to be equaled again.*** [22] **"If those days had not been cut short, no one would survive, but for the sake of the elect those days will be shortened.** [23] **At that time if anyone says to you, 'Look, here is the Messiah!' or, 'There he is!' do not believe it.** [24] **For false**

messiahs and false prophets will appear and perform great signs and wonders to deceive, if possible, even the elect. [25] See, I have told you ahead of time. [26] So if anyone tells you, 'There he is, out in the wilderness,' do not go out; or, 'Here he is, in the inner rooms,' do not believe it. [27] For as lightning that comes from the east is visible even in the west, so will be the coming of the Son of Man. [28] Wherever there is a carcass, there the vultures will gather." This section tells us that times will be so hard that we are warned not to be deceived, not to fall for false messiahs, and not to pay attention to false prophets. The hallmark of false prophets is, when the truth is that extremely hard things lie ahead, they are proclaiming a message of "peace and safety." We are also told clearly here when the gathering of the saints will occur in the remainder of this passage: **"[29] *Immediately after the tribulation of those days* the sun will be darkened, and the moon will not give its light; the stars will fall from heaven, and the powers of the heavens will be shaken. [30] Then the sign of the Son of Man will appear in heaven, and then all the tribes of the earth will mourn, and they will see the Son of Man coming on the clouds of heaven with power and great glory. [31] And He will send His angels *with a great sound of a trumpet,* and *they will gather together His elect* from the four winds, from one end of heaven to the other" (Matthew 24:15-31, emphasis mine).** There is no mistaking from this passage that the rapture, or gathering of the saints, occurs after the tribulation, not before it.

Jesus told us in the passage from Matthew to let those in Judea flee to the mountains. In Daniel, in the passage Jesus is referring to directly, we learn the exact places to which to flee: Edom, Moab, and Ammon, which comprise modern-day Jordan. No other place on earth is specifically described as safe during this time. I want to draw our attention to what is stated by Jesus regarding the rapture in verses 29-31: "And He will send His angels with *a great sound of a trumpet*, and they will gather together His elect from the four winds, from one end of heaven to the other." When did He say this will happen? He says it will occur immediately "after the tribulation of those days." We are told in 1 Thessalonians **"to wait for His Son from heaven, whom He raised from the dead, that is Jesus, who rescues us from the wrath to come" (1 Thessalonians 1:10).** So does He forget to rescue the saints referenced in this Daniel passage? No, Jesus did not forget, and these were not a group of saints who were being punished. The only logical answer is that the tribulation of those days was not God's wrath.

We learn from Daniel 11 that this ruler (the antichrist-beast) shall come to his end without human agency, and no one will help him. This is describing his end and final destruction by Christ Jesus when He comes with His saints, after the resurrection and rapture. How much time passes between the rapture and Lord's return with His saints to vanquish the final beast and set up Jesus' earthly thousand-year reign? As stated before, possibly only a relatively brief time, during which time the saints are in heaven with Christ. The reason I think only a short time elapses between the time we are raptured, taken to heaven for the marriage supper of the Lamb, and then return with Jesus is that I believe these events will occur in a manner that will fulfill the feasts that God instituted after the exodus of the children of Israel from Egypt. He has already fulfilled the Feast of Passover and the Feast of Weeks (Pentecost), setting up Christ as the ultimate fulfillment of these feasts—they were instituted to distinguish the Jewish people as separate from other nations and to point ahead to Christ Jesus. I speculate Jesus may fulfill the Feast of Tabernacles with the marriage supper of the Lamb in heaven. This is the final feast in the fall, and it takes place over an eight-day period. It is soon after this that I anticipate the Lord returns to earth with His saints. You will find a fuller discussion of this in chapter 10 regarding the Jewish Feasts.

Let us now turn our attention back to the antichrist-beast and connect some of the things we have learned of him in Daniel and how he meets his end: In chapter 5 of this book, we looked at the vision of the ram and the goat and learned that it relates to Iran (Persia) at the time of the end, and military engagements related to that event. Returning to Daniel 8 briefly, we see a similar description of him to what we have previously read: "[22] **The four horns that replaced the one that was broken off represent four kingdoms that will emerge from his nation but will not have the same power. [23] In the latter part of their reign, when rebels have become completely wicked, a *fierce-looking king, a master of intrigue*, will arise. [24] He will become very strong, but not by his own power. He will cause astounding devastation and will succeed in whatever he does. He will destroy those who are mighty, the holy people. [25] He will cause deceit to prosper, and he will consider himself superior. When they feel secure, he will destroy many and take his stand against the Prince of princes. Yet he will be destroyed, but not by human power"(Daniel 8:22-25, emphasis mine).** Now please review the same verses from Daniel 8 in the NKJV: "[22] **As for the broken horn and the four that stood up in its place, four kingdoms shall arise out of that nation, but not with its power. [23] "And *in the latter time of their kingdom*, When the transgressors have reached their fullness, *A king shall arise, Having fierce features, Who understands sinister schemes.* [24] His power shall be mighty, but not by his own power [but rather from Satan]; He shall destroy fearfully, And shall prosper and thrive; *He shall destroy the mighty,***

***and also the holy people.* [25] *Through his cunning He shall cause deceit to prosper* under his rule; And he shall exalt himself in his heart. *He shall destroy many in their prosperity*" (Daniel 8: 22-25, NKJV)** (In Appendix 5 of this book you will find a detailed examination of Scripture which points to the destruction of America. Scripture in Revelation 17 and 18 points to the destruction of a very prosperous, wealthy place, one that is the center of world commerce. It is a place where all the world's merchants sell their goods. The destruction of this place comes at the hand of the antichrist-beast in an alliance with ten kings. Here in Daniel, we read of this individual that "He shall destroy many in their prosperity." In other translations it tells us "When they feel secure, he will destroy many.")

This passage above, like the others we have examined in this chapter, also describes the final beast (ruler), but *the four horns* which we are told are the four kingdoms mentioned are all in existence at the same time. (These are different from the four beasts we have previously encountered, as those were sequential, one after another.) Let us sum up what we have observed about the antichrist from the passages we have examined:

- His power shall be mighty, but not by his own power;
- He is fierce-looking and a master of intrigue,
- He shall destroy fearfully,
- And shall prosper and thrive;
- He shall destroy the mighty, and also the holy people.
- He will be destroyed, but not by human power.

Now, let's review our encounter with the antichrist-beast in Revelation 13 which we looked at earlier in this chapter: (My words are in parentheses.)

1 Then I stood on the sand of the sea. And I saw *a beast* rising up out of the sea (This is again, the end time antichrist-beast. However, we read in Revelation 11:7 that this beast came up out of the abyss, here we read he was seen rising up out of the sea, and again we are told in Revelation 17:8 that he comes up out of the abyss)**, *having seven heads*** (Heads are kings, as are horns) ***and ten horns*, and on his horns ten crowns, and on his heads a blasphemous name. 2 Now the beast which I saw was like a leopard, his feet were like the feet of a bear, and his mouth like the mouth of a lion. The dragon gave him his power, his throne, and great authority.** (His power comes from Satan.) **3 And I saw one of his heads as if it had been mortally wounded, and his deadly wound was healed.** (Perhaps this is a counterfeit copy of the death and resurrection of Christ, and that this will be observed to happen to the antichrist-beast) **And all the world marveled and followed the beast. 4 So they worshiped the dragon who gave authority to the beast; and they worshiped the beast, saying, "Who is like the beast? Who is able to make war with him?" 5 And he was given a mouth speaking great things and blasphemies, and he was given authority to continue for forty-two months.** (Forty- two months is three and a half years.) **6 Then *he opened his mouth in blasphemy against God*, to blaspheme His name, His tabernacle, and those who dwell in heaven. 7 *It was granted to him to make war with the saints and to overcome them.* And authority was given him over every tribe, tongue, and nation. 8 All who dwell on the earth will worship him, whose names have not been written in the Book of Life of the Lamb slain from the foundation of the world.** 9 If anyone has an ear, let him hear. 10 He who leads into captivity shall go into captivity; he who kills with the sword must be killed with the sword. Here is the patience and the faith of the saints. (Revelation 13:1-9) It is clear this is the final world ruler, the antichrist-beast. All in the world will worship him except the saints. He blasphemes God. We see the seven heads and ten horns that we have seen repeatedly in other Scriptures associated with him. It is also clear the saints must persevere in their faith whether they are to die or are to be taken into captivity.

We again encounter this same beast, with seven heads, and ten horns, in Revelation 17: 7 **And the angel said to me, "Why do you wonder? I will tell you the mystery of the woman and of the beast that carries her, which has the seven heads and the ten horns.** (Reading further in this passage gives more understanding about the seven heads. We also learn what the purpose of the ten horns are.) 8 **"*The beast* that you saw was, and is not, and is about to come up out of the abyss and go to destruction.**[3] **And those who dwell on the earth, whose name**

---

3 (John is writing this during the reign of Rome. When he states the beast was, and is not, I believe he means this beast who is the antichrist-beast of the end time, comes from one of the previous empires that have been spoken of elsewhere in Scripture. When the fifth trumpet is blown in Revelation 9:1 we read that John sees a "star that fell from heaven, and the key to the abyss was given to him." **"1Then the fifth angel sounded, and I saw a star from heaven which had fallen to the earth; and the key of the bottomless pit was given to him." (Revelation 9:1)** A few verses later in Revelation 9:11, we learn this angel is the king over the locusts that come from the smoke that came from the bottomless pit. He is called the angel of the abyss, which seems to infer that the bottomless pit and the abyss are one and the same. **"11They have as king over them, the angel of the abyss; his name in Hebrew is Abaddon, and in the Greek he has the name Apollyon." (Revelation 9:11)** Just as Satan entered into Judas Iscariot, it may be that this angel, the king of the abyss,

has not been written in the book of life from the foundation of the world, will wonder when they see the beast, that he was and is not and will come. [9] **"Here is the mind which has wisdom.** ***The seven heads are*** **seven mountains on which the woman sits,** [10] **and** ***they are seven kings*****; five have fallen, one is, the other has not yet come; and when he comes, he must remain a little while.** (Keep in mind, John was writing in the first century. I believe "Five have fallen" refers to five kings who headed empires in times past. I believe "One is" speaks of the current head of the empire of Rome, which exists at the time John is writing this. I believe "the beast which was and is not, is himself also an eighth and is one of the seven" tells us the origin of this beast. I believe it will come from one of the previous empires, and is the seventh king, the last and final king of any earthly empire. That this last king gets his power from Satan, perhaps even being indwelt by a fallen angel who is subject to Satan, may be what is inferred by saying "he himself is also an eighth." That "he goes to destruction" confirms this is the antichrist-beast end time ruler who Jesus destroys by casting him into the lake of fire.) [11] **"The beast which was and is not, is himself also an eighth and is one of the seven, and he goes to destruction.** [12] **"*****The ten horns*** **which you saw** ***are ten kings*** **who have not yet received a kingdom, but they receive authority as kings with the beast for one hour.** [13] **"These have one purpose, and** ***they give their power and authority***

enters into the man who is the end time antichrist-beast. That this beast "is not" would seem to indicate that he is not part of the beast that is presently ruling, which is Rome. When he says he is about to come up out of the abyss and go to destruction, he connects us to the beast which comes up out of the abyss and kills the two witnesses of God when they have finished their testimony in Revelation 11:7. John also tells us that he is the end time beast, which Jesus destroys by casting him into the lake of fire.)

to the beast. (These ten kings who give their power and authority to the beast join with him to destroy the place called "Babylon the Great.") [16]**"And the ten horns** (kings) **which you saw, and the beast,** ***these will hate the harlot*** (Babylon the Great) **and will make her desolate and naked, and will eat her flesh and** ***will burn her up with fire.*** [17] ***For God has put it in their hearts to execute His purpose*** **by having a common purpose, and by giving their kingdom to the beast, until the words of God will be fulfilled." (Revelation 17:7–13; 16-17)** (Words in parentheses are mine.) The seven heads are themselves, also seven kings. But they were spread over time, unlike the ten horns (kings) who were all present at the same time. The ten kings exist to give their power to the beast. Acting together, they destroy a wealthy, very prosperous people who live in a place Scripture calls "Babylon the Great." There will still be saints living in this place, for the rapture has not occurred when the destruction of this land occurs. Otherwise, it would not be necessary for the Lord to say to His people who dwell there "come out of her, my people, so that you will not participate in her sins and receive of her plagues." [4]**I heard another voice from heaven, saying, "*Come out of her, my people, so that you will not participate in her sins and receive of her plagues*; (Revelation 18:4)** This reveals to us that the destruction of Babylon the Great we are told about in Revelation 17 and 18 occurs before the events in Revelation 11, when the seventh trumpet is sounded and the rapture takes place. We have found that the saints are rescued from God's wrath and taken to heaven when the seventh trumpet sounds.

Here are the details we have learned about the final ruler, the antichrist-beast, from the prophecies of Daniel and Revelation:

- He has mighty power from Satan and his arrival will include signs and false wonders.
- He will likely survive a mortal wound or perhaps come back from the dead.
- Forces from him will desecrate the sanctuary, put an end to sacrifice and offering, and set up an abomination of desolation.
- He will demand that all people worship him.
- He will crush and trample down all opposition on earth.
- He is deceitful, shrewd, and a master of intrigue, and he understands sinister schemes.
- He has fierce features.
- He will destroy many to an extraordinary degree while they are at ease and feel secure.
- He will wage war against the saints, who have been given into his hand for forty-two months, overcoming them and killing many.
- He will make alterations in times and in law.
- Acting in concert with ten kings, or heads of nations, he will destroy many, including Babylon the Great.
- He is pompous and will utter great boasts. He is proud enough even to oppose and blaspheme the Prince of princes (the Lord). He blasphemes the God of Heaven.
- He is destroyed by Christ Jesus upon His return with His saints and thrown into the lake of fire.

Thus, by combining the study of Daniel with that of Revelation, we are able to get quite a lot of detail concerning what to expect at the end of time, right before the Lord returns for His saints at the resurrection/rapture. These details should aid us in being watchful and ready, so as not to be among those who are deceived by this conniving individual.

Let us study well, preparing our hearts and minds and being watchful, as we are instructed to do as believers in the Lord.

chapter EIGHT
Seventy Sevens

A Little-Known Key to Unlocking Prophecy

About five hundred and fifty years before Christ, the prophet Daniel received a visit from the angel Gabriel. The circumstances of this occurrence are recorded for us in Daniel chapter nine. Daniel was part of the Jewish deportation by Nebuchadnezzar, king of Babylon, when he captured Jerusalem in 606 BC in fulfillment of the prophecy given to Jeremiah (Jeremiah 25:11; 29:10). By looking back at Daniel and his study of the prophecies God had given to Jeremiah, we will discover important truths that pertain to Christ and to the future of the church.

Seventy Years of Exile for Israel to Babylon

Israel had been commanded by God to farm its land for six years and then let the land have a sabbath rest in the seventh year. They were to do this for seven periods of seven years each, then after the forty-ninth year they were to declare a Jubilee year, the fiftieth year, and also give the land an additional sabbath rest, back-to-back with the forty-ninth year's rest. However, the Israelites failed to obey these commands. Because of their disobedience in this and in many other regards, God declared after warning them through His prophets that they would be taken into exile to Babylon for seventy years to give the land all the sabbath rests that it had been denied. We find details recorded in Jeremiah and Chronicles: **"This whole land will be a desolation and a horror, and these nations**

***will serve the king of Babylon seventy years*" (Jeremiah 25:11).** Those who had escaped from the sword he carried away to Babylon; and they were servants to him and to his sons until the rule of the kingdom of Persia, **"[21]to fulfill the word of the Lord by the mouth of Jeremiah, *until the land had enjoyed its sabbaths.* All the days of its desolation it kept sabbath *until seventy years were complete*" (2 Chronicles 36:20–21).**

Daniel's Realization and His Prayer

In Daniel chapter nine, we find that Daniel has been reading the Word of the Lord by the prophet Jeremiah, and he realizes that he and the exiles have now been in captivity for nearly the seventy years that was declared by the Lord. He begins to pray to God about forgiving Israel for His own name's sake and that He would return the people to Jerusalem, which he knows is God's holy city, the place on earth where He declared His name would dwell.

Daniel was focused on prayer regarding the seventy years which were near an end that had been decreed regarding the years of exile in Babylon. In answer to his prayer, the Lord sends the angel Gabriel to answer Daniel, and tells him about a different "seventy." It would be easy to miss the fact that contained in Gabriel's words to Daniel is a prophecy by which God revealed when Christ would come the first time, and when He would be crucified. I believe that gaining an understanding of this truth is key to unsealing much of Daniel as well as Revelation. Of course, this connection was hidden until Jesus had come and was crucified, but the truth that was revealed to Daniel by the angel Gabriel was there in Scripture for over five hundred years in the possession of the scribes. This connection has been known for hundreds of years by many serious students of God's Word. I first came across this when studying the Word in 1971 and was astounded at what it revealed. Isaac Newton, among others, studied this and understood it. Newton was so amazed that he stated he would stake the entire truth of Christianity on this one prophecy which is contained in Daniel chapter nine. Given this astounding declaration, I think it is worth examining the chapter in detail: **"[1]In the first year of Darius the son of Ahasuerus, of the lineage of the Medes, who was made king over the realm of the Chaldeans— [2]in the first year of his reign I, Daniel, understood by the books the number of the years specified by the word of the LORD through Jeremiah the prophet, that He would accomplish seventy years in the desolations of Jerusalem. [3]Then I set my face toward the Lord God to make request by prayer and supplications, with fasting, sackcloth, and ashes. [4]And I prayed to the LORD my God, and made confession, and said, 'O Lord, great and awesome God, who keeps His covenant and mercy with those who love Him, and with those who keep His commandments, [5]we have sinned and committed iniquity, we have done wickedly and rebelled, even by departing from Your precepts and Your judgments. [6]Neither have we heeded Your servants the prophets, who spoke in Your name to our kings and our princes, to our fathers and all the people of the land. [7]O Lord, righteousness belongs to You, but to us shame of face, as it is this day—to the men of Judah, to the inhabitants of Jerusalem and all Israel, those near and those far off in all the countries to which You have driven them, because of the unfaithfulness which they have committed against You. [8]O Lord, to us belongs shame of face, to our kings, our princes, and our fathers, because we have sinned against You. [9]To the Lord our God belong**

mercy and forgiveness, though we have rebelled against Him. [10]We
have not obeyed the voice of the LORD our God, to walk in His laws,
which He set before us by His servants the prophets. [11]Yes, all Israel
has transgressed Your law, and has departed so as not to obey Your
voice; therefore the curse and the oath written in the Law of Moses
the servant of God have been poured out on us, because we have
sinned against Him. [12]And He has confirmed His words, which He
spoke against us and against our judges who judged us, by bringing
upon us a great disaster; for under the whole heaven such has never
been done as what has been done to Jerusalem. [13]As it is written in
the Law of Moses, all this disaster has come upon us; yet we have
not made our prayer before the LORD our God, that we might turn
from our iniquities and understand Your truth. [14]Therefore the
LORD has kept the disaster in mind, and brought it upon us; for the
LORD our God is righteous in all the works which He does, though
we have not obeyed His voice. [15]And now, O Lord our God, who
brought Your people out of the land of Egypt with a mighty hand,
and made Yourself a name, as it is this day—we have sinned, we
have done wickedly! [16]O Lord, according to all Your righteousness,
I pray, let Your anger and Your fury be turned away from Your city
Jerusalem, Your holy mountain; because for our sins, and for the
iniquities of our fathers, Jerusalem and Your people are a reproach
to all those around us. [17]Now therefore, our God, hear the prayer of
Your servant, and his supplications, and for the Lord's sake cause
Your face to shine on Your sanctuary, which is desolate. [18]O my God,
incline Your ear and hear; open Your eyes and see our desolations,
and the city which is called by Your name; for we do not present
our supplications before You because of our righteous deeds, but

because of Your great mercies. [19]O Lord, hear! O Lord, forgive! O Lord, listen and act! Do not delay for Your own sake, my God, for Your city and Your people are called by Your name'" (Daniel 9:1-19). This first section is detailing Daniel's deep conviction and supplication to the Lord, and it is simply the first part of this pivotal conversation. The rest of the exchange reveals the truths we look for, but this context is important so we can see what has been happening and where Daniel's heart is as the Lord reveals new truths to him. Daniel acknowledges God's Holiness and righteousness, and his own and Israel's sin. He appeals to God to act on behalf of Jerusalem for the impact that would have to exalt God's own name. Continue reading through the chapter, and then we will dig through this astonishing conversation:

A New Prophecy about a New "Seventy of Sevens"

[20]Now while I was speaking, praying, and confessing my sin and the sin of my people Israel, and presenting my supplication before the LORD my God for the holy mountain of my God, [21]yes, while I was speaking in prayer, the man Gabriel, whom I had seen in the vision at the beginning, being caused to fly swiftly, reached me about the time of the evening offering. [22]And he informed me, and talked with me, and said, 'O Daniel, I have now come forth to give you skill to understand. [23]At the beginning of your supplications the command went out, and I have come to tell you, for you are greatly beloved; therefore consider the matter, and understand the vision: (Daniel 9:1-23) (NKJV) As stated, Daniel was praying about the seventy years of exile and captivity which he had observed from reading Jeremiah. However, God was going to reveal a different "seventy" to him in response to his prayer.

[24]Seventy 'sevens' are decreed for your people and your holy city to finish transgression, to put an end to sin, to atone for wickedness, to bring in everlasting righteousness, to seal up vision and prophecy and to anoint the most holy. [25]Know and understand this: From the issuing of the decree to restore and rebuild Jerusalem until the Anointed One, the ruler, comes, there will be seven 'sevens,' and sixty-two 'sevens.' It will be rebuilt with streets and a trench, but in times of trouble. [26]After the sixty-two 'sevens,' the *Anointed One* will be cut off and will have nothing. The people of the ruler who will come will destroy the city and the sanctuary. The end will come like a flood: War will continue until the end, and desolations have been decreed. [27]He will *confirm a covenant* with many for one 'seven.' In the middle of the 'seven' he will put an end to sacrifice and offering. And *on a wing of the temple* he will set up an abomination that causes desolation, until the end that is decreed is poured out on him'" (Daniel 9:24–27, NIV84, emphasis mine). We will presently examine this passage to determine the meaning of the new "seventy of sevens" the Lord revealed to Daniel and why it is significant to end times prophecies.

A Day for a Year Prophecy

This conversation between Daniel and Gabriel not only tells, five hundred years ahead of time, exactly when Jesus would come to earth, but it also gives us clues about the other prophecies we are grappling with in this book. Jesus is referred to as the "Anointed One" in some versions, and "messiah" in others. But either way, God disclosed when He would send our Lord. He told Daniel that He would send a messiah who would be "cut off and have nothing" and exactly when that would occur. Then He fulfilled his Word, sending His son Jesus sixty-nine sevens, or 483 years (as reckoned by Jews, having 360 days a year) from the day He made the declaration, marking it by giving a decree through the king to rebuild Jerusalem. (Reckoning according to a Jewish calendar is appropriate as this was written to the Jews, by a Jew. Additionally, the Gregorian calendar with 365 and ¼ days was not adopted at the time of this writing.)

Just like an official at a race with a stopwatch that he punches when the race begins, the Father said to start the watch and begin the count with *a decree to rebuild Jerusalem.* God also told us the second temple-- which had not even been built at the time this prophecy was given-- would itself be destroyed, along with the city of Jerusalem. No one disputes the fact that the Jewish Scriptures which say these things had existed for centuries before these events occurred.

In the Jewish Study Bible, the Tanakh Translation, this passage from Daniel 9 reads: **"25 You must know and understand: From the issuance of the word to restore and rebuild Jerusalem until the [time of the] *anointed leader* is seven weeks; and for sixty-two weeks it will be rebuilt, square and moat, but in a time of distress. 26 And after those sixty-two weeks, *the anointed one* will disappear and vanish. The army of a leader who is to come will destroy the city and the sanctuary, but its end will come through a flood. Desolation is decreed until the end of war" (Daniel 9: 25-26, Jewish Study Bible, emphasis mine).**

First, as we consider these verses, it is important to note that the original text was written by Daniel in Hebrew. Scholars have recognized for centuries that these Scriptures pin-pointed the time of the crucifixion of our Lord Jesus Christ. God sent the angel Gabriel to give this prophecy to Daniel, and we will examine precisely how we have come to know this truth.

To connect the dots, we need to look at a passage of Scripture found in Ezekiel: "**4 Lie also on your left side, and lay the iniquity of the house of Israel upon it. According to the number of the days that you lie on it, you shall bear their iniquity. 5 For I have laid on you the years of their iniquity, according to the number of the days, three hundred and ninety days; so you shall bear the iniquity of the house of Israel. 6 And when you have completed them, lie again on your right side; then you shall bear the iniquity of the house of Judah forty days. *I have laid on you a day for each year"* (Ezekiel 4:4-6, emphasis mine).** What we learn from the previous passage is that God established *a principle* of "a day for a year" prophetically for Israel. Among others, John Wycliffe, Martin Luther, Matthew Henry, and Sir Isaac Newton have written about prophetic "day-years" in previous centuries and have accepted this as a paradigm. This is easy to overlook and just regard as an oddity when we read this portion of Ezekiel, but when we apply this principle of "a day for a year" in regard to the prophecy that Gabriel gave to Daniel, it provides clarity and enables us to finally understand a revelation from God that He had hidden and sealed up.

The Angel's Declaration

Daniel chapter twelve reveals that understanding of these things had been decreed to be sealed up until the end time: "[4]**But as for you, Daniel, conceal these words and *seal up the book until the end of time*; many will go back and forth, and knowledge will increase" […]"[9]He said, 'Go your way, Daniel, for *these words are concealed and sealed up***

***until the end time*'" (Daniel 12:4, 9, emphasis mine).**

As we continue, I will include excerpts from a study guide for his book "Hidden Beast" done by a fellow saint and student of God's Word, Ellis Skolfield.[4] Ellis Skolfield, author of *Hidden Beast,* has remarked on the "day for a year" paradigm along with many others, and thus some excerpts from his book will lend support to this discussion. This key to understanding this prophecy has been written about for centuries. However, as you will learn, the full understanding of the entire book of Daniel has just in our lifetimes been unsealed.

I have chosen to provide excerpts from Skolfield's studies on Daniel and Revelation because I believe he has presented it in a clear and logical manner, supported by Scripture. Much of what follows regarding this key to unsealing Daniel I credit to Skolfield. He explains the principle of "a day for a year" as follows:

When Scripture refers to days in prophecy, *a day equals a year* in our understanding. When the prophecy appears in the Old Testament, we reckon the year as the Jews did, with a prophetic year having twelve months of thirty days each, for a total of 360 days in a prophetic Jewish year. To convert a Jewish prophetic year to one we commonly use, divide 360 by the number of days in a solar year, 365.24. Thus, a prophetic year appearing in Daniel (Old Testament) is .9857 of our standard year.

When the prophecy appears in the New Testament, we use our standard Roman or Gregorian calendar which is based on the earth's solar cycle having 365 and ¼ days per year.

---

4 Hidden Beast 2, 2nd Edition, Revised March 15, 1991. Ellis Skolfield, Copyright 1990 by Fish House, ISBN 0-9628139-0-7

The Meaning of This Prophecy Was Hidden Until It was Fulfilled

We will next examine the prophecy that the angel Gabriel gave to Daniel in the first year of Darius the King, which scholars believe to be 536 BC: I encourage you to go back and read Daniel 9:25-26, which I cited above.

The Hebrew Word for "Seven"

Hebrew has no word that translates into English as "week," thus the Jews call a week a "seven." Elsewhere in the Scriptures, the Hebrew word for week is "shavua."

שְׁבֻעַ֖ם Shavua

In this particular Scripture however, it is different; it is "shavuim," a plural form of the word for seven.

שָׁבֻעִ֑ים Shavuim

Skolfield makes the point that the plural form requires a multiplier, so these are not weeks of ordinary twenty-four-hour days. So first, it is crucial to understand that what is translated as weeks in some versions is actually the Hebrew word for "seven." (The New International Version recognizes this.) We are instructed that six "sevens" plus another sixty-two "sevens" is the period of time from the going forth of a decree to rebuild Jerusalem until the time that the Messiah will be "cut off" or killed. Sixty-nine "sevens" out of the total of seventy "sevens" are fulfilled with the crucifixion of Jesus. It is also important to remember that the prophecy was given to a Jew, about Jerusalem and the Messiah. It was given about five hundred and fifty years before the birth of Christ. At this time, the Jews were in exile in Babylon, and the Romans had not yet come on the scene. Why is this significant? Because today, we use a Roman, or Gregorian, calendar, with 365.24 days per year, in keeping with the solar cycle of the earth. But the Jews kept a different calendar, one with twelve months with thirty days each month. Their "prophetic" calendar contained three hundred sixty days, not 365.24. We discover that using "weeks" of Jewish years, the meaning of the message from God delivered by Gabriel becomes clear. Sixty-nine "weeks" or "sevens" of years is sixty-nine times seven, or four hundred eighty-three Jewish years. With each year having three hundred and sixty days, this is a total time period of 173,880 days. To be able to discern the number of years the way our current calendar reckons years, we must divide the total number of days by the number of days in one of our years, 365.24. When we do this, 173,880 divided by 365.24, we learn that 476 years the way we count time, which equals 483 Jewish prophetic years, is the time that was revealed would elapse from a decree to rebuild Jerusalem until the Messiah would be killed, or "cut off."

The Decree to Rebuild Jerusalem Found in Nehemiah

Now we search the Scriptures and find several different decrees that are similar, but only one of them fits exactly the requirements set forth by Gabriel, "a decree to rebuild Jerusalem:" "[1]**And it came about in the month Nisan, in the twentieth year of King Artaxerxes, that wine was before him, and I took up the wine and gave it to the king. Now I had not been sad in his presence. [2]So the king said to me, 'Why is your face sad though you are not sick? This is nothing but sadness of heart.' Then I was very much afraid. [3]I said to the king, 'Let the king live forever. Why should my face not be sad when the city, the place of my fathers' tombs, lies desolate and its gates have been consumed by fire?' [4]Then the king said to me, 'What would you request?' So**

I prayed to the God of heaven. [5]I said to the king, 'If it please the king, and if your servant has found favor before you, send me to Judah, *to the city* of my fathers' tombs, *that I may rebuild it.*' [Notice that Nehemiah asked *for permission to rebuild Jerusalem,* not the walls or the temple] **[6]Then the king said to me, the queen sitting beside him, How long will your journey be, and when will you return?' So it pleased the king to send me, and I gave him a definite time. [7]And I said to the king, 'If it please the king, *let letters be given me* for the governors of the provinces beyond the River, that they may allow me to pass through until I come to Judah,** (Here Nehemiah asked for letters, he asked for a written "decree" from the king that allowed him to rebuild Jerusalem.) **[8]and a letter to Asaph the keeper of the king's forest, that he may give me timber to make beams for the gates of the fortress which is by the temple, for the wall of the city and for the house to which I will go'" And the king granted them to me because the good hand of my God was on me" (Nehemiah 2:1–8, emphasis mine).**

This passage of Scripture tells us when to begin counting, in the twentieth year of King Artaxerxes, since that is when Nehemiah requested "letters…for the governors and provinces" so that he may rebuild Jerusalem. We learn from scholars that Artaxerxes began to reign in 465 BC, so his twentieth year would have been 445 BC. The King's decree that he put in writing for Nehemiah was to grant him authority to rebuild the "city of his father's tombs" which was none other than Jerusalem.

Using what we reviewed previously, we must count 476 of our years reckoned according to our current Gregorian calendar forward from 445 BC to find the time when Jesus, the anointed one, the Messiah, was to be killed or "cut off." Doing so puts the date of the crucifixion at 31 AD. It is possible that we may have a historical error in when Artaxerxes began his reign, or we may have error when we start counting as the birth year of Christ our Lord, but I believe if there is an error it is with man's counting and historical record, not with God's Word. When you consider that this prophecy was given over five hundred years before Christ, this represents remarkable precision. I say we "may have an error" in one of these two dates, but I personally believe Jesus was born in 2 BC, and crucified in 31 AD. I believe there are astronomical events in the heavens in 2 BC that tie to the star of Bethlehem which was seen by the shepherds.

The Events that Would Unseal the Meaning of Daniel's Prophecy

So the question we should be asking is, "how does this provide a key to unlocking the meaning of other prophecies, whether they be in Daniel or Revelation?" As we have seen, the "weeks" are weeks of years, (and specifically years as reckoned by the Jewish calendar, not our Gregorian calendar) not weeks of days. So, we might ask if God meant for a day to represent a year in this particular prophecy in Daniel, did He also intend for us to use "a day for a year" to unlock other prophecies in Daniel? The short answer is " yes." I believe what we discover may be another example of dual fulfillment of prophecy. When we examine the results of using a day for a year closely, we find that the Lord did just as the angel Michael said in Daniel 12: He sealed up these prophecies until the time of the end. Beginning with the last verifiable date that sacrifices were offered in Jerusalem by priests, who were the only ones permitted by God to offer them, we are led to the following possible conclusions:

- The date that Jerusalem was returned to the people of Israel after having been trampled under foot of the Gentiles was hidden in Scripture, but was revealed once that date was reached, in much the same way that the date of Jesus's crucifixion was hidden until the appointed time for His death.
- The date that Israel was allowed to become a nation once again on the land God gave to Abraham and his descendants was hidden in Scripture and has since been revealed.
- The date the abomination of desolation "was set up on a wing of the temple" was hidden in Scripture.

A thorough investigation of how these dates were revealed is found in appendix 3 if you care to study it. I emphasize that while I find the revelation of these dates to be remarkable and beyond coincidence, I still believe they are likely only part of the story, that some or all of them may be dual fulfilled in the seven-year period right before the Lord returns for His saints. If so, just as is the case with the unveiling of these dates regarding the nation of Israel, the city of Jerusalem, and the abomination of desolation, we will find that it will not be until they are completely fulfilled that we see all that God has hidden.

chapter NINE
The Millennial Reign

The Great Harlot is Judged Before the Rapture

To lay the groundwork for understanding the reign of Jesus on earth depicted in Revelation 20, it will help to summarize what Revelation 19 reveals to us. It provides a look back to a time prior to the gathering of the saints which took place when the seventh angel sounded, in Revelation 11:15. In verses 1 through 6 we learn that God has judged the great harlot who was described in Revelation 17 through 18, "[2]**for true and just are his judgments. He has condemned the great prostitute who corrupted the earth by her adulteries. He has avenged on her the blood of his servants" (Revelation 19:2, NIV84).** This destruction of the great harlot, Babylon the Great, took place while the saints were still on the earth. We can reason this to be the case because of the verse found in Revelation 18 instructing God's people to come out of her, or they will share in her sins (Revelation 18:4). It would not be necessary to warn them to "come out" if Jesus had already rescued them in the rapture before this destruction occurs.

When Are Men Judged?

Scripture tells us regarding judgement, **"[27]And inasmuch as it is appointed for men to die once and after this comes judgment" (Hebrews 9:27).** We learn here that men face judgement after they die. Aside from telling us that men only live one time (discrediting reincarnation as a belief system), we all face judgement. Christians have been credited with the righteousness of Christ Jesus, thus when God looks at us regarding judgment, He sees the righteousness of His son so we do not need to fear judgment. However, we are judged for rewards. The unbelieving remainder of mankind will come to life in the second resurrection to face the great white throne judgment of Christ after His thousand-year reign on earth. Thus, every man will face judgement. Jesus warned us, **[36]"But I tell you that every careless word that people speak, they shall give an accounting for it in the day of judgment. [37]For by your words you will be justified, and by your words you will be condemned" (Matthew 12:36–37).** Even though Christians have been given the righteousness of Christ, we still will reap what we have sown. We have eternal life with Jesus, but Christ will still judge all men and reward them accordingly: "**[10]For we must all appear before the judgment seat of Christ, so that each one may be recompensed for his deeds in the body, according to what he has done, whether good or bad" (2 Corinthians 5:10)**.

Nations Must Be Judged While They Still Exist

How does all of this relate to the judgement of Babylon the Great? God makes it plain that men face judgement after they die. However, unlike men, nations do not come to life in a resurrection to face judgement, rather they face judgement for their acts in their present existence: **"He makes the nations great, then destroys them; He enlarges the nations, then leads them away" (Job 12:23).**

God uses the nations to accomplish His intended purposes, whether they are God-fearing nations or not. God had warned Israel of judgement over and over if they did not repent and obey His commandments. After many warnings, He first sent Assyria against Israel to take them into captivity about 700 BC. But even though the Lord used Assyria as His tool, He did not hold them guiltless. Read in Isaiah the Lord's response to Assyria: **"[5]Woe to Assyria, the rod of My anger And the staff in whose hands is My indignation" (Isaiah 10:5).** God said when He was finished using Assyria to accomplish His work against Israel, He would punish them for their arrogance: **"[12]So it will be that when the Lord has completed all His work on Mount Zion and on Jerusalem, He will say, 'I will punish the fruit of the arrogant heart of the king of Assyria and the pomp of his haughtiness'" (Isaiah 10:12).**

Almost a century later, he sent Babylon against Judah to punish them and take them into captivity for seventy years. He also proclaimed He would judge Babylon as a nation in Jeremiah 25:12. **'Then it will be when seventy years are completed I will punish the king of Babylon and that nation,' declares the Lord, 'for their iniquity, and the land of the Chaldeans; and I will make it an everlasting desolation. (Jeremiah 25:12)** God likewise judged Babylon for what they had done to His people. In just the same way, before the time when Jesus returns to gather His saints, God will bring judgement on another nation, one that Scripture calls "the great harlot, mystery Babylon the Great." You may read the details of this judgment in Appendix 5. He informs us in Revelation 17 that He will use ten kings who will give their power to the beast (the antichrist) to punish the great harlot:, "Babylon the Great." **"[12]The ten horns which you saw are ten kings who have not yet received a kingdom, but they receive authority as kings with the beast for one hour. [13]These have one purpose, and they give their power and authority to the beast. […] [16] And *the ten horns*** [kings] ***which you saw on the beast*, these will hate the harlot, make her**

desolate and naked, eat her flesh *and burn her with fire*" (Revelation 17:12–13,16, emphasis mine).

The timing of this judgment we are told will happen to Babylon the Great is relevant to our understanding of when Christ will return. We know the antichrist-beast "will destroy many while they are at ease" (Daniel 8:25). Because the destruction of Babylon the Great is a joint endeavor involving "ten kings" in an alliance with the beast, it is likely that the timing for this event falls in the final forty-two months immediately preceding the Lord's return. We have examined Scripture in chapter one indicating that it is not improbable that Jesus may return in the early 2030's, though I have stipulated it is not certain He will return then. As the time draws nearer, if He is going to return in this time frame, we have been promised in Scripture that we who are His followers will know it but that the man of lawlessness must be revealed first if this is to happen. Likewise, Scripture informs us of judgment that is coming to a nation called "Babylon the Great," and it will take place before the Lord returns. Therefore, if Jesus is to return in eight to ten years, the destruction of this nation will occur prior to then, likely between 2028 and 2031. If God purposes for Jesus to tarry for longer, then the destruction of Babylon the Great would be delayed as well because its destruction comes at the hand of the antichrist and ten kings, all of which is part of a countdown, so to speak, to the day of the Lord. But keep in mind that its destruction occurs before Jesus raptures His saints.

As we continue to move forward in Revelation 19 toward the beginning of the millennial kingdom, we read about the marriage supper of the Lamb. We can see in verses 7-9 that the marriage supper of the Lamb has already taken place "[7]'**Let us rejoice and be glad and give the**

glory to Him, for the marriage of the Lamb has come and His bride has made herself ready.' [8]It was given to her to clothe herself *in fine linen, bright and clean; for the fine linen is the righteous acts of the saints.* [9]Then he said to me, 'Write, "Blessed are those who are invited to the marriage supper of the Lamb."' And he said to me, 'These are true words of God'" (Revelation 19:7–9). In the verses which follow below, you will read about the armies that accompany the Lord. The reference to the fine linen, bright and clean in verse eight confirms for us that as we continue to read the armies with the Lord are in fact, His saints.

As we continue in Revelation verses 11 through 19, we see heaven opened, and discern that Jesus is returning to earth to wage war: "[11]**And I saw heaven opened, and behold, a white horse, and He who sat on it is called Faithful and True, and in righteousness He judges and wages war. [12]His eyes are a flame of fire, and on His head are many diadems; and He has a name written on Him which no one knows except Himself. [13]He is clothed with a robe dipped in blood, and His name is called The Word of God. (Revelation 19:11–13)** We read His armies in heaven are with Him, clothed in fine line, white and clean: [14]**And the armies [we the saints] which are in heaven, *clothed in fine linen, white and clean*, were following Him on white horses" (Revelation 19:14).** Thus, I believe all the saints who were raptured when the seventh angel sounded went to heaven with Jesus, participated in the marriage supper of the Lamb, and return with Him to wage war on the earth. We then pick back up with the destruction of the antichrist-beast and the false prophet when Jesus casts them into the lake of fire at the end of Revelation 19. As we move into chapter 20, we will read that a group of saints come to life and reign with Him for a thousand years.

What Does the Bible Teach about the Thousand-Year Reign of Christ on Earth?

We begin to learn about this period in Revelation, right after the beast and the false prophet are thrown alive into the lake of fire at the end of Revelation 19:11-21 when the Lord Christ returns from heaven with His armies.

As we discussed in chapter two of this book, some people have theorized that the thousand-year reign of Jesus is not literal, but figurative, and that it began right after the cross when Jesus ascended to heaven. The view that the thousand years is just an indeterminate length of time also holds that Jesus began His reign at his resurrection and ascension and that since that time, Satan has been bound and unable to deceive the nations. But this theory ignores the context around the verse (that Jesus reigns for a thousand years), which makes it clear that the beast and the false prophet were just thrown into the lake of fire. (Revelation 19:20) According to Scripture, the beast and the false prophet are not on the earth until the time of the end and the great tribulation. Their theory ignores the preceding verses at the beginning of Revelation 19 which reveal that Jesus has just come back from heaven, that the marriage supper of the Lamb has taken place (Revelation 19:7), and that Jesus has brought with Him armies, clothed in “fine linen, white and clean,” suggesting the judgment and absolution of the saints has already occurred (Revelation 19:14). We have shown that these armies that are with Him are His saints who were at the marriage supper. Their theory requires that we accept that Satan is currently bound and cannot deceive the nations and has been since the cross. Perhaps most significantly, their theory ignores the necessity of Jesus reigning physically on earth with His saints, because Scripture states plainly that Satan gathers the nations *on earth* to wage war against the saints, indicating that Jesus has been on earth reigning with His saints for the previous thousand years. It also ignores the statement that follows that event which tells us that after Satan is released for a short time, he will be cast into the lake of fire where the beast and false prophet "are also" (Revelation 20:10). Their interpretation also ignores the statement that those who do not take the mark of the beast come to life and reign with Jesus during this period. The beast had not appeared before the cross, and the mark of the beast had not been given for saints to refuse. In effect, the proponents of this theory that the thousand years is just a long time, and it started at the cross, must also interpret the references to the destruction of the beast and the false prophet metaphorically. I believe a literal interpretation is more consistent with Scripture here than a figurative one. Revelation chapter 20 teaches us more about this thousand-year period, sometimes referred to as the "millennial reign." Perhaps the most significant flaw in this theory we have discussed is that they assert that Jesus began reigning over the kingdoms of the world when He ascended into heaven after His resurrection. Yet Jesus told Pilate right before He was crucified, **"'My kingdom is not of this world. If My kingdom were of this world, then My servants would be fighting so that I would not be handed over to the Jews; but as it is, My kingdom is not of this realm'" (John 18:36).** Clearly His earthly kingdom was not yet beginning prior to the cross. In fact, we are told *when* the kingdoms of this world become the kingdoms of the Lord and of His Christ: "[15] **Then the seventh angel sounded: And there were loud voices in heaven, saying, "The kingdoms of this world *have become* the kingdoms of our Lord and of His Christ, and He shall reign forever and ever!" (Revelation 11:15).** The kingdoms of this world become the kingdoms of the Lord and of His Christ at this event. This is declared by loud voices from heaven, at the sounding of the seventh angel, when the last trumpet is blown, and the Lord gathers His saints. Belief in this theory requires assuming that much of prophecy is a metaphor rather than assuming it is to be taken at face value. As we have seen earlier, when prophecy contains a metaphor, such as in the beginning of Revelation when we see seven lampstands, Scripture will usually tell us shortly after what the metaphor represents, or we can search previous Scripture and find the same image such as fig trees or lampstands used where their meaning is disclosed. Regarding the lampstands, Scripture told us "The seven lampstands are the seven churches." In Daniel, the Word tells us that "four beasts are four kings" and "the four horns are four kings." Even when the meaning of the symbol is not immediately revealed, we find if we search the remainder of God's Word, it will often reveal the meaning to us.

Who Comes to Life to Reign with Christ?

Assuming Revelation 20 is speaking of literal events, let's examine it
more carefully: "1**Then I saw an angel coming down from heaven,**
having the key to the bottomless pit and a great chain in his hand.
2He laid hold of the dragon, that serpent of old, who is the Devil
and Satan, and bound him for a thousand years; 3and he cast him
into the bottomless pit, and shut him up, and set a seal on him, so that he should deceive the nations no more till the thousand years were finished. But after these things he must be released for a little
while. 4And I saw thrones, and they sat on them, and judgment was committed to them. Then I saw the souls of those who had been beheaded for their witness to Jesus and for the word of God, who had

not worshiped the beast or his image, and had not received his mark on their foreheads or on their hands. And they lived and reigned with Christ for a thousand years" (Revelation 20:1-4,NKJV).

The last portion of this passage can be a source of confusion for many: Do only saints who were martyred by beheading in the great tribulation come to life and reign with Jesus during this period? No, all saints are there with Him. Scripture informs us that once the rapture occurs, we shall always be with the Lord: "[16]**For the Lord Himself will descend from heaven with a shout, with the voice of the archangel and with the trumpet of God, and the dead in Christ will rise first. [17]Then we who are alive and remain will be caught up together with them in the clouds to meet the Lord in the air, *and so we shall always be with the Lord*" (1 Thessalonians 4:16–17).** All believers are there at the marriage supper of the Lamb, and they all come back with Him as His armies. This would include all those saints from Old Testament times, such as Abel, Enoch, Noah, Job, Abraham, Isaac, Jacob, Moses, Joshua, Samuel, David, Elijah, as well as all the apostles, and all the saints who have died in Christ right up to the point of His return. All of these He first raises from the dead, then those saints who are alive and remain on earth are all caught up to meet Him in the air when the seventh angel sounds. All of these together then participate in the marriage supper of the Lamb in heaven while the wrath of God is poured out from the seven bowls of wrath on those dwelling on the earth, and then all the saints return with Him as His armies.

When Do the Rest of the Dead Come to Life?

"[5]But the rest of the dead did not live again until the thousand years were finished. This is the first resurrection. [6]Blessed and holy is he

who has part in the first resurrection. Over such the second death has no power, but they shall be priests of God and of Christ, and shall reign with Him a thousand years. [7]Now when the thousand years have expired, Satan will be released from his prison [8]and will go out to deceive the nations which are in the four corners of the earth, Gog and Magog, to gather them together to battle, whose number is as the sand of the sea. [9]They went up on the breadth of the earth and surrounded the camp of the saints and the beloved city. And fire came down from God out of heaven and devoured them. [10]The devil, who deceived them, was cast into the lake of fire and brimstone where the beast and the false prophet are. And they will be tormented day and night forever and ever" (Revelation 20:5-10, NKJV). The rest of the dead are the unsaved, who come to life to face judgment before the great white throne of Christ after the thousand years are ended.

The last verse, verse 10, conclusively ties this passage to the final verses of chapter 19 of Revelation which we just read where the beast and the false prophet were thrown into the lake of fire. The events described in verses 1-10 of Revelation 20 follow chronologically the destruction of the beast and the false prophet. In verse 4, we find that some of the dead come to life. They were praised for not taking the mark of the beast. Clearly, they were on the earth when the mark of the beast was given to those who worshiped him or his image during the great tribulation. We learn in verses 4 and 5 when those who did not take the mark were killed and then "came to life" that this was the *first resurrection*. We know from elsewhere in Revelation that those who have faith in Christ as their savior and are alive at His return are not caught up to meet him in the air *before the dead in Christ rise first*. Therefore, the "rapture" (the gathering of the saints) has not occurred before the great tribulation, because this is described as *the first resurrection*, and these who were beheaded did not die until the great tribulation. In this passage we see that only once the number of them that are to die is complete according to God's predetermined plan will the Lord come to gather all His saints, raising the dead first, which includes those killed for their faith during the years of tribulation. To assert that there has been a resurrection prior to this one forces us to say that we should not believe Scripture means what it says. In other words, we would have to claim Scripture can't mean that this the first resurrection, even though it says that it is. If it were not the first resurrection, Scripture would say, "these also came alive" but it would not tell us something that is not true. Those who insist there must be a pre-tribulation rapture are forced to tell us this Scripture does not mean what it says.

The second resurrection, that of the unsaved, takes place when they are raised to stand before the great white throne to be judged. It takes place after Satan is cast into the lake of fire at the end of the thousand-year reign of Christ. The next section of Revelation 20 describes this judgment: "[11]**Then I saw a great white throne and Him who sat on it, from whose face the earth and the heaven fled away. And there was found no place for them. [12]And I saw the dead, small and great, standing before God, and books were opened. And another book was opened, which is the Book of Life. And the dead were judged according to their works, by the things which were written in the books" (Revelation 20:11–12,NKJV).**

The first resurrection is *the only resurrection* of the saints. It takes place when the seventh angel sounds. Included in it are these saints who will be beheaded for their testimony of Jesus during the great tribulation, and for not taking the mark of the beast. (I believe Scripture tells us this is the first resurrection so we understand clearly that the saints are not gathered before these saints die in the great tribulation for their testimony.)

Once the Lord Jesus begins to reign on earth, He does so for a thousand years while Satan is bound. While Scripture says here that those who were beheaded for not taking the mark of the beast will rise to reign with Jesus, *it does not say* that *they are the only ones who rise from the dead.* I believe that Peter, John, James, Paul, Titus, Timothy, Mary, the mother of Jesus, and all the Old Testament saints are raised at this time. I believe *all saints*, including Old Testament saints (for example, King David, Daniel, Job, Noah, Moses, Joshua, etc.) will be included in this *first resurrection.* The second resurrection of the dead is for all those who are not saved and is for the purpose of standing before the great white throne judgement of Jesus. During this time of the thousand-year reign of Jesus on earth, the Word declares that Satan cannot deceive the nations. During this time, Jesus reigns with those who have risen at the first resurrection.

Whom Does Jesus Rule over with a "Rod of Iron"?

Are there also still mortal unbelievers on earth with Jesus and the saints, all of whom are now immortal, during this time? Daniel 7 reveals that there are indeed: "[11]**Then I kept looking because of the sound of the boastful words which the horn was speaking; I kept looking until the beast was slain, and its body was destroyed and *given to the burning fire.*** [12]**As for the rest of the beasts, *their dominion was taken away, but an extension of life was granted to them for an appointed period of time*" (Daniel 7:11–12).** Verse 11 describes the same event that we see in Revelation 19:20 when Jesus casts the beast and the false prophet into the lake of fire. Verse 12 tells us that "the rest of the beasts" (referring to descendants of peoples from previous empires such as the Persian, Greek, and Roman empires) who were unbelievers that survived the wrath of God (were granted an extension of life). These unbelievers are the nations that Jesus *rules over with a rod of iron* during His millennial reign.

If there are not unbelievers living on the earth at this point, then who is deceived when Satan is released for a short season at the end of the thousand years to deceive the nations and gather them for war? I believe that not every living soul who was left on the earth will perish when the wrath of God is poured out on those remaining. Those unbelievers who survive will be the ones who Jesus, together with His saints, reign over for a thousand years. Verse 6 in Revelation 20 tells us we reign with Christ for a thousand years. What else does Scripture reveal about our reign with Christ? For one thing, we will be judges: "[2]**Or do you not know that *the saints will judge the world?* If the world is judged by you, are you not competent to constitute the smallest law courts?" (1 Corinthians 6:2).** We get more insight from Daniel on this time and our role: "[22]**until the Ancient of Days came and judgment was passed in favor of the saints of the Highest One, and the time arrived when the saints took possession of the kingdom. […] [27]'Then the sovereignty, the dominion and the greatness of all the kingdoms under the whole heaven will be given to the people of the saints of the Highest One; His kingdom will be an everlasting kingdom, and *all the dominions will serve and obey Him*'" (Daniel 7:22,27)** This reign is over all the kingdoms under heaven, all dominions, which were formerly under the control of the Prince of the power of the air, but are now under the sovereign reign of Christ, from whose **"mouth comes a sharp sword, so that with it He may strike down the nations, and *He will rule them with a rod of iron*; and He treads the wine press of the fierce wrath of God, the Almighty" (Revelation 19:15).** If the Lord just destroyed all sinners left on earth after the tribulation and rapture outright, he would not rule over them, for they would be dead and gone.

Different Life Spans

The idea that we will reign with Christ for one thousand years begs the question, will the span of life be different after the rapture and the supper of the Lamb? In Isaiah we learn the following"[18]**But be glad and rejoice forever in what I create; For behold, I create Jerusalem as a rejoicing, And her people a joy. [19]I will rejoice in Jerusalem, And joy in My people; The voice of weeping shall no longer be heard in her, Nor the voice of crying. [20]'No more shall an infant from there live but a few days, Nor an old man who has not fulfilled his days; For the child shall die one hundred years old, But the sinner being one hundred years old shall be accursed. [21]They shall build houses and inhabit them; They shall plant vineyards and eat their fruit. [22]They shall not build and another inhabit; They shall not plant and another eat; For as the days of a tree, so shall be the days of My people, And My elect shall long enjoy the work of their hands. [23]They shall not labor in vain, Nor bring forth children for trouble; For they shall be the descendants of the blessed of the LORD, And their offspring with them. [24]"It shall come to pass That before they call, I will answer; And while they are still speaking, I will hear. [25]The wolf and the lamb shall feed together, The lion shall eat straw like the ox, And dust shall be the serpent's food. They shall not hurt**

nor destroy in all My holy mountain,' Says the LORD" (Isaiah 65:18-25,NKJV).

Notice, it speaks of people living exceedingly long lives during this time, but still eventually dying. We know that saints cannot die again. Scripture says the second death cannot harm the saints. So, who dies during this period, even though people live routinely for over a hundred years? Those who die during the millennial reign of Christ are the mortals who survived the wrath of God and who remain opposed to him. Also, during this period, animals in nature, the wolf and the lamb coexist and the wolf does not prey on the lamb.

The verse that precedes this passage we just examined is verse **17: "For behold, *I create new heavens and a new earth*; And the former things will not be remembered or come to mind" (Isaiah 65:17).** I am inclined to think that the description *that follows this verse*, which we read just before this still refers to the thousand-year reign of Christ on earth. This is before the New Jerusalem comes down from heaven, and when there is no more sun nor moon needed to light the city and no sea. I think Isaiah 65:20-25 describes the period of Jesus' millennian reign. It is then followed by a final war, then the creation of a new heaven and new earth, and last, the Father brings the heavenly Jerusalem down to earth and Jesus hands over the kingdom to Him.

We find the description of the new heaven and new earth in Revelation 21: **"[1]Now I saw a new heaven and a new earth, for the first heaven and the first earth had passed away. Also there was no more sea. [2]Then I, John, saw the holy city, New Jerusalem, coming down out of heaven from God, prepared as a bride adorned for her husband. [3]And I heard a loud voice from heaven saying, 'Behold, the tabernacle of**

God is with men, and He will dwell with them, and they shall be His people. God Himself will be with them and be their God. [4]And God will wipe away every tear from their eyes; there shall be no more death, nor sorrow, nor crying. There shall be no more pain, for the former things have passed away'" (Revelation 21:1-4,NKJV). Note in verse 4 there shall be no more death. Compare this to the passage in Isaiah 65:20 which states that "the youth will die at age one hundred, and the one who does not reach the age of one hundred Will be thought accursed."

In the new heavens and new earth, there will be no death, but before that there is a period when life will be greatly extended, and the one living only one hundred years would be thought of as accursed. This sounds remarkably similar to the long-life spans that we read about in the period before the flood and the judgment on the world in the days of Noah.

The "Prince" in Ezekiel 44

We learn more about the millennial reign when we read the final chapters of Ezekiel from chapter 40 through 48. Beginning in Ezekiel 40 and continuing through 42, we are given detailed measurements of a new temple in Jerusalem. Scripture tells us elsewhere this temple will be built by Branch (Jesus): **"[12]Then say to him, 'Thus says the Lord of hosts, "Behold, a man whose name is Branch, for He will branch out from where He is; and He will build the temple of the Lord"'" (Zechariah 6:12).** We also read this about him in Jeremiah: **"[5]'Behold, the days are coming,' declares the Lord, 'When I will raise up for David a righteous Branch; And He will reign as king and act wisely And do justice and righteousness in the land'" (Jeremiah 23:5).**

The temple described here in Ezekiel is larger than either of the two temples that existed before in Jerusalem. The dimensions are so large that some scholars question how it could be that large. Yet, the detail is specific and very comprehensive, so it is not logical to think this portion of Scripture is symbolic and not literal. In addition, there is a massive wall all around this new temple which did not surround either of the first two temples in Jerusalem, and it is approximately twelve feet high and twelve feet thick. Furthermore, the wall forms a square around the temple, and it is approximately 6,000 feet in length on each side, or over a mile. The present temple mount in Jerusalem is not large enough for this complex. In Ezekiel 43 we read that "[4] **And the glory of the Lord came into the temple by way of the gate which faces toward the east. [5] The Spirit lifted me up and brought me into the inner court; and behold, the glory of the Lord filled the temple" (Ezekiel 43:4-5).** In the next chapter we learn of "the prince" (who we will learn is the resurrected King David): " [1] **Then He brought me back to the outer gate of the sanctuary which faces toward the east, but it was shut. [2] And the Lord said to me, 'This gate shall be shut; it shall not be opened, and no man shall enter by it, because *the Lord God of Israel has entered by it*; therefore it shall be shut. [3] As for the *prince, because he is the prince*, he may sit in it to eat bread before the Lord; he shall enter by way of the vestibule of the gateway, and go out the same way'" (Ezekiel 44:1-3,NKJV).** It is noteworthy that in giving instructions concerning the priests who will minister before the Lord in this new temple, it tells us *the priests will marry:* **"[22] They shall not take as wife a widow or a divorced woman, but take virgins of the descendants of the house of Israel, or widows of priests" (Ezekiel 44:22, NKJV)** Remember, Jesus told us that *in heaven* we will be like the angels, neither marrying nor giving in marriage. But this passage is not describing heaven. At this time, people are still marrying, having children, and dying. Yet, we know that saints are here in this time, reigning with Christ Jesus. These saints have already died once and were raised from the dead, never to die again. Those who are dying are the survivors of the wrath of God, over whom Jesus is reigning.

Note that during this time, sacrifices are being offered in the temple. Naturally, this raises the question why? Didn't we learn in Hebrews that **" [26] it was fitting for us to have such a high priest, holy, innocent, undefiled, separated from sinners and exalted above the heavens; [27] who does not need daily, like those high priests, to offer up sacrifices, first for His own sins and then for the sins of the people, because *this He did once for all when He offered up Himself*" (Hebrews 7:26-27)?** Jesus is our high priest when He is in heaven. But now He is on earth, as King of Kings, and Lord of Lords, and we are with Him. But look at what Scripture says about Jesus being on earth: **[4]Now *if He were on earth, He would not be a priest at all*, since there are those who offer the gifts according to the Law;" (Hebrews 8:4).** Also, careful study of the temple described in Ezekiel which Jesus builds will reveal that this temple *has no veil separating the Holy of Holies from the remainder of the temple*. It has no dividing wall, no ark of the covenant. The sacrifices are not offered at all the same times formerly required by the law; they are only offered at two times of the year: at the feast of Passover, and at the feast of Tabernacles. These sacrifices which are being offered in this millennial temple are in remembrance of what has been done and are sacrifices of thanksgiving. *They are not sacrifices for sin*. Also, orthodox Jews would not build a temple without a veil and without a dividing wall, nor would they worship in it.

With Jesus now back on earth and reigning as King over all the earth, it appears He is not acting as a priest, for He is King over all the earth. I believe this may be why we learn of priests who still offer sacrifices in this temple which remains to be built to fulfill prophecy. This temple will be in existence during the millennial reign. Because sacrifices are still being offered in this temple, I believe it is to teach the unbelieving nations and to serve as a reminder of His sacrifice, and as sacrifices of thanksgiving to honor Him.

At the end of Ezekiel 44, we learn that an inheritance in the land is to be apportioned out to each of the tribes of Israel, and in 45 that the Lord himself has a designated portion. Once again, the priests get no land, as the Lord himself is their inheritance: "**And *when you divide by lot the land for inheritance*, you shall *offer an allotment to the Lord, a holy portion of the land*; the length shall be the length of 25,000 cubits, and the width shall be 20,000. It shall be holy within all its boundary round about" (Ezekiel 45:1).** Next, we learn that "the prince" shall have a separate designated inheritance. Scripture indicates that the prince referred to here is the risen King David: "[23]**Then I will set over them one shepherd, *My servant David*, and he will feed them; he will feed them himself and be their shepherd.** [24]**"And I, the LORD, will be their God, *and My servant David will be prince among them*; I the LORD have spoken" (Ezekiel 34:23–24).** It is clear that a distinction is made between the Lord Jesus and the prince when the land is apportioned for an inheritance during this period, for it says "***The prince shall have land on either side of the holy allotment* and the property of the city, adjacent to the holy allotment and the property of the city, on the west side toward the west and on the east side toward the east, and in length comparable to one of the portions, from the west border to**

the east border" (Ezekiel 45:7). The prince will have children and can give his sons a portion of his inheritance: **"Thus says the Lord God, 'If the prince gives a gift out of his inheritance to any of his sons, it shall belong to his sons; it is their possession by inheritance'" (Ezekiel 46:16).** Finally, the rest of the land is allotted to the tribes of Israel: **"This shall be his land for a possession in Israel; so My princes shall no longer oppress My people, but they shall give the rest of the land to the house of Israel according to their tribes" (Ezekiel 45:8).**

Water Flowing from the Sanctuary

In Ezekiel 47, we learn of miraculous water that flows from under the altar. Up to now, as we have progressed through the final chapters of Ezekiel, we have discovered details of God's plan during the reign of Jesus that are specific to the redeemed remnant of Israel. However, by revealing this miraculous river we learn that God's blessings pertain not just to Israel, but to all believers. I believe the description of this unique river indicates that it is indeed real and not a figurative representation of something else. It starts as a trickle and becomes a river that cannot be forded, and **"[9] It will come about that every living creature which swarms in every place where the river goes, will live. And there will be very many fish, for these waters go there and the others become fresh; so everything will live where the river goes. [12] By the river on its bank, on one side and on the other, will grow all kinds of trees for food. Their leaves will not wither and their fruit will not fail. They will bear every month because their water flows from the sanctuary, and their fruit will be for food and *their leaves for healing*" (Ezekiel 47: 9,12).** Among other things, we learn in Ezekiel 48 the dimensions of the city of Jerusalem: **"The city shall be 18,000 cubits round about;**

and the name of the city from that day shall be, 'The Lord is there.' " (Ezekiel 48:35)

Is Zechariah 14 Referring to the Millennial Reign of Christ?

"[16] And it shall come to pass that *everyone who is left of all the nations* which came against Jerusalem *shall go up from year to year to worship the King, the LORD of hosts, and to keep the Feast of Tabernacles.* [17] And it shall be that whichever of the families of the earth do not come up to Jerusalem to worship the King, the LORD of hosts, *on them there will be no rain.* [18] If the family of Egypt will not come up and enter in, *they shall have no rain*; they shall receive the plague with which the LORD strikes the nations who do not come up to keep the Feast of Tabernacles. [19] This shall be the punishment of Egypt and the punishment of all the nations that do not come up to keep the Feast of Tabernacles" (Zechariah 14:16-19). There are survivors of the battle described in Zechariah 14 in which nations come against Jerusalem, so we know this battle must occur prior to the beginning of the millennial reign, because the battle that will occur when Satan gathers the nations at the end of the Lord's reign will have no survivors. I believe this passage reflects the rebelliousness of man and the patience of the Lord. Jesus is reigning on earth, with perfect wisdom, justice, and righteousness, ruling not imperfectly as men have ruled for thousands of years, but with the perfection that only God can demonstrate. Nevertheless, when Satan is released at the end of Jesus's thousand-year reign, most if not all mortals will again demonstrate that man is corrupt and evil, and will follow Satan.

By studying prophecy in Scripture, we learn that saints will be on the earth during the great tribulation until the Lord returns unless they are killed, which happen to many (probably most). They must persevere in faith and resist taking the mark of the beast. If necessary, we must give up our lives for the testimony of Jesus and the Word of God. We learn that we are not destined for the wrath of God,

but wrath is something altogether different than suffering or persecution for our faith in Christ, which we are guaranteed to endure to some degree even before the time of the end. We learn that there is a one-thousand-year earthly reign of the Lord Christ here on earth before the final judgment of unbelievers. The saints reign with Him on earth over all the nations and all the peoples, and He reigns with a "rod of iron." At the end of this period, Satan is let loose for a brief time during which he deceives the nations one last time and gathers them to war against the Lord and His saints. Satan and all the rebellious are destroyed by God when this last war occurs. It is at this time that the Lord destroys the current heavens and earth before creating a new heavens and new earth where those who trust in Christ will live with him forever.

Let us examine briefly what the Scripture says about what occurs there at the end of "the day of the Lord" before he creates the new heavens and new earth: **"[10]But *the day of the Lord* will come like a thief, in which the heavens will pass away with a roar and the elements will be destroyed with intense heat, and the earth and its works will be burned up" (2 Peter 3:10).** As we have talked about, "the day of the Lord" is one-thousand years long and comes after six other one-thousand year "days" are completed. We are presently remarkably close to the end of the sixth "thousand-year day." We remember that Scripture tells us just two verses prior to the one above the following: "[8]**But do not let this one fact escape your notice, beloved, that with the Lord** ***one day is like a thousand years, and a thousand years like one day*****" (2 Peter 3:8)**. As previously noted, I believe *it is at the very end of this one-thousand-year day that the Lord burns up the earth, destroying it with intense heat.* This is the culmination of Jesus' millennial reign on the earth, right after Satan is released for a short season to gather the nations to war against the Lord Jesus and His saints. Even though this fiery destruction comes at the end of the day, it is still included in "the day of the Lord."

There is a saying regarding our theology: "In the essentials, unity; in all else, grace and liberty." Faithful, godly saints often differ over points of theology that are not essential to our salvation. As I consider the idea of the thousand-year reign of Christ on the earth (which is not an "essential" in terms of salvation theology) and tying these Scriptures in Ezekiel, Isaiah, and Zechariah to that period, I must admit, I may be wrong. I continue to ponder these Scriptures and ask the Lord to reveal to me what they mean.

chapter TEN Jewish Feasts

How Do the Jewish Feast Days Relate to End Time Events?

I presume that most of you who are reading this book are Christian, but that few if any of you are Jewish. Scripture refers to Jews and Gentiles. Everyone in the world who is not a Jew is by definition a Gentile. As a Gentile myself, who is now a Christian, I never gave much thought to the Jewish festivals that the Jews are commanded to observe and which are listed in Leviticus chapter 23. However, I noticed a pattern that caused me to consider the deeper meaning of these festivals.

The Feast of Passover

The first festival of the year is Passover, held on the fourteenth day of the first month in the Jewish calendar, Nissan. The Jews were told by Moses to kill an unblemished, year-old lamb and put its blood on their doorposts and the lintel so that the destroying angel would "pass over" their dwellings in Egypt when God sent him out to slay the firstborn son in every household in Egypt. It is obvious that the crucifixion of the Lord on Passover, together with Jesus being called the Lamb of God, is the fulfillment of the Passover Feast. Just like the lamb in Exodus was sacrificed, so also was Jesus, the Lamb of God, sacrificed. The blood of that lamb, which was slain in Egypt, caused the angel of death to "pass over" the homes of the Israelites, saving their lives. The blood of the lamb of God who was slain saves our lives. The Jews have been observing a prophetic picture of the Lord fulfilling this festival for thousands of years. Many believers recognize this feast fulfillment and recognize its connection to communion when we remember Christ's sacrifice as our Passover Lamb and partake in his "body" and his "blood," which also points us ahead toward the marriage supper of the Lamb when we will no longer "do this in remembrance" of him (Luke 22:20), but rather we will feast with him. So we as believers already incorporate a Jewish feast day into our corporate worship, but there may be more parallels among the other feast days which could help illuminate what God will do in the end times.

Jesus continued the fulfillment of the Feast of Unleavened Bread by being placed in the grave during the first days of this feast. Jesus' sinless life is a fulfillment of the extended metaphor of bread without leaven which God spoke of to the Israelites back in Exodus. Leaven is a representation of sin in the Scriptures, and the command to eat unleavened bread during this feast was meant to point their attention to their own sins and their need for rescue.

Next, when Christ arose from the dead on "the day after the Sabbath," He arose on the Feast of First Fruits, fulfilling that feast. We are told about this particular feast in Leviticus, where God instructs that "11 **'He shall wave the sheaf before the LORD for you to be accepted; *on the day after the sabbath* the priest shall wave it" (Leviticus 23:11).** Jesus arose on the day after the sabbath, mirroring the timing of this feast as well. Additionally, Scripture informs us that Christ is the *first fruits*: **"But now Christ has been raised from the dead, the *first fruits* of those who are asleep" (1 Corinthians 15:20).** Many different words could have been used here to describe Christ and his resurrection, but the particular term "first fruits" is meant to connect Jesus's resurrection with yet another Jewish feast._

The Feast of Weeks (Pentecost)

Fifty days later, (seven sabbaths plus one day), the giving of the Holy Spirit on Pentecost fulfilled the Feast of Weeks: **"[1] When the day of Pentecost had come, they were all together in one place. [4]And they were all filled with the Holy Spirit..."**

The Feast of Trumpets

I believe the fall feast of Trumpets (prophetically a picture just like all the others) will be the day the Lord returns to rapture the saints. We are told in the Word that He comes with a great trumpet blast. We do not know what year, or even what day or hour, because of the fluctuation of the start of the Jewish year and the uncertainty over when the month of Nissan begins. The start of the other months are all determined afterward for the year, based on the first month, and everything is counted from the first of Nissan going forward. Modern day Jewish observance of these dates may be different from that of Jesus' day from a calendar perspective. Many Scriptures informing us about when He returns mention a trumpet, and in 1 Corinthians 15 we learn he comes at *the last trumpet*: **"[52] in a moment, in the twinkling of an eye, *at the last trumpet.* For the trumpet will sound, and the dead will be raised incorruptible, and we shall be changed" (1 Corinthians 15:52).** Some say it cannot be so simple that the Lord will come on the Feast of Trumpets, which is the first day of the seventh Jewish month, Tishrei. You will recall that in Hebrews 4, we examined the concept of entering God's rest, and made the connection between that terminology and the "seventh day," which Scripture calls "a sabbath rest." Throughout this book, you have seen Scripture that supports the concept of "the day of the Lord" being one thousand years in duration and being called a sabbath rest. In keeping with these same Scriptural indications, I find the New King James Version of the description of the Feast of Trumpets, found in Leviticus 23, to be clearer with regard to return of the Lord on the Feast of Trumpets: **"[24]Speak to the children of Israel, saying: 'In the seventh month, on the first day of the month, *you shall have a sabbath-rest*, a memorial of blowing of trumpets, a holy convocation" (Leviticus 23:24, NKJV, emphasis mine).** I find it noteworthy that the Feast of Trumpets, of all the annual feasts instituted in Leviticus 23 for the Jews to keep, is the only feast connected with the term "sabbath rest" -- the same phrase used in Hebrews 4 to describe the ultimate rest that will belong to the believers at the end. The Hebrew word used in Leviticus 23:24 for "Sabbath-rest" is "Shabbaton" (ןוֹתָּבַשׁ). It is derived from the word "Shabbat" which means "Sabbath" or "rest", and carries the additional meaning of a "solemn rest" or "special rest".

Doesn't Scripture tell us, "No man knows the day or the hour?" Jewish law determines the start of the month by the sighting of the new moon. It requires that two Rabbi see the new moon from Jerusalem as witnesses before the start of the new month can be proclaimed. If the sky is overcast, regardless of modern astronomical charts, the month cannot be proclaimed. Thus, even if we can tie these prophecies to a potential prediction of when Christ might return, still "no man knows the day or the hour." In fact, if you search for it, you will discover that the Jews have called the feast of trumpets "no man knows the day or the hour" for many years. In Matthew 24 Jesus tells us: "[29] ***But immediately after the***

tribulation of those days **THE SUN WILL BE DARKENED, AND THE MOON WILL NOT GIVE ITS LIGHT, AND THE STARS WILL FALL from the sky, and the powers of the heavens will be shaken. [30] And then the sign of the Son of Man will appear in the sky, and then all the tribes of the earth will mourn, and they will see the SON OF MAN COMING ON THE CLOUDS OF THE SKY with power and great glory. [31] And He will send forth His angels with A GREAT TRUMPET and THEY WILL GATHER TOGETHER His elect from the four winds, from one end of the sky to the other" (Matthew 24:29-31).**

At a great trumpet is when the angels gather his elect, and this is the rapture. Note the first words in verse (29) above, "*Immediately after the tribulation.*" When the seventh angel sounds Jesus takes the saints to heaven for the marriage supper of the Lamb: **"[9]Then he said to me, 'Write, "Blessed are those who are invited to the *marriage supper of the Lamb.*"' And he said to me, 'These are true words of God'" (Revelation 19:9)**. We are not on the earth for a time after the great tribulation, and we have learned that the wrath of God begins to be poured out on those who dwell on the earth immediately after we are raptured when the seventh angel sounds. We go to heaven, but we know that Jesus comes back to earth after some interlude and brings us with Him to wage war against the beast and his armies. It is logical from the Scripture, and the placement of the verse above in Revelation 19 to conclude we have been at the marriage supper of the Lamb.

The Day of Atonement

Ten days after the Feast of Trumpets comes the Day of Atonement. The time in between is what the Jews refer to as "the days of awe." Because of this terminology, I believe this ten-day period could be when the saints are off the earth in heaven and when the "bowls of wrath" are poured out on the earth on those remaining. This period is detailed beginning in Revelation 14:19 through Revelation chapter 16. So just as Jesus the Messiah has fulfilled the spring feasts, I believe he will fulfill both the *Feast of Trumpets*, the *Day of Atonement*, and the *Feast of Tabernacles*.

The Feast of Tabernacles

When Jesus returns for the saints "at the last trumpet," I believe it will be on the day of the Feast of Trumpets, and He will thus fulfill that feast. Five days after the Day of Atonement, which is fifteen days after the Feast of Trumpets, marks the beginning of the Feast of Tabernacles in Jewish tradition. This feast lasts from Sabbath to Sabbath, plus one more day, for a total of eight days. I believe Jesus will then return soon after the Feast of Trumpets, perhaps about three weeks after the last day of the Feast of Tabernacles, together with His now immortal risen saints to destroy the antichrist-beast and begin His thousand-year reign. That leaves just the final feast of the annual Jewish festivals in Leviticus 23 unaccounted for, the Feast of Tabernacles, also called the Feast of Booths or Succoth. This feast is a grand celebration, as noted above, lasting from Sabbath to Sabbath plus one more day, making it an eight-day celebration. I believe the marriage supper of the Lamb, in which the "bridegroom celebrates His marriage to His bride," the body of believers, will be celebrated in heaven during this period.

Additionally, I believe I may have found evidence that Jesus may have been born on the last day of the Feast of Tabernacles. If I am right, then Jesus has already partially fulfilled this feast as well. Regarding His birth, consider the following: **"[14] And the Word became flesh, and *dwelt* among us, and we saw His glory, glory as of the only begotten from the Father, full of grace and truth" (John 1:14).** The word *dwelt* according to Strong's Greek dictionary, is σκῆνος (G4636). Strong's goes on to say that Biblical usage is to fix one's *tabernacle,* have one's tabernacle, abide (or live) in a tabernacle (or tent), tabernacle. Young's Literal Translation gives us this: "[14] **And the Word became flesh and did *tabernacle* among us, and we beheld his glory, glory as of an only begotten of a father, full of grace and truth.** So, it is reasonable to consider that Jesus "made his tabernacle" with us when He came to earth being born of a woman to put on flesh. Thus, it may be that God has already partially fulfilled the Feast of Tabernacles, the final remaining Jewish festival of the year. I believe every single one of the feasts proclaimed in Leviticus 23 will be fulfilled by God, with the only ones remaining to be fulfilled being the Feast of Trumpets, the Day of Atonement, and the Feast of Tabernacles.

chapter ELEVEN Israel's Future

Is God Finished with Israel?

Even though some try to say that the church has now replaced Israel, it becomes clear when reading Scripture and encountering language like "I will gather them from the nations where I have scattered them," and "They will look on Him who they pierced," and "He will cause them to dwell again in their own land," that He is referring to the nation of Israel and not the church. We will examine Scripture to see if it becomes clear that God still has prophecy that must yet be fulfilled regarding Israel.

Consider the Jews today, in 2023. As of the end of 2022, they number only about 15.2 million people world-wide, with about half being in the United States and half in Israel. Today, the Jews number only fifteen million out of a world population of eight billion, about two tenths of one percent of the world population. The Jews are barely visible as a percentage of the world population. Now think about the fact that God said 2500 years ago that He would *gather them from all the nations* where He had scattered them and cause them to dwell in the land he had given to Abraham.

In Jeremiah 32 we read: "[37] **Behold, I will *gather them out of all the lands* to which I have driven them in My anger, in My wrath and in great indignation; and *I will bring them back to this place* and *make them dwell in safety*. [38] They shall be My people, and I will be their**

God; [39] and I will give them one heart and one way, that they may fear Me always, for their own good and for *the good of* their children after them. [40] I will make an everlasting covenant with them that I will not turn away from them, to do them good; and I will put the fear of Me in their hearts so that they will not turn away from Me. [41] I will rejoice over them to do them good and will faithfully plant them in this land with all My heart and with all My soul. [42] For thus says the Lord, 'Just as I brought all this great disaster on this people, so I am going to bring on them all the good that I am promising them'" (Jeremiah 32:37-42, emphasis mine). In verse 37 above, God said He would make them dwell in safety, and if we trust that all Scripture must be fulfilled, we know God will fulfill His word. They will yet dwell in safety.

The Remnant

In Ezekiel 11 Scripture says: "[17] **Therefore say, 'Thus says the Lord God, "*I will gather you from the peoples* and assemble you out of the countries among which you have been scattered, and *I will give you the land of Israel.* [18] When they come there, they will remove all its detestable things and all its abominations from it. [19] And I will give them one heart, and put a new spirit within them. And I will take the heart of stone out of their flesh and give them a heart of flesh, [20] that they may walk in My statutes and keep My ordinances and do them. Then they will be My people, and I shall be their God"'" (Ezekiel 11:17-20, emphasis mine).** God put a new spirit in all those who believe that He raised Jesus from the dead and confess Him as Lord with their mouth. He gave us the Holy Spirit to dwell in us and He will do likewise with the remnant of Israel when he removes the veil over their eyes. We read in Romans that "[2]**God has not rejected His people whom He foreknew. Or do you not know what the Scripture says in the passage about Elijah, how he pleads with God against Israel? [3]'Lord, THEY HAVE KILLED YOUR PROPHETS, THEY HAVE TORN DOWN YOUR ALTARS, AND I ALONE AM LEFT, AND THEY ARE SEEKING MY LIFE.' [4]But what is the divine response to him? 'I HAVE KEPT for Myself SEVEN THOUSAND MEN WHO HAVE NOT BOWED THE KNEE TO BAAL.' [5]In the same way then, there has also come to be at the present time a remnant according to God's gracious choice" (Romans 11:2–5).**

Had you considered during the Middle Ages the prophecy regarding gathering Israel back on the land He gave to Abraham, you would in all likelihood have scoffed. At the beginning of the nineteenth century, it is estimated that less than ten thousand Jews lived in Israel. It would have seemed just as unlikely during the American revolution in 1776, during the civil war, World War I, or World War II. Yet in 1948, a miracle occurred, and God caused the rulers of the nations to give the Jews back their homeland in Israel. It is apparent He has begun gathering them from the nations where He scattered them, just as the Scripture said. *It is not finished yet,* but He is fulfilling His word.

Why Would God Show Favor to the Jews?

Here is a question sometimes asked: "Why would God show favor to the Jews? Didn't they reject His son, their messiah, and cause him to be crucified?" God answers the question for us: it is not because of any goodness in them that He does these things, but *for His own name's sake*: "[27] **'When I bring them back from the peoples and gather them from the lands of their enemies, *then I shall be sanctified through them in the sight of the many nations.* [28] Then they will know that I**

am the Lord their God because I made them go into exile among the nations, and then gathered them *again* to their own land; and I will leave none of them there any longer. [29] I will not hide My face from them any longer, for I will have poured out My Spirit on the house of Israel,' declares the Lord God" (Ezekiel 39:27-29) Scripture informs us that God will bring honor and glory to His own name through what He will do through Israel. It will be for His own name's sake.

Arguably, the present nation of Israel does not fit that Scripture because He has not poured out His spirit on them on the whole. In fact, many of them are atheists, and He has not gathered all of them. Some claim instead that God already gathered them after the Babylonian exile, and that fulfilled the prophecy concerning them. These people assume God will no longer favor Israel.

Thousands of years ago, the kingdom of Israel was split into two, with separate capitals and separate kings. They became known as the ten northern tribes which continued to be called Israel, and the two southern tribes which were subsequently called Judah. Samaria was the capital of Israel, and Jerusalem the capital of Judah. Two thousand seven hundred years ago, the Lord sent Assyria against the northern tribes, Israel, and carried them away as captives. There were dispersed throughout the Assyrian empire. A century later, God sent a different nation, Babylon, ruled by Nebuchadnezzar, to carry Judah into captivity in Babylon.

The following passage from Ezekiel informs us that even though for centuries the nation of Israel was split into two separate kingdoms, God plans to unite them into one kingdom again. Ephraim refers to the ten northern tribes, and Judah represents Judah and Benjamin:

"[15]The word of the LORD came again to me saying, [16]'And you, son of man, take for yourself one stick and write on it, "For Judah and for the sons of Israel, his companions"; then take another stick and write on it, "For Joseph, the stick of Ephraim and all the house of Israel, his companions." [17]Then join them for yourself one to another into one stick, that they may become one in your hand. [18]When the sons of your people speak to you saying, "Will you not declare to us what you mean by these?" [19]say to them, "Thus says the Lord GOD, 'Behold, I will take the stick of Joseph, which is in the hand of Ephraim, *and the tribes of Israel, his companions*; and I will put them with it, *with the stick of Judah*, and make them one stick, *and they will be one in My hand.*'[20]"The sticks on which you write will be in your hand before their eyes. [21]Say to them, "Thus says the Lord GOD, 'Behold, I will take the sons of Israel from among the nations where they have gone, and I will gather them from every side and bring them into their own land; [22]and I will make them one nation in the land, on the mountains of Israel; and one king will be king for all of them; and *they will no longer be two nations and no longer be divided into two kingdoms.* [23]'They will no longer defile themselves with their idols, or with their detestable things, or with any of their transgressions; but I will deliver them from all their dwelling places in which they have sinned, and will cleanse them. And they will be My people, and I will be their God'"'" (Ezekiel 37: 15-23, emphasis mine)

Scripture here reveals that David will be king over the reunited kingdoms. I believe this refers to the resurrected King David during the millennial reign of Christ on earth. The people of Israel will all be gathered into the land of Israel. Continuing, we read:

"[24]*My servant David will be king over them*, and they will all have one shepherd; and they will walk in My ordinances and keep My statutes and observe them. [25]*They will live on the land that I gave to Jacob My servant*, in which your fathers lived; and they will live on it, they, and their sons and their sons' sons, forever; and *David My servant will be their prince forever.* [26]I will make a covenant of peace with them; it will be an everlasting covenant with them. And I will place them and multiply them, and will set My sanctuary in their midst forever. [27]My dwelling place also will be with them; and I will be their God, and they will be My people. [28]And *the nations will know that I am the Lord who sanctifies Israel*, when My sanctuary is in their midst forever" (Ezekiel 37:24–28, emphasis mine).

Some might think this passage above refers to the exiles from Babylon who were allowed to go back to Israel. But we read that there is to be a second gathering of the Lord's banished ones of Israel, leaving no doubt this refers not to the church, but to the nation of Israel, but more specifically to a chosen remnant of the nation.

"[11]Then it will happen on that day that the Lord Will again recover *the second time with His hand The remnant of His people*, who will remain, From Assyria, Egypt, Pathros, Cush, Elam, Shinar, Hamath, And from the islands of the sea. [12]And He will lift up a standard for the nations And assemble *the banished ones of Israel*, And will gather the dispersed of Judah From the four corners of the earth" (Isaiah 11:11–12).

These who are gathered are in addition to "those already gathered," as noted in Isaiah 56:

“8The Lord GOD, who gathers the dispersed of Israel, declares, ’Yet others I will gather to them, to those already gathered’” (Isaiah 56:8).

This next portion of Scripture seems to indicate something that frankly I find myself puzzling over. It seems to describe a time after the Lord Jesus has returned from heaven with the saints and begun His reign on earth. Careful reading seems to indicate that at this time, the remnant of Israel is still dispersed throughout the earth, and will now be gathered. Perhaps I am failing to understand this properly, but this is what it seems to indicate.

18“For I know their works and their thoughts; the time is coming to gather all nations and tongues. And they shall come and see My glory. 19“*I will set a sign among them* and will send survivors from them to the nations: Tarshish, Put, Lud, Meshech, Tubal and Javan, to the distant coastlands that have neither heard My fame nor seen My glory. And they will declare My glory among the nations. 20“Then *they shall bring all your brethren from all the nations* (This seems to indicate the brethren are Jews) **as a grain offering to the LORD, on horses, in chariots, in litters, on mules and on camels, to My holy mountain Jerusalem,” says the LORD, “just as the sons of Israel bring their grain offering in a clean vessel to the house of the LORD. 21“I will also take some of them for priests and for Levites,” says the LORD. 22“For just as the new heavens and the new earth Which I make will endure before Me,” declares the LORD, “So your offspring and your name will endure. 23“And it shall be from new moon to new moon And from sabbath to sabbath, All mankind will come to bow down before Me,” says the LORD. 24“Then they will go forth and**

look On the corpses of the men Who have transgressed against Me. For their worm will not die And their fire will not be quenched; And they will be an abhorrence to all mankind." (Isaiah 66:18–24)

In the previous passage, in verse 19 it says "I will set a sign among them." The next passage seems to say something similar, that the Lord will "set up My standard to the peoples."

[22]Thus says the Lord GOD, "Behold, I will lift up My hand to the nations And *set up My standard to the peoples*; And they will bring your sons in their bosom, And your daughters will be carried on their shoulders. [23]"Kings will be your guardians, And their princesses your nurses. They will bow down to you with their faces to the earth And lick the dust of your feet; And you will know that I am the LORD; Those who hopefully wait for Me will not be put to shame. [24]"Can the prey be taken from the mighty man, Or the captives of a tyrant be rescued?" [25]Surely, thus says the LORD, "Even the captives of the mighty man will be taken away, And the prey of the tyrant will be rescued; For I will contend with the one who contends with you, And I will save your sons. [26]"I will feed your oppressors with their own flesh, And they will become drunk with their own blood as with sweet wine; And all flesh will know that I, the LORD, am your Savior And your Redeemer, *the Mighty One of Jacob*." (Isaiah 49:22–26)

The following passages from Isaiah chapter 43 all focus on the fact that God is making it known that He is the God of Israel, the God of Jacob. He is informing us that He will glorify Himself and His name by what He demonstrates to all the nations through His favor and salvation to this remnant of Israel. He calls himself **"the LORD, your Creator, *O***

***Jacob*, And He who formed you, O Israel,"** and tells them, **"'Do not fear, for I have redeemed you; I have called you by name; you are Mine! [...]**

3For I am the LORD your God, *The Holy One of Israel*, your Savior; I have given Egypt as your ransom, Cush and Seba in your place.

4Since you are precious in My sight, Since you are honored and I love you, I will give other men in your place and other peoples in exchange for your life. 5Do not fear, for I am with you; I will bring your offspring from the east, And gather you from the west. 6I will say to the north, 'Give them up!' And to the south, 'Do not hold them back.' Bring My sons from afar And My daughters from the ends of the earth, [...]

8Bring out the people who are blind, even though they have eyes, And the deaf, even though they have ears'" (Isaiah 43:1,3-6,8)

These verses all demonstrate the tenderness the Lord has toward his chosen nation of Israel as well as the lengths he will go to in order to draw them back to himself.

I believe God has begun fulfilling the Scripture relating to gathering Israel back to the land He gave them but is not yet finished. He said He will be glorified through Israel (Ezekiel 39:27). He is ultimately going to use Israel again *to bring glory to His own name*, just as He did once before when He demonstrated His power against Pharaoh in Egypt using Moses. In Exodus chapter 10, we are told, **"And the LORD said unto Moses, Go in unto Pharaoh: for I have hardened his heart, and the heart of his servants, that I might shew these my signs before him: And that thou mayest tell in the ears of thy son,**

and of thy son's son, what things I have wrought in Egypt, and my signs which I have done among them; that ye may know how that I *am* the LORD" (Exodus 10:1-2, emphasis mine).

A few chapters later, God states: "[17] **And I indeed will harden the hearts of the Egyptians, and they shall follow them. So I will gain honor over Pharaoh and over all his army, his chariots, and his horsemen. [18] Then the Egyptians shall know that I am the LORD, when *I have gained honor for Myself* over Pharaoh, his chariots, and his horsemen" (Exodus 14:17-18, emphasis mine).** Paul addressed this particular instance of God gaining glory for his own name in Romans chapter 9: **"For the Scripture says to the Pharaoh, 'For this very purpose I have raised you up, that I may show My power in you, and *that My name may be declared in all the earth*'" (Romans 9:17).**

God will demonstrate at the end of time not just to Egypt, but to all the nations, to all the peoples, through Israel that He is God. He will cause His name to be magnified and exalted.

The following prophecy concerning Israel makes it emphatically clear that God promises Israel will always be His people. He will make a new covenant with them, which is not dependent on them doing anything: **"[31] 'Behold, days are coming,' declares the Lord, 'when I will make a new covenant with the house of Israel and with the house of Judah, [32] not like the covenant which I made with their fathers in the day I took them by the hand to bring them out of the land of Egypt, My covenant which they broke, although I was a husband to them,' declares the Lord. [33] 'But this is the covenant which I will make with the house of Israel after those days,' declares the Lord, 'I will put My law within them and on their heart I will write it; and I will**

be their God, and they shall be My people. [34] They will not teach again, each man his neighbor and each man his brother, saying, "Know the Lord," for they will all know Me, from the least of them to the greatest of them,' declares the Lord, 'for I will forgive their iniquity, and their sin I will remember no more.' [35] Thus says the Lord, who gives the sun for light by day And the fixed order of the moon and the stars for light by night, Who stirs up the sea so that its waves roar; The Lord of hosts is His name: [36] 'If this fixed order departs from before Me,' declares the Lord, 'Then the offspring of Israel also will cease From being a nation before Me forever.' [37] Thus says the Lord, 'If the heavens above can be measured And the foundations of the earth searched out below, Then I will also cast off all the offspring of Israel For all that they have done,' declares the Lord" (Jeremiah 31:31-37). We see in verse 34 above that God is going to make it so all in Israel "know the Lord." However, I am reminded that He only saves a remnant, therefore, this language that sounds inclusive of "all Israel" means "all of the remnant." He has not fulfilled this prophecy yet, but He will.

God Will Use Israel to Exalt His Name in All Nations

God clearly has deep tenderness in his heart for Israel and promises to preserve a part of that nation for himself. However, God also says he will **"gather all the nations"** and use them to **"enter into judgment with them there On behalf of My people and My inheritance, Israel, Whom they have scattered among the nations" (Joel 3:2).**

Again, concerning Israel, He revealed through the prophet Zechariah the following: "[1] **The burden of the word of the Lord concerning Israel. *Thus* declares the Lord who stretches out the heavens, lays**

the foundation of the earth, and forms the spirit of man within him,
2 'Behold, I am going to make Jerusalem a cup that causes reeling to
all the peoples around; and when the siege is against Jerusalem, it
will also be against Judah. 3 It will come about in that day that I will
make Jerusalem a heavy stone for all the peoples; all who lift it will
be severely injured. And all the nations of the earth will be gathered
against it. 4 'In that day,' declares the Lord, 'I will strike every horse
with bewilderment and his rider with madness. But I will watch
over the house of Judah, while I strike every horse of the peoples
with blindness. 5 Then the clans of Judah will say in their hearts,
"A strong support for us are the inhabitants of Jerusalem through
the Lord of hosts, their God." 6 In that day I will make the clans
of Judah like a firepot among pieces of wood and a flaming torch
among sheaves, so they will consume on the right hand and on the
left all the surrounding peoples, while the inhabitants of Jerusalem
again dwell on their own sites in Jerusalem. 7 ***The Lord also will***
save the tents of Judah first**, so that the glory of the house of David**
and the glory of the inhabitants of Jerusalem will not be magnified
above Judah. 8 In that day the Lord will defend the inhabitants
of Jerusalem, and the one who is feeble among them in that day
will be like David, and the house of David ***will be*** **like God, like the**
angel of the Lord before them. 9 And in that day I will set about to
destroy all the nations that come against Jerusalem. 10 I will pour
out on the house of David and on the inhabitants of Jerusalem, the
Spirit of grace and of supplication, so that they will look on Me
whom they have pierced; and they will mourn for Him, as one
mourns for an only son, and they will weep bitterly over Him like
the bitter weeping over a firstborn'" (Zechariah 12:1-10, emphasis

mine). Due to the fact that the subject of this prophecy from Zechariah is indicating from verse three that "all the nations of the earth will be gathered against it" referring to Jerusalem, it seems to indicate that this is pointing to the time right before the Lord's return. Because the focus throughout this prophecy is Judah and the house of David, it may be that the other tribes, Israel, have not been gathered at this point as is indicated will take place in other Scripture (such as in Ezekiel 37:15-28 or Isaiah 66:18-24). This raises the question, "when does the Lord complete the gathering of the remainder of Israel back to the land?" Isaiah 66:20 gives the impression that men of other nations, having been conquered and humbled, transport all the remaining people of Israel back to the land. This would seem likely only after the Lord returns from heaven with His saints and destroys the beast and the false prophet and establishes His reign on earth. I have to admit, this is puzzling to contemplate and perhaps I am missing instruction from other Scripture that provides more clarity on this matter.

This next passage of Scripture gives us a glimpse of how all the nations on earth will travel to Israel to worship the Lord in Jerusalem. If they fail to observe this, they will suffer the penalty of having no rain on their land. This is an annual requirement. Rather than being finished with Israel, God will establish his earthly rule there during the millennium: "[16] Then it will come about that any who are left of all the nations that went against Jerusalem will go up from year to year to worship the King, the Lord of hosts, and to celebrate the Feast of Booths. [17] **And it will be that whichever of the families of the earth *does not go up to Jerusalem to worship the King, the Lord of hosts, there will be no rain on them*" (Zechariah 14:16-17, emphasis mine).** Moreover, we know that Jesus will reign over all the earth for a thousand years, and

His saints reign with Him. He will not have as His global capital city London, or New York, or Moscow, or Beijing. Christ will reign from Jerusalem. Consider these verses from Isaiah 2: **"[2]Now it will come about that In the last days The mountain of the house of the LORD Will be established as the chief of the mountains, And will be raised above the hills; And all the nations will stream to it. [3]And many peoples will come and say, 'Come, let us go up to the mountain of the LORD, To the house of the God of Jacob; That He may teach us concerning His ways And that we may walk in His paths.' For the law will go forth from Zion And the word of the LORD from Jerusalem. [4]And He will judge between the nations, And will render decisions for many peoples; And they will hammer their swords into plowshares and their spears into pruning hooks. Nation will not lift up sword against nation, And never again will they learn war" (Isaiah 2:2–4).**

Scripture makes it plain in Romans that God has a plan to save Israel: **"[25]For I do not want you, brethren, to be uninformed of this mystery—so that you will not be wise in your own estimation—that a partial hardening has happened to Israel until the fullness of the Gentiles has come in; [26]and so all Israel will be saved;** [we must read this "all the remnant of Israel"] **just as it is written, "THE DELIVERER WILL COME FROM ZION, HE WILL REMOVE UNGODLINESS FROM JACOB." [27]"THIS IS MY COVENANT WITH THEM, WHEN I TAKE AWAY THEIR SINS." [28]From the standpoint of the gospel they are enemies for your sake, but from the standpoint of God's choice they are beloved for the sake of the fathers; [29]for the gifts and the calling of God are irrevocable" (Romans 11:25–29).**

Many believers like to interpret all mentions of Israel in the Bible as referring to the church body as a whole now, and apply them as such, but I believe that is an over-simplification and ignores the specific plans God has declared he has for the nation of Israel. While it is true that the family of God has expanded through Jesus and his saving work to include Gentiles as well, and thus some passages that refer to "my people" can and do indicate all believers, it does not do justice to God's clear intentions toward Israel to simply conflate "Israel" and "the church." This is a nuanced conversation, and I have only begun to scratch the surface of it in this chapter, but I hope that examination of these verses will cause my reader to see that God has not completely turned away from Israel as a people. While we may not know yet how he plans to use them in the future or how he will re-gather his chosen remnant, we see that he will somehow do those things because he has told us in his Word that he will.

chapter
TWELVE
Takeaways

A Timeline Summary

Here are how events unfold based on what Scripture teaches regarding the time of the end.

1. We know the apostasy (a falling away of the faith, people who had professed Christ abandoning their faith) will come first. (In fact, I believe we are already witnessing the beginning of the apostasy.)

2. Next, the final ruler, called the antichrist-beast, of a worldwide empire will be revealed. His emergence is due to the power of Satan, with signs and false wonders that will deceive many. He will make war with the saints and prevail over them. The Bible calls this coming ruler various things, including the man of lawlessness, the son of perdition, and the beast. The Word says this about this antichrist-beast: **"[9]that is, the one whose coming is in accord with the activity of Satan, with all power and signs and false wonders" (2 Thessalonians 2:9).**

3. At Some point after the antichrist-beast is revealed, the Scriptures indicate the antichrist will persecute the saints. When this happens, the great tribulation has begun. The saints have been given into his hand, and during the great tribulation he will prevail over them and kill very many or most of them. **"[24]His**

power will be mighty, but not by his own power, And he will destroy to an extraordinary degree And prosper and perform his will; *He will destroy mighty men and the holy people*" (Daniel 8:24).

4. The Word tells us we must endure to the end, that it is he who endures that will be saved. But tribulation is not the same as God's wrath. God's wrath is for those who are not saved, for those who have rejected the truth. The wrath comes, but has not come yet and will not come until the Lord rescues His saints, taking them from the earth at the last trumpet.

5. A detailed analysis in Appendix 5 at the end of this book indicates that *a land of great wealth, called mystery "Babylon the Great" (America) will be destroyed* by the alliance of ten kings or heads of nations who give their power to this ruler, the antichrist-beast. Unmistakable direct parallels exist between this wealthy land in the end time and ancient Babylon. These are examined in appendix 6 of this book. God's people are still present on the earth when this destruction occurs. He warns His people to "come out of her, my people," speaking of this place.

6. There is no widespread revival leading to repentance going on during this time. The Word tells us that "because of lawlessness, the love of most will grow cold." We know that the antichrist-beast cannot be revealed until there is a great apostasy, so rather than many people coming to faith in a great revival, most are doing the opposite, abandoning faith in a great apostasy. Further, there is no mention in Revelation or elsewhere in the Word of anyone repenting and coming to salvation through faith from the opening

of the seals through the sounding of the trumpets, or when God's wrath comes on the earth. Instead, we are told three times, "the rest of mankind did not repent," and "men did not repent."

7. When the number of those who are to be killed for their faith is complete (see Revelation 6:11), then the Lord Jesus comes in the clouds with His mighty angels. He sends His angels over all the earth to gather them and take them to heaven for the marriage supper of the Lamb, and this is the "rapture of the saints." The Word of God tells us the Lord comes to gather His saints at the last trumpet.

8. Then the wrath of God comes and is poured out on those who dwell on the earth. The saints have been rescued and are in heaven with the Lord, at the marriage supper of the Lamb. These last two events begin "the day of the Lord." Simultaneously the Lord snatches His saints from the earth, and His angels begin pouring out the wrath of God upon those who dwell on the earth. This "day of the Lord" lasts for a thousand years. These two events, the gathering of the saints, and God's wrath upon those who dwell on earth, occur at the very beginning of the day of the Lord.

As we have discussed, there are a number of perspectives on end times prophecies, especially with regard to how much we can know about when Christ will return and whether there will be a rapture before that event. All the varying ideas can certainly be confusing. We also know that these issues are not core issues of our faith and should not impede our unity as a body. So if we are not going to agree on every aspect of these prophecies and what they mean, and we may not even be able to know what time they pertain to, what is the point of studying these things? I believe there are a number of valid reasons we should spend time studying these (often confusing) Scriptures:

- God has revealed to us through His Word what His plan is by declaring the end from the beginning.
- We must prepare our hearts for what lies ahead. Consider this verse from Psalms 78: **"[8]And not be like their fathers, A stubborn and rebellious generation, A generation *that did not prepare its heart And whose spirit was not faithful to God*" (Psalm 78:8, emphasis mine).** This verse contains a clear warning not to be like those who did not prepare their hearts and consequently were not faithful to God.
- We have been told that we must remain steadfast in our faith and endure unto the end.
- We have been told that He will rescue us from the wrath to come.
- He has revealed to us definite things that must take place before Jesus returns and warns us not to be deceived by false claims that He has already come. He also warns of false prophets who would come, and to avoid being deceived we must know the truth. We cannot simply wait for Jesus' return to happen at any time; these events must occur beforehand.
- Scripture has revealed to us that an evil ruler, the antichrist-beast, will arise, coming with false signs and wonders with the power of Satan, and he will force everyone to worship himself or be killed or imprisoned. The beast will be accompanied by the most convincing of all false prophets, deceiving all but God's people,

who will work signs and false wonders on his behalf. We must be ready to resist regardless of the cost.

- God will send a great delusion on those who did not love the truth so that they will believe the lie. They will be fooled by the antichrist as a result.

- Over centuries, every time some individual proclaimed that Jesus was going to come back at such-and-such a date it has proven to be false. If for no other reason than this fact, I am emphatically stating that I am not predicting the Lord's return in the early 2030's. What I am saying is that the Scriptures indicate that when the time for His return is near, *we will know it* because "we walk in the light, and not in darkness." We need to be watchful from now until 2028 and possibly several years beyond that for the signs we have been told to look of His return. In the meantime, we must still work diligently at whatever things the Lord has given us individually to do. We must not simply become fixated on the hope of His return and neglect our roles as God's lights in a dark world, our roles as fathers and mothers, as husbands and wives, as faithful workers in the workplace, and as providers for our families. In light of those callings, I want to leave you with this passage to ponder:

"[23]Let us hold unswervingly to the hope we profess, for he who promised is faithful. [24]And let us consider how we may spur one another on toward love and good deeds. [25]Let us not give up meeting together, as some are in the habit of doing, but let us encourage one another—and all the more as you see the Day approaching" (Hebrews 10:23–25, NIV84).

Appendix 1

How Are We Saved?

On the chance that some of you may read this book out of curiosity but have not yet come to faith in Jesus Christ, I have included this section.

Q. How are we saved? Do we have to earn it? If I believe sincerely in another religion, treat people as I would want to be treated, and strive to be devout in my faith, though it is not Christian, can I be saved?

A. According to the Bible, we are saved by believing that God sent His son, Jesus, to die for us and that God raised Jesus from the dead. **Mark 16:16** says, "**He who believes and is baptized will be saved; but he who does not believe will be condemned.**" Salvation from our sins, and the promise of eternal life, are a result of faith-- believing God, trusting that He will do what He promises

A passage of Scripture that many people are familiar with says: "[16] **For God so loved the world that He gave His only begotten Son, that whoever believes in Him should not perish but have everlasting life. [17] For God did not send His Son into the world to condemn the world, but that the world through Him might be saved. [18] He who believes in Him is not condemned; but he who does not believe is condemned already, because he has not believed in the name of the only begotten Son of God" (John 3:16-18).**

We must first recognize we need saving, which means we know we are sinners and need forgiveness from the perfect, righteous God who made us. If we believe we are sinners, *we must repent of our sin.* We learn more about repentance in Matthew 4 when Jesus travels to Galilee and preaches to the crowds, saying that **"the kingdom of God is at hand. Repent, and believe in the gospel". (Matthew 4: 15).** Repentance means we acknowledge God to be right and ask Him to help us turn away from sin. Without faith in Christ, we will not have the power to defeat sin in our lives.

We also must tell someone of our faith, in other words, "confess with our mouth" what we believe: [9] **that if you confess with your mouth the Lord Jesus and believe in your heart that God has raised Him from the dead, you will be saved. [10] For with the heart one believes unto righteousness, and with the mouth confession is made unto salvation. [11] For the Scripture says, "Whoever believes on Him will not be put to shame." (Romans 10:9-11)**

Q. What if I want to believe, but I am having difficulty doing so?

A. We find in Scripture an example of a man with a child who desperately wanted Jesus to heal him. Now granted, this specifically relates to healing, but it was recorded for us to read for a much broader reason. It is to let us know that God understands our weaknesses and He stands ready to help us. Read this excerpt from Mark 9: " [23] Jesus said to him, **'If you can believe, all things are possible to him who believes.' [24] Immediately the father of the child cried out and said with tears, 'Lord, I believe; help my unbelief!'" (Mark 9:23-24).**

My advice to you is to remember that Scripture says, "seek, and you shall find, knock, and it shall be opened unto you." Cry out in prayer to God and ask Him to give you the faith you need to believe in His son Jesus as your Lord, and that God raised him from the dead.

Q. Do we have to earn salvation?

A. No, in fact, you cannot earn it. The Word of God tells us: **"[8] For by grace you have been saved through faith, and that not of yourselves; *it is* the gift of God, [9] not of works, lest anyone should boast" (Ephesians 2:8-9).**

This is what differentiates saving faith in Christ from all other religions. All other religions at their core involve people striving to do good things to please God to earn favor with Him (or to advance themselves toward greater spirituality). But the one true God requires that we believe Him and trust Him: **"[3]For what does the Scripture say? 'ABRAHAM BELIEVED GOD, AND IT WAS CREDITED TO HIM AS RIGHTEOUSNESS.'" (Romans 4:3) .**

God made it very plain through the requirement of sacrifices of animals and the shedding of their blood in the Old Testament that sin was abhorrent to Him. Then He showed us that Jesus, who had never sinned, *died once for all as a blood sacrifice* to meet His requirement to take our sins away: "**For every high priest taken from among men is appointed for men in things *pertaining* to God, that he may offer both gifts and sacrifices for sins" (Hebrews 5:1).** But regarding Jesus, Hebrews later tells us that "**Jesus does not need daily, as those high priests, to offer up sacrifices, first for His own sins and then for the people's, for this He did once for all when He offered up Himself" (Hebrews 7:27).**

Being made acceptable to God is not about our behavior but rather about believing what God did on our behalf to reconcile us to Himself. When we come to believe and understand that God saves us by His grace and mercy, not because we deserve it, then we want to please Him and keep His commandments.

We just must accept that truth, and trust Jesus Christ as our Lord. This means submitting to him as best we can in obedience. Otherwise, we have not trusted Him. We have only intellectually assented to the idea that Jesus is real and is God's son, but we are not letting that change our behavior. If we do not unite the Word with faith and walk in obedience to it, then it profits us not at all. Intellectual assent will not save us, but faith in the Word will. We do not earn salvation with the right behavior, or obedience to the Word of God. Instead, obedience is the true indicator to each one of us personally of our faith, evidence that we are saved, have eternal life, and are a new creation in Christ. It is our own personal test that we are truly His. Scripture says the demons believe, and shudder. We cannot say that Jesus is our Lord and go on intentionally sinning. Does that mean we will not sin? No, but we cannot continue to purpose to sin: "[6] **If we say that we have fellowship with Him, and walk in darkness, we lie and do not practice the truth. [7] But if we walk in the light as He is in the light, we have fellowship with one another, and the blood of Jesus Christ His Son cleanses us from all sin. [8] If we say that we have no sin, we deceive ourselves, and the truth is not in us. [9] If we confess our sins, He is faithful and just to forgive us our sins and to cleanse us from all unrighteousness. [10] If we say that we have not sinned, we make Him a liar, and His word is not in us" (1 John: 6-10).** The Word goes on to assure us: "[1] **My little children, these things I write to you, so that you may not sin. And if anyone sins, we have an Advocate with the Father, Jesus Christ the righteous. [2] And He Himself is the propitiation for our sins, and not for ours only but also for the whole world.**

[3] Now by this we know that we know Him, if we keep His commandments. [4] He who says, 'I know Him,' and does not keep His

commandments, is a liar, and the truth is not in him. [5] But whoever keeps His word, truly the love of God is perfected in him. By this we know that we are in Him. [6] He who says he abides in Him ought himself also to walk just as He walked" (1 John 2:1-6)

Q. Is there truly only one path to salvation? Does it have to be only through Jesus Christ, the son of God?

A. Before looking at Scripture, I ask you to consider the following: Suppose you consider the facts, and you believe Jesus was a real person, who lived 2000 years ago, and not just a fantasy, or myth. Suppose as is reported by many eyewitnesses and recorded in multiple verified and trusted historical documents, you believe He worked miracles, giving sight to a blind person, healing a person born lame, restoring hearing to the deaf, healing lepers, and feeding thousands from just a tiny bit of fish and bread that He miraculously multiplied. Not to mention walking on water, or commanding the wind and waves to be still. We have a record of much of his teaching, and it is without dispute very wise. In fact, people were amazed at the authority with which he spoke and taught.

Now at this point, let us suppose we change the account of His life. Let us suppose at the end of His life, he told his followers, "I have shown you how powerful I am, and proven that I came from God. I have told you how you should live, so now, I am leaving. You just need to do as I have taught you, and you will live forever with God in His kingdom." But what we will change is in this new account is that we have Him skip dying on the cross. We would then have the classic "God grades on the curve" approach to who lives forever and who does not. In other words, God compares me to the rest of mankind, and on average, I'm fairly good, so I must be acceptable to Him. Just be good enough, and you live forever.

But the son of God, the Lord Jesus Christ, did not skip the cross. Why? Because His suffering in our place was necessary to save us. If it were not essential, then wouldn't it be cruel of God the Father to put Jesus His son through that agonizing pain, suffering, and humiliation if there was another way? But there was no other way.

Scripture says in 1 Corinthians 1: "[23] **but we preach *Christ crucified*, to the Jews a stumbling block and to the Greeks foolishness, [24] but to those who are called, both Jews and Greeks, Christ the power of God and the wisdom of God" (1 Corinthians 1:23-24).** Christ's death on the cross, and His resurrection from the dead by God, are at the very heart and core of the truth of the gospel. No other religion has someone who gave themselves as a perfect, sinless sacrifice to pay the justly required price for sin to save others. Moreover, no other religion has an empty tomb that demonstrates victory over death, and the promise of eternal life by the eternal Almighty God. So no, being spiritual and a good person will not save you. Holding onto that belief is only holding onto one's own pride and rebellion against our Creator. Realize that you, like all men, have sinned. Repent of your sin, and rather than trusting in your own goodness, accept the free gift of God who wants to bestow His love on you forever. To accept this free gift by God's grace, you must believe you have sinned and tell Him you repent of it. If you do not think you have sin, you are deceiving yourself. If you think you have no sin, Scripture says you deceive yourself. If you do believe yourself to be a sinner in need of forgiveness, all you need to do is confess your sin to God and ask Him to forgive you: "[8]**If we say that we have no sin, we are deceiving ourselves and the truth is not in us. [9]If we confess our sins, He is faithful and righteous to forgive us our sins and to cleanse us from all unrighteousness. [10]If we say that we have not sinned, we**

make Him a liar and His word is not in us" (1 John 1:8–10).

If you have not done so before, stop and pray now, acknowledge that you are a sinner, repent, and ask God to give you faith in his son Jesus, and receive God's free gift of His grace. You do not deserve it; no one does. Don't think you have to clean up your life before you can ask God for this gift of faith. You don't. If you deserved it, it would be what you are entitled to, and it would not be a gift.

If you have not believed in Christ Jesus, that He died and that God raised him from the dead, and confessed it with your mouth, you have not yet entered into eternal life. You have not yet been born again of His Spirit. You have not yet received from God the gift of His Holy Spirit to live within you, inside you, in your body. Without His Spirit to reveal the things of God to you, you will continue to fail to understand the things of God. You will continue to be perplexed and walk in darkness. You are what Scripture calls a natural man. As such, you cannot understand the things of God. Read what Scripture says about this condition: "[7] **But we speak the wisdom of God in a mystery, the hidden *wisdom* which God ordained before the ages for our glory, [8] which none of the rulers of this age knew; for had they known, they would not have crucified the Lord of glory. [9] But as it is written: *'Eye has not seen, nor ear heard, Nor have entered into the heart of man The things which God has prepared for those who love Him.'*[10] But God has revealed *them* to us through His Spirit. For the Spirit searches all things, yes, the deep things of God. [11] For what man knows the things of a man except the spirit of the man which is in him? Even so no one knows the things of God except the Spirit of God. [12] Now we have received, not the spirit of the world, but the Spirit who is from God, that we might**

know the things that have been freely given to us by God. [13] These things we also speak, not in words which man's wisdom teaches but which the Holy Spirit teaches, comparing spiritual things with spiritual. [14] But the *natural man* does not receive the things of the Spirit of God, for they are foolishness to him; nor can he know *them, because they are spiritually discerned*" (1 Corinthians 2:7-14).

Once you surrender the desire to rule your own life and trust in Christ Jesus to rule you as your saving Lord, you will be given the Holy Spirit to dwell within you, and you will become a new creation in Christ Jesus. He told us to cast our burden on Him, that His yoke is easy. He is a perfect and loving master and demonstrated His love and faithfulness by suffering and dying to redeem us. As the Scripture above says, you have no comprehension of what God has in store for you once you put your trust in Him through faith in Jesus His son. Don't wait. Act immediately if you have not yet confessed out loud that you trust in Him, in His death and resurrection from the dead, and that you need him to be your Lord to save you. Then you can have eternal life, and victory over sin in your life. Then you can begin the most amazing journey, one that you have not begun to imagine. Once you believe and confess Him, the following will be true of you: **"Or do you not know that your body is the temple of the Holy Spirit who is in you, whom you have from God, and you are not your own?" (1 Corinthians 6:9).**

What is spoken of above has not happened for you if you have not put your complete faith and trust in the Lord Jesus Christ as the risen son of the only true God. Once you do trust him, He will send His Holy Spirit to live and dwell in your body. You will enter into eternal life.

Appendix 2

Doubts About One's Own Salvation

Are we supposed to know for certain that we are saved?

Recently I was surprised and startled by a conversation I had during a Bible study and fellowship time with three other men that I have known for decades and have been meeting with for years on almost a weekly basis. We were talking about a question that I once heard Doctor D. James Kennedy, the former long-time pastor of a large church in the Coral Gables Florida area, use in teaching evangelism to his congregation. The question was, "If you died last night, and then stood before God and He asked you, 'Why should I let you in My heaven?' What would be your answer?" Generally, you get one of two answers to this question. As we discussed the answers, which I will come back to, it led to the question, "*Can you know for certain you are saved*? If so, how?" The answer is yes, Scripture says you can know for sure. At this point in our discussion, one of the men said, "I believe, but I often doubt my salvation. I would like to know for sure I am saved." Immediately one of the other men said, "Me too." So together we decided to go to the Word and learn how we can know for sure that we are saved and have eternal life. . Now I will come back to the two different answers to the hypothetical question God might ask about why He should let you in heaven. But first let's consider if you can know for certain that you are saved, that you have eternal life, and what the Word tells us about that question.

Peter, the chief of the Apostles, wrote to believers *to make certain about their calling*. He would not have instructed believers in this way unless it was possible *to be certain about our calling.*

Consider this Scripture from 2 Peter 1:

> **"[10]Therefore, brethren, be all the more diligent to make certain about His calling and choosing you; for as long as you practice these things, you will never stumble; [11]for in this way the entrance into the eternal kingdom of our Lord and Savior Jesus Christ will be abundantly supplied to you." (2 Peter 1:10–11)**

Do each of us want this personal assurance? Of course. What comes before the "therefore?" Listen to what it says:

- **[8]For *if these qualities are yours and are increasing*, they render you neither useless nor unfruitful in the true knowledge of our Lord Jesus Christ. [9]For he who lacks these qualities is blind or short-sighted, having forgotten his purification from his former sins. (2 Peter 1:8–9)** (If we lack these qualities, we are told we are blind or short sighted about our being called and chosen by God. That would be a serious, even a grave concern.)

What qualities? So we must back up a little more in the passage. How is entrance into the eternal kingdom *abundantly supplied to us*? We will come back to answer this question.

Are we supposed to know we have eternal life? In the discussion with my three long-time friends I mentioned the following verse:

- **[13]These things I have written to you who believe in the name of the Son of God, *so that you may know that you have eternal life.* (1 John 5:13)**

I mentioned that what each of the men said surprised and startled me. The reason I was surprised is because I know how grounded in the Word and in the Lord these men are, and I never expected this response. Maybe some of you reading this now, even though you are long time believers and are grounded in the Word just like these men, would also like *more assurance of your salvation*. Hopefully, as we examine the Word together here, you will find exactly that assurance. If you are not saved, then you will hear how you can be.

As we proceed, let's go back to the question about what would you say to God if he asked you why should I let you in heaven? One of the two answers most commonly given is something like "well, I do my best, I don't steal or lie, I haven't killed anyone, or committed adultery, and I go to church regularly, and try to be kind, and so forth. I hope you will let me in." Let me tell you, before we are finished here, you will know that this is not the answer. But what is?

The word says without faith it is impossible to please God.

- **Hebrews 11:6** says: [6]**And *without faith it is impossible to please Him*, for he who comes to God must believe that He is and that *He is a rewarder of those who seek Him.***

Who was the father of our faith? Abraham. For a little background, Abraham was the father of Isaac, who was the father of Jacob. Jacob had twelve sons, and was given the name Israel by God. He and his family went down to Egypt, after the brothers sold Joseph into slavery and he rose to be second only to Pharoah. Their descendants lived there for over four hundred years, until Moses led them out. Now the ten commandments, the law, were not yet given until the time of Moses, who received them on the mountain. So, there was no law in the time of Abraham. He lived almost five hundred years before the law was given. If there is no law, you cannot break the law. The word says in Romans 4:15, "where there is no law, there is also no violation." Think of it like a speed limit law on a road. If there is no speed limit, you can't be given a citation for going over the limit. Going back to Abraham, if there was no law in his time, no rules, Abraham could not say "Hey God, I kept the rules, you have to let me in."

Scripture says in **Romans 4:3, "Abraham believed God, and it was *credited to him as righteousness*."** How so?

God told Abraham to leave his home and go where he would lead him, that he would give him and his descendants a land as a possession forever, and He promised to make a great nation of Abraham. He further told him the promise would come through a son that would be born to Sarah, his wife. At her age 90, and his age 100, sure enough, she had a son, and he was named Isaac. Then about 12 years later, God told Abraham to sacrifice his son. What did Abraham do? He proceeded to do just that.

- Scripture tells us in Hebrews 11 that: [17]**"By faith Abraham, *when he was tested*, offered up Isaac, and he who had received the promises was offering up his only begotten son; [18]it was he to whom it was said, "In Isaac your descendants shall be called." [19]*He considered that God is able to raise people even from the dead*, from which he also received him back as a type." (Hebrews 11:17-19)**
- We find more of this explained in Romans 4: [2]**For if Abraham**

> **was justified by works, he has something to boast about, but not before God. [3]For what does the Scripture say? "ABRAHAM BELIEVED GOD, AND IT WAS CREDITED TO HIM AS RIGHTEOUSNESS." [4]Now to the one who works, his wage is not credited as a favor, but as what is due. [5]But to the one who does not work, but believes in Him who justifies the ungodly, his faith is credited as righteousness, [6]just as David also speaks of the blessing on the man *to whom God credits righteousness apart from works*: [7]"BLESSED ARE THOSE WHOSE LAWLESS DEEDS HAVE BEEN FORGIVEN, AND WHOSE SINS HAVE BEEN COVERED. [8]"BLESSED IS THE MAN WHOSE SIN *THE LORD WILL NOT TAKE INTO ACCOUNT*." (Romans 4:2–8)**

Please forgive me for repeating this if you have previously encountered this in reading this book, but let me pose a hypothetical to you. Suppose we change just one thing about the Gospel, the good news about Jesus. This hypothetical goes like this, suppose Jesus did all the same mighty miracles that He did, gave sight to the blind, healed lepers and the sick, caused the lame to walk, walked on water, stilled the waves and wind with a word, fed thousands with just a few loaves and fish, and raised the dead. He still taught us to love God with all our heart, and our neighbor as ourself. He taught us to love our enemies and pray for them. But at the end of His ministry, imagine that He skipped the cross, and just said to His disciples, now go do as I have taught you. Then we would have a circumstance where it might be that God would grade on a curve, and if you were good enough, He would let you in. But how good is good enough? If it were possible to be saved by being good enough, why would Christ have to suffer and die on the cross? Wouldn't that be cruel of God to make his only son die, unless that was absolutely necessary?

Some people say they think Christ was a great man, or a good teacher, and it is good to follow His example. But they stop short of believing He died and that God raised Him from the dead, and that He must be obeyed as Lord.

But Christ *was crucified.* He did not skip the cross. Listen to this next passage:

- **[21]For since in the wisdom of God the world through its wisdom did not come to know God, God was well-pleased through the foolishness of the message preached to save those who believe. [22]For indeed Jews ask for signs and Greeks search for wisdom; [23]but *we preach Christ crucified,* to Jews a stumbling block and to Gentiles foolishness, [24]but to those who are the called, both Jews and Greeks, Christ the power of God and the wisdom of God. (1 Corinthians 1:21–24)**

The word says in Hebrews, "Without the shedding of blood, there is no forgiveness of sin."

- **[22]And according to the Law, one may almost say, all things are cleansed with blood, and *without shedding of blood there is no forgiveness.* (Hebrews 9:22)**

While Israel was still in slavery in Egypt, for the final demonstration of His power, God told Moses to have all the people to take a one-year-old, *unblemished lamb*, and kill it, and put *its blood* over the door that was the entrance to their dwelling, and on the sides of the doorposts. They were to then roast the lamb, and eat its flesh before morning, and not to go out of the door. The angel of the Lord would then *pass over* their homes and spare them, but would take the life of every first born

Egyptian both of man and beast. This was called *the Passover*, and Jews were commanded to keep it perpetually at the same time of year throughout all generations. When Jesus appeared to be baptized by John the Baptist, he proclaimed, "behold *the lamb of God*, who takes away the sin of the world." Jesus was crucified, His blood shed, He was *the unblemished lamb*, and was slain on the Jewish Passover.

Now let's go back to how you can know you have eternal life. It is a gift, not based on works, on our effort. Following are some Scriptures that give us clarity on salvation and assurance of our faith:

- **8But God demonstrates His own love toward us, in that while we were yet sinners, Christ died for us. 9Much more then, having now been *justified by His blood*, we shall be saved from the wrath of God through Him. 10For if while we were enemies we were reconciled to God through the death of His Son, much more, having been reconciled, we shall be saved by His life. (Romans 5:8–10)**
- **23For the wages of sin is death, but *the free gift of God* is eternal life in Christ Jesus our Lord. (Romans 6:23)**
- **1And you were dead in your trespasses and sins, 2in which you formerly walked according to the course of this world, according to the prince of the power of the air, of the spirit that is now working in the sons of disobedience. 3Among them we too all formerly lived in the lusts of our flesh, indulging the desires of the flesh and of the mind, and were by nature *children of wrath, even as the rest.* 4But God, being rich in mercy, because of His great love with which He loved us,**

[5]**even when we were dead in our transgressions, made us alive together with Christ (by grace you have been saved),** [6]**and raised us up with Him, and seated us with Him in the heavenly places in Christ Jesus,** [7]**so that in the ages to come He might show the surpassing riches of His grace in kindness toward us in Christ Jesus.** [8]**For by grace you have been saved through faith; and that not of yourselves, *it is the gift of God*;** [9]**not as a result of works, so that no one may boast. (Ephesians 2:1–9)**

You must believe in your heart *that God raised Jesus from the dead.* If Christ is not raised, our faith is worthless.

- We read in 1 Corinthians 15: [16]**For if the dead are not raised, not even Christ has been raised;** [17]**and if Christ has not been raised, your faith is worthless; you are still in your sins. (1 Corinthians 15:16–17)**

You may say, "I believe." Well, demons also believe, and they shudder.

- In James 2 we read: [19]**You believe that God is one. You do well; the demons also believe, and shudder. (James 2:19)**

We will come back to this verse. To be saving faith, or "belief that saves," you must *join your faith with obedience.* Listen to this next passage:

- John 3 says: [4]**Everyone who *practices sin* also practices lawlessness; and sin is lawlessness.** [5]**You know that He appeared in order to take away sins; and in Him there is no sin.** [6]***No one who abides in Him sins*; no one who sins has seen Him or knows Him.** [7]**Little children, make sure no one deceives you; *the one who practices righteousness is righteous*, just as He is righteous;** [8]***the one who practices sin is of the devil*; for the devil**

has sinned from the beginning. The Son of God appeared for this purpose, to destroy the works of the devil. [9]*No one who is born of God practices sin,* because His seed abides in him; and he cannot sin, because he is born of God. [10]*By this the children of God and the children of the devil are obvious: anyone who does not practice righteousness is not of God, nor the one who does not love his brother.* (1 John 3:4–10)

Again I ask the question, If God said "Why should I let you in My heaven?" what would be your reply?

Jesus said, Many will say "Lord, Lord, but I will say depart from me, I never knew you…"

- Jesus said: **[16]"You will know them by their fruits. Grapes are not gathered from thorn bushes nor figs from thistles, are they? [17]"So every good tree bears good fruit, but the bad tree bears bad fruit. [18]"*A good tree cannot produce bad fruit, nor can a bad tree produce good fruit.* [19]"Every tree that does not bear good fruit is cut down and thrown into the fire. [20]"So then, you will know them by their fruits. [21]"Not everyone who says to Me, 'Lord, Lord,' will enter the kingdom of heaven, but he who does the will of My Father who is in heaven will enter. [22]"Many will say to Me on that day, 'Lord, Lord, did we not prophesy in Your name, and in Your name cast out demons, and in Your name perform many miracles?' [23]"And then I will declare to them, 'I never knew you; DEPART FROM ME, YOU WHO PRACTICE LAWLESSNESS.' (Matthew 7:16–23)**

You should be able to look at your own life, at the way you treat others, and how you live, and examine your "fruit." Are you producing good fruit, or bad fruit? This self-examination is not your "justification" that you are worthy of the kingdom; rather, it is a self-test, to inform you whether you need to repent, or not. Is what you live day-to-day lining up with what you say you believe? Do you obey the teachings of Jesus? If not, you are walking in disobedience, practicing "lawlessness," and you need to repent. If you need to repent, but do not, you will not have eternal life with Christ in His kingdom.

Does God grade on a curve? No, he doesn't. How good is good enough? *Perfect righteousness is required, something we humans are not capable of.* So, God gave Jesus, the *perfect unblemished lamb*, to die, to shed His blood on our behalf. When we believe, He *credits us with His righteousness*.

How are we saved? The word says believe in your heart that God raised Jesus from the dead, and confess with your mouth Jesus as Lord.

- Listen to Romans 10: **8But what does it say? "THE WORD IS NEAR YOU, IN YOUR MOUTH AND IN YOUR HEART"—that is, the word of faith which we are preaching, 9that if you *confess with your mouth Jesus as Lord*, and *believe in your heart that God raised Him from the dead, you will be saved*; 10for *with the heart a person believes, resulting in righteousness*, and *with the mouth he confesses, resulting in salvation.* 11For the Scripture says, "WHOEVER BELIEVES IN HIM WILL NOT BE DISAPPOINTED." 12For there is no distinction between Jew and Greek; for the same Lord is Lord of all, abounding in riches for all who call on Him; 13for "WHOEVER WILL CALL ON THE NAME OF THE LORD WILL**

BE SAVED."[14]How then will they call on Him in whom they have not believed? How will they believe in Him whom they have not heard? And how will they hear without a preacher? [15]How will they preach unless they are sent? Just as it is written, "HOW BEAUTIFUL ARE THE FEET OF THOSE WHO BRING GOOD NEWS OF GOOD THINGS!" [16]However, *they did not all heed the good news*; for Isaiah says, "LORD, WHO HAS BELIEVED OUR REPORT?" (Romans 10:8–17)

There is a warning contained in this last verse. Not everyone who heard the good news heeded it. This passage ends with… **[17]So faith comes *from hearing*, and hearing by the word of Christ**.

In Hebrews, we find more sobering words concerning our salvation.

- Hebrews 4 says: **[1]Therefore, *let us fear if*, while a promise remains of entering His rest, any one of you may seem to have come short of it. […][7]He again fixes a certain day, "Today," saying through David after so long a time just as has been said before, "TODAY *IF YOU HEAR HIS VOICE*, DO NOT HARDEN YOUR HEARTS." […][16]Therefore let us draw near with confidence to the throne of grace, so that we may receive mercy and find grace to help in time of need. (Hebrews 4:1, 7, 16)**

The Word says "*Today, if you hear my voice*." Is God stirring something in your heart? What do you do?

You Repent. Right after Jesus went into the wilderness to be tempted by the Devil, we read from Matthew:

- **[17]From that time Jesus began to preach and say, "*Repent*, for the kingdom of heaven is at hand." (Matthew 4:17)**

Jesus went on to elaborate about the need for repentance.

- Listen to Luke 13: [1]**Now on the same occasion there were some present who reported to Him about the Galileans whose blood Pilate had mixed with their sacrifices.** [2]**And Jesus said to them, "Do you suppose that these Galileans were greater sinners than all other Galileans because they suffered this fate?** [3]**"I tell you, no, *but unless you repent*, you will all likewise perish.** [4]**"Or do you suppose that those eighteen on whom the tower in Siloam fell and killed them were worse culprits than all the men who live in Jerusalem?** [5]**"I tell you, no, *but unless you repent*, you will all likewise perish." (Luke 13:1–5)**

If you repent, there is good news.

- John 3 says: [16]**"For God so loved the world, that He gave His only begotten Son, that whoever believes in Him shall not perish, but have eternal life.** [17]**"For God did not send the Son into the world to judge the world, but that the world might be saved through Him. (John 3:16–17)**

From the very beginning of the Gospel and the church, **believing was accompanied by obedience**. The first step in obedience was *to be baptized.*

- Hear this from Acts 2:38: [38]**Peter said to them, "Repent, and *each of you be baptized in the name of Jesus Christ for the forgiveness of your sins*; and you will receive the gift of the Holy Spirit.**

- Acts 2:40–41 shows what happened: [40]**And with many other words he solemnly testified and kept on exhorting them,**

saying, "Be saved from this perverse generation!" [41]So then, *those who had received his word were baptized;* and that day there were added about three thousand souls. (Acts 2:40–41)

Does obedience save us? No, but if we are truly His, we will obey Him because we understand what He has done for us by His grace and mercy, and out of overflowing gratitude we want to please Him. John 3:36 contains a warning about obedience:

- **[6]"He who believes in the Son has eternal life; *but he who does not obey the Son will not see life*, but the wrath of God abides on him." (John 3:36)**

Are there many alternate paths to eternal life? Listen to what the Word says:

- In Acts 4:12 we read: **[12]"And there is salvation in no one else; for there is no other name under heaven that has been given among men by which we must be saved." (Acts 4:12)**
- 1 Timothy 2:5 tells us more: **[5]For there is one God, and *one mediator also between God and men, the man Christ Jesus*, (1 Timothy 2:5)**
- John 5:12 makes it plain. Listen to what this Scripture says: **[12]He who has the Son has the life; he who does not have the Son of God does not have the life. (John 5:12)**

And now we come back to answer one of the questions I left open when I started. How can you have assurance of your salvation?

- I will leave you with a final passage to examine: **[1]Simon Peter, a bond-servant and apostle of Jesus Christ, *To those who have received a faith of the same kind as ours*, by the righteousness**

> **of our God and Savior, Jesus Christ: [2]Grace and peace be multiplied to you in the knowledge of God and of Jesus our Lord; [3]seeing that His divine power has granted to us everything pertaining to life and godliness, through the true knowledge of Him who called us by His own glory and excellence. [4]For by these He has granted to us His precious and magnificent promises, so that by them you may become partakers of the divine nature, having escaped the corruption that is in the world by lust. [5]Now for this very reason also, *applying all diligence, in your faith supply moral excellence, and in your moral excellence, knowledge, [6]and in your knowledge, self-control, and in your self-control, perseverance, and in your perseverance, godliness, [7]and in your godliness, brotherly kindness, and in your brotherly kindness, love. [8]For if these qualities are yours and are increasing*, they render you neither useless nor unfruitful in the true knowledge of our Lord Jesus Christ. [9]For he who lacks these qualities is blind or short-sighted, having forgotten his purification from his former sins.**

- **[10]Therefore, brethren, be all the more diligent to make certain about His calling and choosing you; for as long as you practice these things, you will never stumble; [11]for *in this way the entrance into the eternal kingdom of our Lord and Savior Jesus Christ will be abundantly supplied to you.* (2 Peter 1:1–11)**

You start with faith, provided only by the grace of God. Then by the indwelling of the Holy Spirit, you begin to see a progression of increasing fruit of that Spirit in your life as evidence of your true faith. If you look at your life, and you see a trend which gives evidence to this progression, after having believed in Jesus for your salvation, then you have assurance you are His, and are certain of your eternal life with Him. If you think you have made a profession of faith in Jesus, and you in the privacy of your own heart examine your life since then, and do see these qualities where before they were absent, you have certainty you are a "new creation in Christ Jesus" by God's grace. But if you do not see these qualities, I urge you to repent and cry out to Jesus to be your Lord while there is still time.

In summary, we cannot earn our salvation, for we are saved by *faith*. The object of our faith is *Christ*, more specifically, His shed blood on our behalf, His death in our place, and His resurrection by God. We must believe this in our heart, and make him our Lord, our master. And we must confess it with our mouth before men. Our *assurance* comes as we examine ourselves. Are we good trees, producing good fruit? Are we seeing more of this good fruit in ourselves over time and is it increasing? Are you being diligent to make certain about his calling and choosing you? You are either practicing righteousness, because the spirit of Christ now dwells in you, or you are still practicing lawlessness and sin, because you have refused to hear the call of God and repent and be saved. Think about the parable of the Sower and the seed. Do not let the word be choked out and prevented from bearing good fruit because of worries about the world and cares about riches. If you examine yourself, do you see good fruit, and is it increasing? If you do, you know Christ is in you, and you have eternal life. If you do not, then do not wait. Believe and repent, confess Jesus as your Lord, and be saved.

Finally, what is the answer to the hypothetical question, why should I let you in heaven? Father, it is because I believe in your only begotten son,

Jesus, as my Lord. He shed his blood and died to take away my sins. You raised Him from the dead, and will raise me. I am your adopted son or daughter through Him, and He lives in me. Like all the rest, I was dead in my sins, but You have saved me by your grace and mercy.

Appendix 3

Other "Day for a Year" Applications

Let us look at Daniel chapter twelve, specifically at verses eleven and twelve: [11]"***From the time that the regular sacrifice is abolished and the abomination of desolation is set up*, there will be 1,290 days. [12]"How blessed is he who keeps waiting and attains to the 1,335 days." (Daniel 12:11–12)**

Skolfield[5] noted that it is possible to determine when the original practice of sacrifices stopped and that God gave us a precise date in Scripture. It is important to note that under the law, *only priests were empowered and recognized by God as being allowed to offer sacrifices.* We find this first set forth in Exodus 30: **[19]"Aaron and his sons shall wash their hands and their feet from it; [20]when they enter the tent of meeting, they shall wash with water, so that they will not die; or when they approach the altar to minister, by offering up in smoke a fire sacrifice to the LORD. [21]So they shall wash their hands and their feet, so that they will not die; and it shall be a perpetual statute for them, for Aaron and his descendants throughout their generations." (Exodus 30:19-21)**

If there were no priests to offer sacrifices, then the sacrifices must cease. The offering of sacrifices did not require a temple to be standing, for they offered sacrifices in a tent, called the tabernacle before the temple was ever built by Solomon. Knowing this, we can turn to Scripture and find three separate deportations of the Jews by Nebuchadnezzar. The first has

---

5 Hidden Beast 2, 2nd Edition, Revised March 15, 1991. Ellis Skolfield, Copyright 1990 by Fish House, ISBN 0-9628139-0-7

been widely accepted by scholars to have occurred in the year 606 BC when King Nebuchadnezzar laid siege to Jerusalem, captured the city, and deported most of the captives to Babylon. This is recorded in the following Scripture: [10]**At that time the servants of Nebuchadnezzar king of Babylon went up to Jerusalem, and the city came under siege. [11]And Nebuchadnezzar the king of Babylon came to the city, while his servants were besieging it. [12]Jehoiachin the king of Judah went out to the king of Babylon, he and his mother and his servants and his captains and his officials. So the king of Babylon took him captive *in the eighth year of his reign.* [13]He carried out from there all the treasures of the house of the Lord, and the treasures of the king's house, and cut in pieces all the vessels of gold which Solomon king of Israel had made in the temple of the Lord, just as the Lord had said. [14]Then he led away into exile all Jerusalem and all the captains and all the mighty men of valor, ten thousand captives, and all the craftsmen and the smiths. None remained except the poorest people of the land. (2 Kings 24:10–14)**

Then Nebuchadnezzar installed a new king over the remnant left in Jerusalem and named him Zedekiah. But Zedekiah rebelled after a few years, so Nebuchadnezzar returned. He once again took the city and this time he killed all of Zedekiah's children before his eyes, then he put out Zedekiah's eyes and put him in shackles, and deported him and all but the poorest of the people to Babylon. But the question remains, had the sacrifices ceased? We learn from reading Jeremiah that they had not ceased, but were finally caused to cease when the final group which contained priests was deported from the land and taken to Babylon. We read in Jeremiah about offerings being brought before the Lord:

[4]Now it happened on the next day after the killing of Gedaliah, when no one knew about it, [5]that *eighty men came from Shechem*, from Shiloh, and from Samaria with their beards shaved off and their clothes torn and their bodies gashed, *having grain offerings and incense in their hands to bring to the house of the Lord*. (Jeremiah 41:4-5) Only priests were permitted to offer sacrifices at the altar. But Jeremiah 41:4-5 was written six to ten months after the temple had been destroyed, showing that sacrifices were still being offered at the temple site, where the altar had been in the house of the Lord. So, sacrifices had not yet ceased.

In the final chapter of Jeremiah, in Jeremiah 52:28-30 we find recorded *the final deportations of exiles* under Nebuchadnezzar: "**[28]These are the people whom Nebuchadnezzar carried away into exile: in the seventh year 3,023 Jews; [29]in the eighteenth year of Nebuchadnezzar 832 persons from Jerusalem; *[30]in the twenty-third year of Nebuchadnezzar*, Nebuzaradan the captain of the guard carried into exile 745 Jewish people; there were 4,600 persons in all." (Jeremiah 52:28–30)** We note from the above verses that it is in the twenty-third year of Nebuchadnezzar's reign that the final deportation is recorded. It follows that this is when any remaining priests were exiled and the sacrifices ceased, in the year of 583 BC. This would mark the date regular sacrifices were abolished because no more priests remained to offer them.

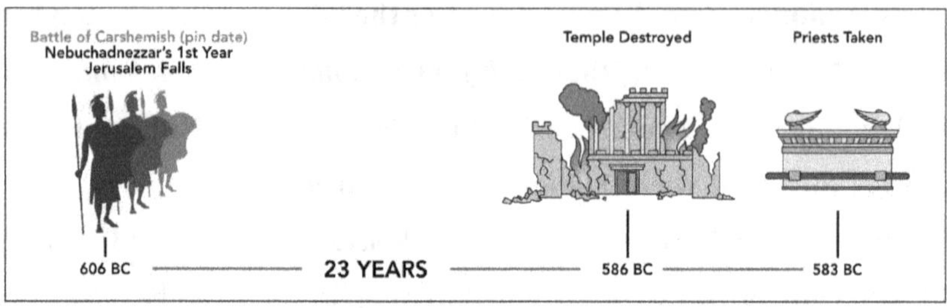

Therefore, because it is appropriate to reckon "a day for a year" when determining when Jesus was to be crucified, something we have verified from Daniel chapter nine, then it is consistent to do the same when seeking to understand another prophecy in Daniel found in chapter twelve. When we do that, we find something that many Bible scholars have overlooked. It would appear that the Dome of the Rock could be an abomination of desolation. (Perhaps this prophecy has a dual fulfilment. It may have been a foreshadowing of a fulfilment of this prophecy at a later date. Remember, *Jesus told the disciples that John the Baptist was Elijah* **(Matthew 11:14 [14]"And if you are willing to accept it, John himself is Elijah who was to come.),** then later on after John had been beheaded said that *Elijah was still to come* **(Matthew 17:11–13: [11]And He answered and said, "Elijah is coming and will restore all things; [12]but I say to you that Elijah already came, and they did not recognize him, but did to him whatever they wished. So also the Son of Man is going to suffer at their hands." [13]Then the disciples understood that He had spoken to them about John the Baptist.**). This is an example of a prophecy with *dual fulfilment.*) You will see as you continue reading why this seems worth considering.

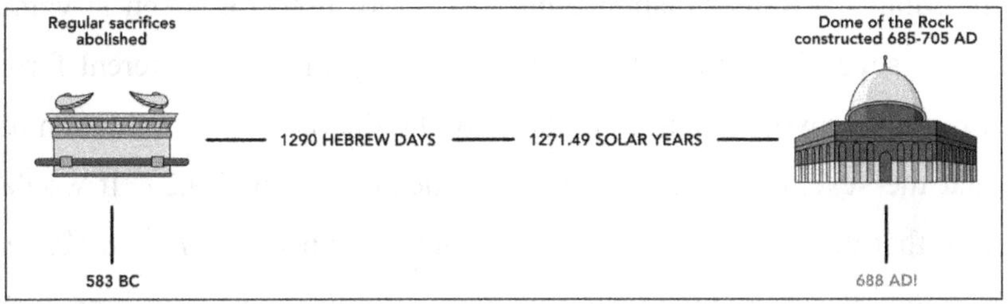

You may be wondering "what about the reference in this verse to waiting until the 1335 days? Well, 1290 days plus 45 days (totaling 1335 days) or 45 years after the Dome of the Rock was set up, Charles Martel succeeded in defeating the Muslims at the battle of Tours, halting the spread of Islam across Europe. (This is one possible explanation.)

What about the seventieth seven of Daniel 9:27? We have accounted for the first seven sevens and the next sixty-two sevens, for a total of sixty-nine sevens or 483 Jewish years. These stretched from the decree to rebuild Jerusalem given in Nehemiah chapter two to the crucifixion of our Lord Jesus in thirty-one AD. What is the meaning of the final or seventieth seven? It is possible that it is a final seven years just like the first sixty-nine sevens of years? Only in this case, the fulfilment has been suspended, *with a gap in time* that is now approaching two thousand years. Is it the case that when other events that are decreed to happen begin to unfold, we will then know that the final seven years of this prophecy have begun? Or could there be another interpretation of this last or seventieth seven? To uncover its meaning, we must carefully consider the text of the original language in which Daniel recorded this prophecy given to him by the angel Gabriel. We read it in English, which has been translated from the original Hebrew. It turns out that the Hebrew word form for seven in this verse changes from the verses preceding it. Rather than shavuim, the word used for seven in verse twenty-seven is shavua. So, it would be logical that a different form of multiplier would be used in determining the proper interpretation of what the seventieth "seven" the Lord meant in Daniel 9:27. It would seem that the seventieth "seven" is being described *as a time different from the other sixty-nine sevens of years*. But the question is how long a time is being indicated? I confess, with regard to the interpretation of this seventieth seven I remain unconvinced. I am inclined to take this unfulfilled seven to mean "a literal seven years." But Skolfield offers an alternative, and I consider that this may be a case of the *dual fulfillment of prophecy.* Perhaps what Skolfield shows has in fact been hidden in God's word, having *been sealed up as promised in Daniel* and now revealed at the end of time. As you read further, you will see why this may be the case, for it pertains to Israel and things we could not have understood until they occurred. One has to do with Israel being allowed to become a nation again and to resettle in their land in 1948. The other has to do with Israel regaining control over Jerusalem in 1967. Until these events had transpired, that they were contained in the prophecy had been sealed up. We may also discover right before the Lord Jesus returns that another truth has also been hidden which will be revealed. Skolfield posits we need to look to a pattern established in the Levitical Code found in the Law of Moses, in Leviticus 25: [1]**The Lord then spoke to Moses at Mount Sinai, saying, [2]"Speak to the sons of Israel and say to them, 'When you come into the land which I shall give you, then *the land shall have a sabbath to the Lord.* [3]'Six years you shall sow your field, and six years you shall prune your vineyard and gather in its crop, [4]*but during the seventh year the land shall have a sabbath rest*, a sabbath to the Lord; you shall not sow your field nor prune**

your vineyard. [5]'Your harvest's aftergrowth you shall not reap, and your grapes of untrimmed vines you shall not gather; the land shall have a sabbatical year. [8]'*You are also to count off seven sabbaths of years* for yourself, *seven times seven years*, so that you have the time of the seven sabbaths of years, namely, *forty-nine years.* [9]'You shall then sound a ram's horn abroad on the tenth day of the seventh month; on the day of atonement you shall sound a horn all through your land. [10]'*You shall thus consecrate the fiftieth year* and proclaim a release through the land to all its inhabitants. It shall be a jubilee for you, and each of you shall return to his own property, and each of you shall return to his family.[11]'You shall have the fiftieth year as a jubilee; you shall not sow, nor reap its aftergrowth, nor gather in from its untrimmed vines. (Leviticus 25:1–5, 8-11)

The pattern we observed from the Levitical Code was:

1. One seven of years
2. Followed by six more sevens of years
3. Last, a final unique Jubilee year with 360 Sabbaths

Remember we began Daniel 9 with Daniel having noted from reading Jeremiah that the time of the captivity was to have been seventy years, the number of Sabbaths that the land had been denied since the Jews did not obey this command from the Lord. The "seventy-sevens" are related to this in that they were given in response to Daniel's prayer. Skolfield posits that a similar pattern is in evidence to that seen above in the Levitical Code.

The pattern of the "seventy-sevens":

1. Seven sevens of weeks, seven Shavuim

2. Followed by sixty-two more sevens of weeks, sixty-two Shavuim

3. Last, a final unique week, a Shavua

Since the time of the crucifixion of Jesus, we have been able to discern what the first seven plus sixty-two sevens, totaling sixty-nine sevens mean, for God has revealed it. But He has forced us to wait until the time of the end, as stated in Daniel 12:4, 9 to understand the last seven. We have been waiting on events ordained by God to occur to unseal prophecy. We found in Daniel chapter twelve that the angel Michael told Daniel to "seal up the book until the time of the end." We shall shortly see that only after certain events pertaining to Israel and Jerusalem had occurred were we able to understand and interpret things that were previously hidden in Daniel, and it turns out, also in Revelation. The prophecy in Daniel 9:27 also references an abomination: "**He will confirm a covenant with many for one 'seven.' In the middle of the 'seven' he will put an end to sacrifice and offering. And *on a wing of the temple* he *will set up an abomination that causes desolation*, until the end that is decreed is poured out on him." (Daniel 9:27) (NIV)**

We find identical references to the *abomination* and *desolation* in Daniel 12:11: "**From the time that the daily sacrifice is abolished and the *abomination* that causes *desolation* is set up, there will be 1,290 days." (Daniel 12:11) (NIV)** Skolfield believes the Muslim "Dome of the Rock" which stands on the temple mount in Jerusalem *is the abomination of desolation*, or as the NIV translates it, "an abomination that causes desolation." Again, this prophecy may be another example of dual fulfillment.

Here is what we discover when we look carefully at the original Hebrew in both Daniel 9:27 and 12:11:

The Hebrew word translated "abomination" is shiqquts. (Strong's No. 8251)

שִׁקּוּצִם shiqquts

The Hebrew word translated "desolation" is shaw-man. (Strong's No. 8074)

מְשֹׁמֵם shaw-man

In Daniel 12:11, we find the abomination that maketh desolate is "shiqquts ha shaw-man." Since "shiqquts and shaw-man" refers to the Dome of the Rock in Daniel 12:11, then it follows logically that "shiqquts and shaw-man" also refer to the Dome of the Rock in Daniel 9:27. Since it states in 9:27

"He will confirm a covenant with many for one 'seven.' In the middle of the 'seven,' he will put an end to sacrifice and offering. And *on a wing of the temple, he will set up an abomination that causes desolation*, until the end that is decreed is poured out on him."(NIV) Therefore, the week must stretch into the past and the future from the time of its construction in 688 AD. Skolfield posits that the numerical progression in the Levitical Code and the Seventy-Sevens is the same, i.e., one seven, a multiple of sevens, with a unique time in the end. He suggests specifically:

1. The Levitical Code had a unique end, the Jubilee year, with 360 Sabbaths
2. The Seventy-sevens also has a unique end, a seven, each year of which might have 360 Sabbaths.

So, he suggests multiplying seven times 360, which results in 2520 prophetic years, or 2484 Solar years.

This produces a result that could not have been seen until the event occurred. With the Dome of the Rock being constructed in the middle of the week (seven), 2484 years by our calendar stretches from 536 BC to 1948 AD, *the birth of the new nation of Israel.* As 606 BC is commonly accepted as the date that began the exile, 536 BC is the seventy-year end of that exile per the decree of Cyrus. Certainly, Israel is recognized as a nation again and the gathering of Jews to the land that is prophesied in Scripture is not to be lightly regarded. Is this the correct interpretation of the last week, the seventieth week, of this passage of Scripture? There are certainly strong indicators that it may be. Also, it could be that this passage has more than one meaning or dual fulfillment as we have noted elsewhere in Scripture to be the case. The "weeks" of Daniel 9:24-27 require a multiplier, and a Jubilee year has 360 days which are all Sabbaths. Perhaps the multiplier for the seventieth week described in verse 27 is 360 times seven, which equals 2520 prophetic years, the equivalent of 2484 Solar years.

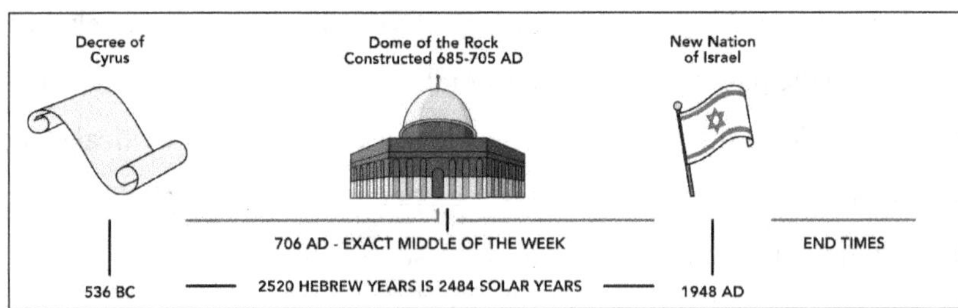

Until the new nation of Israel was established after World War II in 1948, we would have had no clue as to any significance regarding the interpretation of the seventieth week in this manner. However, how does the covenant being confirmed relate to this possibility? God made a covenant with Abraham that we read about in Genesis 15: "[18]**On that day the LORD made a covenant with Abram, saying, "To your descendants I have given this land, From the river of Egypt as far as the great river, the river Euphrates." (Genesis 15:18)** We may view the second birth of the nation of Israel in 1948, which is the end of this "seven," as a confirmation. The Lord was confirming that indeed, He will in fact accomplish His Word and give the land to Israel which He swore He would give to Abraham and his descendants. Additionally, we read in Daniel 12: [11]**"From the time that the daily sacrifice is abolished and the abomination that causes desolation is set up, there will be 1,290 days. [12]Blessed is the one who waits for and reaches the end of the 1,335 days. (Daniel 12:11–12 NIV84)** The New American Standard 1995 translation gives us this for the same verses: [11]**"From the time that the regular sacrifice is abolished and the abomination of desolation is set up, there will be 1,290 days. [12]"How blessed is he who keeps waiting and *attains to* the 1,335 days! (Daniel 12:11–12)** In Daniel 12:12, the word that is translated as "attains" in English is the Hebrew word קִיַּחֲזִי (yachaziq). This word comes from the root קָזָח (chazaq), which means "to be strong, powerful, firm, or steadfast." In this context, it is often translated as "endures" or "perseveres." Therefore, a possible translation of Daniel 12:12 could be: "Blessed is the one who waits and reaches (or endures to) the end of the 1,335 days." We have seen that it is possible that one interpretation of the abomination of desolation that was set up "on a wing of the temple" is that it is the Dome of the Rock on the temple mount. Construction began on the Dome in 688 AD, and some scholars believe it took seven years to complete the building, making the completion date about 695 AD. If we add 1335 "day-years" we arrive at 2030. This date is again consistent with the range of dates in which we may see the return of the Lord. How blessed is he who keeps waiting and attains to the 1,335 days! The Lord has told us, we will not know the day or the hour of His return, but as it draws nearer, we will very certainly know the season. So perhaps this prophecy will be dual fulfilled. We may discover both this explanation and a literal fulfillment of seven years that God will yet reveal will be the case when He completes the unsealing of these prophecies.

Nevertheless, there are additional things to consider regarding this interpretation that do lend further credibility to it being correct. As noted, the New International Version translation of Daniel 9:27 makes a distinction not found in other translations in that it says "on a wing of the temple he will set up an abomination."

Let's examine Scripture further to try and gain insight into this reference about "a wing of the temple." In Mark 13 we read: [1]As He was going out of the temple, one of His disciples said to Him, "Teacher, behold what wonderful stones and what wonderful buildings!" **[2]And Jesus said to him, "Do you see these great buildings? Not one stone will be left upon another which will not be torn down." (Mark 13:1-2)** About forty years after Jesus said these words, the Roman general Titus sacked Jerusalem and destroyed the temple, tearing it down to the bedrock. As a result, the location of the temple was lost. Until 1983, when Israeli archeologists discovered the exact location once again. So, where was the temple exactly? Before we examine the evidence discovered in 1983 by Israeli archeologists, let's lay some groundwork from Scripture.

David purchased the temple site and that fact is recorded for us: **[22]Then David said to Ornan, "Give me the site of this *threshing floor*, that I may build on it an altar to the Lord; for the full price you shall give**

it to me, that the plague may be restrained from the people." [23]Ornan said to David, "Take it for yourself; and let my lord the king do what is good in his sight. See, I will give the oxen for burnt offerings and the threshing sledges for wood and the wheat for the grain offering; I will give it all." [24]But King David said to Ornan, "No, but I will surely buy it for the full price; for I will not take what is yours for the Lord, or offer a burnt offering which costs me nothing." [25]So David gave Ornan 600 shekels of gold by weight for the site. [26]Then David built an altar to the Lord there and offered burnt offerings and peace offerings. And he called to the Lord and He answered him with fire from heaven on the altar of burnt offering. (1 Chronicles 21:22–26)
Note that this site was a "threshing floor." We find that David's son, King Solomon, built the first temple on this site which David purchased. **Then Solomon began to build the house of the Lord in Jerusalem on Mount Moriah, where the Lord had appeared to his father David, at the place that David had prepared *on the threshing floor* of Ornan the Jebusite. (2 Chronicles 3:1)**

Again, the threshing floor is noted. This is important because a threshing floor is flat. It must be so to enable the threshing of the grain on it. The Dome of the Rock which is on the temple mount is not on a flat site but is instead on one which has deep rocky crevasses beneath it. These can be seen from pictures of the inside of the building itself. It turns out, the Dome of the Rock is built to the side of the original temple site, "on a wing of the temple" but not on the site of the temple structure itself. Now we turn to Revelation chapter eleven for a reference to the temple. We also find included in this passage a similar use of a time given for an event to occur, as we find in Daniel chapter nine and again in chapter twelve. **"Leave out the court which is outside the temple and do not**

measure it, for it has been given to the nations; and they will *tread under foot the holy city for forty-two months.* (Revelation 11:2)

The New International Version gives even more insight into this passage: **2 *But exclude the outer court*; do not measure it, *because it has been given to the Gentiles.* They *will trample on the holy city for 42 months.* (Revelation 11:2) (NIV)** You will recall that Jesus, when telling the disciples about the signs of His return, said in Luke 21 **"Jerusalem will be trampled under foot of the Gentiles until the times of the Gentiles be fulfilled." (Luke 21:24)**

John wrote Revelation about ninety AD, and the Dome of the Rock was built almost six-hundred years later. It was built *in the court which is outside the temple*. John wrote in a time when the Romans used a calendar just like ours today, the Gregorian calendar, so it is not necessary to do any conversion of "day-years" to Jewish standards as with Daniel. We use days to equal solar years instead. So, what could the event be that would tie to the temple, have something to do with the court outside the temple, and relate to the holy city (Jerusalem) being "tread under foot for forty-two months?" To gain further insight, note that Jesus used the same phrase, "tread under foot" regarding Jerusalem. We find it in Luke chapter twenty-one. Jesus is answering the question put to him by his disciples as to what will be the signs of your return and the end of the age. **(Luke 21:24) and they will fall by the edge of the sword, and will be led captive into all the nations; and Jerusalem will be *trampled under foot by the Gentiles* until the times of the Gentiles are fulfilled.** The Dome of the Rock is built on "a wing of the temple" and was an abomination that was "set up" that caused desolation.

Did God cause any event to occur that would *unseal prophecy* whose interpretation had previously been hidden? Jerusalem was removed from Jewish control and trampled under foot (controlled by Gentile nations) by the Gentiles from the time Nebuchadnezzar took it in about 600 BC until the Jews regained control of it in the "Six-day war" in June of 1967. However, tied to the exact prophecy of Revelation 11:2, you will see that "forty-two months" (using a "day for a year") after the construction of the Dome of the Rock, Jerusalem passed back into Jewish control fulfilling prophecy.

The graphic below shows the location that archeologists now believe the temple formerly occupied.

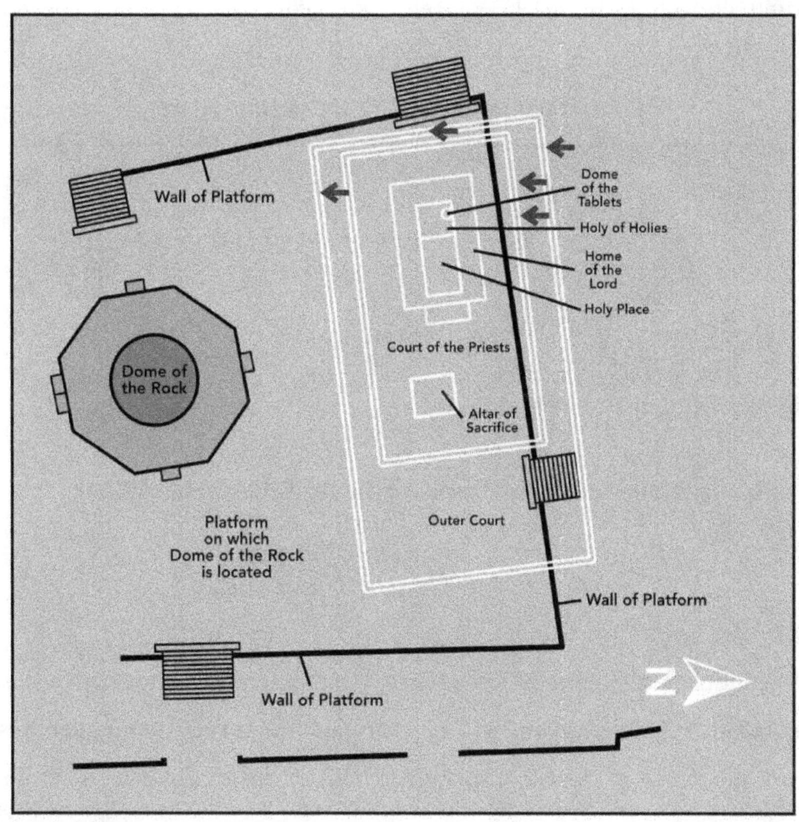

Revelation 11:2 addresses two different events:

1. The temple's court will be given over to the Gentiles.
2. Jerusalem will be under Gentile control for forty-two months. Gentile control over Jerusalem ended with the end of the "Six days war" when on June 6th, 1967.

How many "prophetic days" are in forty-two months? Dividing our Solar year of 365.24 days by twelve gives us 30.437 days in a month. Forty-two months times 30.437 days equal 1278.34 days. Prophetically, forty-two months is equal to 1278.34 day-years. Construction of the Dome of the Rock began in 685 and was completed in 705 AD. Subtracting 1278 from 1967 places us at…689.

Forty Two Months is 1278.34 Day-Years

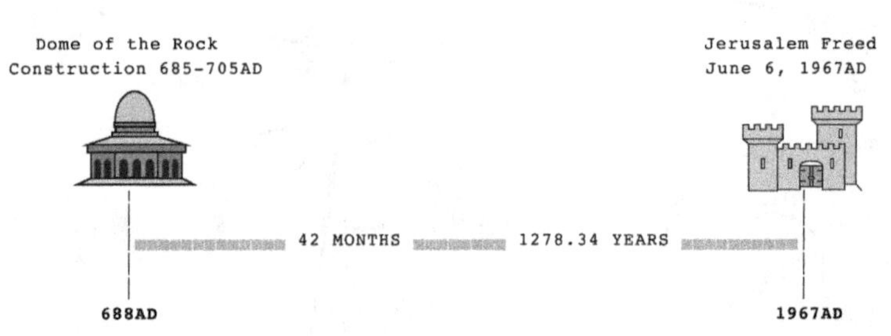

Construction of the Dome of the Rock began in 688AD.

Exactly 1278.34 years after 688 A.D.,
Jerusalem was freed of Gentile control!

A significant statement by Jesus tied to this event must be noted. He said in Luke 21:24 "Jerusalem will be trampled under foot by the Gentiles *until the times of the Gentiles be fulfilled.*" So, what comes after the "times of the Gentiles?" I suggest that after the "times of the Gentiles" comes "the last generation." Jesus went on in the passage recorded in Luke chapter twenty-one to say: **(Luke 21:32) "Truly I say to you, *this generation will not pass away until all things take place.*** I believe Jesus was indicating to us that *the generation of those alive when Jerusalem is no longer trampled under foot by the Gentiles will be the last generation before he returns.* This milestone was reached in 1967. As of this writing in 2023, we are fifty-six years into the possible final generation, marking the "time of the end" frequently referred to in Daniel.

In summary, we observed that using a day for a year, from the going forth of a decree to rebuild Jerusalem (in 445 B.C.), we arrived at 31 A.D. as the date the anointed one or messiah would be cut off and have nothing. It seems reasonable to examine other applications of a prophetic day for a year from both Daniel and Revelation to see if noteworthy events were revealed. The connection to the rebirth of Israel in 1948 seems to fit when using a day for a year. Similarly, the return of Jerusalem to the control of the Jews in 1967 using this same measure seems to be too much of a coincidence to ignore. But for now, it is worth reflecting on. I also emphasize that this may be only the first part of what we discover is a prophecy with dual fulfillment. Will there still prove to be a literal seven years related to this prophecy in Daniel 9:26 that is fulfilled, right before the return of the Lord Jesus? This may still prove to be the case.

Regardless of whether Skolfield is correct in interpreting the Scripture regarding this seventieth seven from Daniel 9:26, I believe that the return of control of Jerusalem to the Jews in 1967 represents the end of the time Jesus spoke of in Luke 21:24 when he said "Jerusalem will be trampled under foot of the Gentiles until the times of the Gentiles be fulfilled."

Appendix 4

Signs Relating to the Sun and Moon at the Opening of the Sixth Seal

Upon the opening of the sixth seal, we read: **[12]I looked when He broke the sixth seal, and there was a great earthquake; and the sun became black as sackcloth made of hair, and the whole moon became like blood; (Revelation 6:12)** This verse points us back to the Old Testament, where we find numerous references to the coming "day of the Lord." Among others, we find this from the prophet Joel: **[31]"*The sun will be turned into darkness And the moon into blood* Before the great and awesome day of the LORD comes." (Joel 2:31)** In the passage above from Joel, it clearly states "Before" *the great and awesome day of the Lord comes*. It does not say "on the day of the Lord."

Returning to the discussion of the passages that tell us the sun and moon will show signs, these Scriptures *do not state that when we see these signs, all the things pertaining* to the day of the Lord follow immediately. There are other examples of signs that occur where the signaled event does not follow immediately. For example, Jesus said the following about his return in Matthew 24: **6 And you will hear of wars and rumors of wars. See that you are not troubled; for all these things must come to pass, but *the end is not yet.* 7 For nation will rise against nation, and kingdom against kingdom. And there will be famines, pestilences, and earthquakes in various places. 8 *All these are the beginning* of sorrows. (Matthew 24:6-8)** Just as Jesus said with regard to these signs, "the end is not yet," we will see that is also the case here.

Some believe because we see prophecies in the Old Testament that describe events of *the day of the Lord* which are fulfilled in the opening of the sixth seal, that *the day of the Lord* follows immediately. But that is not necessarily the case. Let's look at Joel chapter 2: **(10) Before them the earth quakes, The heavens tremble, The *sun and the moon grow dark* And the stars lose their brightness. (11) The LORD utters His voice *before His army*; Surely *His camp is very great*, For strong is he who carries out His word. *The day of the LORD* is indeed great and very awesome, And who can endure it? (Joel 2:10-11**) This passage from Joel tells us *both the sun and moon grow dark.* Further on in the same chapter, Joel tells us "*the sun is turned into darkness, but the moon shows its light, for it is red.*" (Joel 2:31) These two passages, though in close proximity to one another, describe two different events. To understand them, let us take a look at Isaiah 13: **[9]Behold, the day of the LORD is coming, Cruel, with fury and burning anger, To make the land a desolation; And He will exterminate its sinners from it. [10]For the stars of heaven and their constellations Will not flash forth their light; *The sun will be dark when it rises* And *the moon will not shed its light.* (Isaiah 13:9–10)** Here, the passages in Joel 2:10 and Isaiah 13:10 agree that both the sun and moon are dark, as opposed to the moon being red. Consider also the words of Jesus,

[29]"*But immediately after the tribulation of those days* THE SUN WILL BE DARKENED, AND THE MOON WILL NOT GIVE ITS LIGHT, AND THE STARS WILL FALL from the sky, and the powers of the heavens will be shaken. (Matthew 24:29) These words of Jesus also tell us that both the sun and moon are dark and that it is immediately after the tribulation. Then it goes on to say that **"He will send forth His angels with A GREAT TRUMPET and THEY WILL GATHER TOGETHER His elect from the four**

winds, from one end of the sky to the other." (Matthew 24:31)

Now, let's go back and read the context before and after the verse in Joel 2:10 where the sun and moon both grow dark. **[2]A day of darkness and gloom, A day of clouds and thick darkness. As the dawn is spread over the mountains, So there is a great and mighty people; There has never been anything like it, Nor will there be again after it To the years of many generations. [3]A fire consumes before them And behind them a flame burns. The land is like the garden of Eden before them But a desolate wilderness behind them, And nothing at all escapes them. [4]Their appearance is like the appearance of horses; And like war horses, so they run. [5]With a noise as of chariots They leap on the tops of the mountains, Like the crackling of a flame of fire consuming the stubble, Like a mighty people arranged for battle. [6]Before them the people are in anguish; All faces turn pale. [7]They run like mighty men, They climb the wall like soldiers; And they each march in line, Nor do they deviate from their paths. [8]They do not crowd each other, They march everyone in his path; When they burst through the defenses, They do not break ranks. [9]They rush on the city, They run on the wall; They climb into the houses, They enter through the windows like a thief. [10]Before them the earth quakes, The heavens tremble, *The sun and the moon grow dark* And the stars lose their brightness. [11]*The LORD utters His voice before His army; Surely His camp is very great,* For strong is he who carries out His word. The day of the LORD is indeed great and very awesome, And who can endure it? (Joel 2:2–11)** When you read the entire passage, you find you are reading about the Lord and His army. This parallels the Scripture in Revelation 19:11-14 which tells us the Lord brings His armies with Him when He returns from heaven to wage war against the beast and the false prophet:. *His armies are clad in fine linen, white and clean.* [11]**And I saw heaven opened, and behold, a white horse, and He who sat on it is called Faithful and True, and in righteousness He judges and wages war.** [12]**His eyes are a flame of fire, and on His head are many diadems; and He has a name written on Him which no one knows except Himself.** [13]**He is clothed with a robe dipped in blood, and His name is called The Word of God.** [14]**And *the armies which are in heaven, clothed in fine linen, white and clean, were following Him on white horses.* (Revelation 19:11–14)** This event happens after we have been raptured and have participated in the marriage supper of the Lamb. Now Jesus is returning to wage war, and we are His armies. He destroys all the armies of the antichrist-beast and cast him and the false prophet into the lake of fire. Then He reigns on earth for a thousand years, and we reign with Him.

The other passage in Joel 2:31 is similar but describes a totally different time. [31]**"The sun will be turned into darkness And the moon into blood Before the great and awesome day of the LORD comes.** [32]***And it will come about that whoever calls on the name of the LORD Will be delivered*; For on Mount Zion and in Jerusalem There will be those who escape, As the LORD has said, Even among the survivors whom the LORD calls. (Joel 2:31-32)** Verse 32 tells us, "whoever calls on the name of the Lord will be delivered." This is the time of the sixth seal. There is still time left; if men repent, they can still be saved. But will any repent? We know this is a time when the love of most grows cold. We know this is a time when many are abandoning the faith. Scripture tells us the beginning of wisdom is the fear of the Lord. Perhaps, some will fear Him and cry out to Him to save them. This is before the Lord has sent His angels out to gather His elect. Once the seventh angel sounds, there is no more time left. Then comes the rapture, and with it the wrath of God on those who refused His offer of salvation in His son Jesus. We go to the marriage supper of the Lamb, but those still on earth experience His wrath. Then we come back with Jesus and He finishes the wrath of God. **[15]From His mouth comes a sharp sword, so that with it He may strike down the nations, and He will rule them with a rod of iron; and *He treads the wine press of the fierce wrath of God*, the Almighty. (Revelation 19:15)** We read in the last portion of this verse, "He treads the wine press of the fierce wrath of God, the Almighty." Here is where Jesus finishes the wrath of God, which began to be poured out on mankind when the seventh angel sounded.

Appendix 5

America in the End Times

"He makes the nations great, then destroys them; He enlarges the nations, then leads them away. (Job 12:23)

A word of caution is in order: What follows next is going to be deeply unsettling for most who read it. I believe I have been faithful to the Word in sharing this, but of course I cannot be sure of my interpretation. These events will not occur until the antichrist comes on the scene, the man of sin who must be revealed before the Lord Jesus returns. Scripture indicates that this individual will be aided by ten kings who will give their power and authority to him because it is God's plan for them to do so. Therefore, it will not happen until the antichrist has formed an alliance with these ten kings. Before you continue, fix in your mind that what is described next regarding the fate of the great harlot, Babylon the Great, will not happen until the last half of the great tribulation. I believe the Lord will give us clarity as to the timing regarding this prophecy which His Word tells us must be fulfilled before the Lord returns and gathers His saints. As you learned in chapter one, the Lord could return as soon as 2031, which means the seven-year period prior to His return would begin in 2024. The fulfillment of the following prophecy could therefore occur as soon as approximately 2028, but I believe the Lord would make things more clear to His saints as the time draws near. If He tarries, this event would also be delayed until the sometime in the 42 months just prior to His return.

America as we think of it was begun by people who migrated from Europe. The first settlers made their way here in sailing ships beginning in the late fifteenth century and a by a century later in 1600 the non-native population is estimated to have still been only about 10,000. By the late eighteenth century at the time of the American Revolutionary War, the numbers had swelled to around 2.5 million, including both free and enslaved people. As we approach the 250th anniversary of the time of American independence from England, the population is a little more than 330 million, or about 5% of the world's total population.

It may be that the end of America is approaching. This end as portrayed in Scripture would likely reduce the population to less than 10% of its current level, amounting to the death of some 300 million people.

Revelation 17 describes an alliance of ten kings who give their power and authority to the beast, the antichrist. Together they will attack and destroy a place about which a great amount of detail is provided. This attack will occur suddenly and will accomplish this destruction in such a brief period that Scripture describes it as taking place "in one hour."
[12]"The ten horns which you saw are ten kings who have not yet received a kingdom, but they receive authority as kings with the beast for one hour. [13]"These have one purpose, and they give their power and authority to the beast. (Revelation 17:12–13)

The Man of Lawlessness, the Antichrist

It is essential to know that the Bible refers to the final world ruler as the beast or the antichrist in the books of Revelation and Daniel. He is also referred to as "the man of sin, the son of perdition." We have seen that Scripture tells us that the Lord cannot return and gather his saints until the "man of sin, the son of perdition" is revealed: "**Let no one deceive you by any means; for *that Day will not come* unless**

the falling away comes first, and *the man of sin is revealed, the son of perdition*," (2 Thessalonians 2:3). Some translations call this man "the man of lawlessness." A few verses later we read: "**Then *that lawless one* will be revealed whom the Lord will slay with the breath of His mouth and bring to an end by the appearance of His coming;" (2 Thessalonians 2:8).**

To accomplish His purpose, God will put it in the heart of ten kings to align with this individual (Revelation 17:17) who gets his power from Satan. The Scripture tells us plainly that this final world ruler, the beast, and the ten kings who align with him, will ultimately destroy with fire a very wealthy place.

Prophecies Relating to America

We learn that this wealthy place is one which influences the rest of the world and is called "Babylon the Great." This destruction is first referenced in Revelation 14:8: **"[8]And another angel, a second one, followed, saying, "Fallen, fallen is *Babylon the great*, she who has made all the nations drink of the wine of the passion of her immorality." (Revelation 14:8)** We get the sense that through its influence this place has spread immorality throughout the world. The remainder of the world sells its goods to the people of this place. Scripture states their destruction comes about because God wills it; it fulfills His purpose and is swift and terrible in its consequences. The place that before was exceedingly wealthy is ruined and laid waste, and it becomes a home for vultures and other birds that feed on dead bodies. Industry in this place ceases; the sound of a mill is not heard in this place ever again. Musical ensembles no longer play in the land, and men are no longer concerned about getting married, for life has changed so radically that marriage is the farthest thing from their minds. (Revelation 18:22-23) Commerce and trade with other peoples and lands cease. Electricity ceases to flow in the power lines, so the lights go out, and do not come back on again, for the power is not ever restored again. When this place is burned up, it happens so swiftly that Scripture says *in one hour it is burned up*. The thing to notice about the smoke from the fire is unique, such that ships off the coast of this place stay far out to sea because *they fear the smoke of her burning*. Normally, people do not fear the smoke of a fire that is burning. In past times, when a city caught fire, people formed bucket brigades and passed water person to person to those closest to the flames to fight the fire. However, the type of burning that would be the result of missiles with nuclear warheads would certainly cause people to stand far off because of radiation danger and from the fallout ash. (The reference to ships staying far out to sea leads us to consider major cities that are on a seacoast would be among the primary targets of this place. Some commentators have speculated that Rome, Italy is a candidate because of the heretical teaching of the Catholic Church, but I believe they ignore many of the other descriptions that help us to identify the harlot, the mystery "Babylon the Great" of the end time. I believe an inland city like Rome is ruled out because the smoke of their burning could not be viewed burning from ships at sea.) Also, note that this place is described in such a way as to indicate that it is the foremost place in the world where all other nations and their merchants sell their goods. The people of this place are the world's foremost consumers. This place influences kings and nations all over the world to follow in her immorality; This place "exports" immorality. It is critical to note that Scripture warns God's people "come out of her my people, that you may not receive of her plagues."

The Antichrist and Ten Kings

Now, read carefully the Scripture below which deals with the end of time. It describes a destruction of such magnitude that it is hard to imagine, and it indicates this is God's will, but we know the Lord warned His people to flee this place beforehand. Just as the Lord did in ancient times, He uses other nations to judge and destroy this place, which is a nation, a land. *The Lord uses ten nations that He causes to align with the antichrist-beast to destroy these people.* We read again in Revelation 17: **12"The ten horns which you saw are ten kings who have not yet received a kingdom, *but they receive authority as kings with the beast for one hour.*** (They receive authority for "a short time.") **13"These have one purpose, and *they give their power and authority to the beast.* 17"For *God has put it in their hearts to execute His purpose* by having a common purpose, and *by giving their kingdom to the beast, until the words of God will be fulfilled.* (Revelation 17:12-13, 17)** (Words in parentheses are mine.)

(The *beast is also a king*. In this case, this beast is the antichrist, the final world ruler. We learned previously that Scripture uses the term "beast" in prophecy to describe kings or heads of empires. i.e., **Daniel 7:17 'These great *beasts*, which are four in number, *are four kings* who will arise from the earth.'** I discussed the antichrist in chapter seven.)

We learn that this alliance of ten kings in cooperation with the beast *will burn up another place with fire*, a place called "Babylon the Great" and a harlot. (Note, they are not just attacking an institution or an ideology, such as the Catholic Church.) In this present day and age, I believe America is the most obvious candidate for "Babylon the Great." Now if the Lord waits to come for His saints, and he may, this could change.

Fifty years from now it might be London or Singapore. But as things currently stand, as you will shortly see, America is likely the mystery "Babylon the Great." Read and judge for yourself.

[16] And *the ten horns [kings] which you saw on the beast,* these will hate the harlot, make her desolate and naked, eat her flesh *and burn her with fire.* [17] *For God has put it into their hearts to fulfill His purpose,* to be of one mind, and *to* give their kingdom to the beast, until the words of God are fulfilled. [18] And the woman whom you saw is that great city [not just one city] **which reigns over the kings of the earth." (Revelation 17:16-18)**

We see the woman, the harlot, is a place. This place is called "that great city that reigns over the kings of the earth." . In the Bible, Babylon was a city, but Babylon was used to refer to the entire land of Babylon, and its people. It was an empire, ruled by Nebuchadnezzar, king of Babylon. Likewise, Rome was a city, and it was also used to describe the entire empire. I believe the destruction of this great city also includes the destruction of the major cities of the land (or empire-nation) of which it is a part. For complete Scripture support that the major cities of this land are also destroyed, see Appendix 6 at the end of this book. We learn of the fate of this end-time Babylon the Great (also called the harlot) which is destroyed by the antichrist-beast and ten kings in alliance with him. As I explained previously in chapter five where we looked at the vision of the goat and the ram found in the book of Daniel in chapter eight, we gain insight into where the *antichrist-beast* comes from. It says the goat (a ruler and the empire he controls) is broken at the height of its power; then four nations (or nation alliances) come from the former empire of the goat, and the antichrist-beast arises from one of those four nations. It is the antichrist in alliance with ten kings in Revelation 17 that burn up the harlot with fire.

Let's explore more in-depth the Scripture that leads me to conclude that America will be the target of nuclear weapons when "ten kings burn up the harlot with fire."

[12] "*The ten horns* which you saw *are ten kings* who have received no kingdom as yet, but *they receive authority for one hour as kings with the beast.* [13] These are of one mind, and they will give their power and authority to the beast. [14] These *will make war with the Lamb*, and the Lamb will overcome them, for He is Lord of lords and King of kings; and those who are with Him are called, chosen, and faithful." (Revelation 17: 12-14)

A Very Wealthy Place and its Quick Destruction

A careful reading of all the Scripture dealing with the ten kings and the beast reveals that these "make war with the Lamb" as indicated in verse 14 above. But first they attack the harlot, Babylon the Great, and burn this place and the inhabitants up with fire. John the apostle, who many scholars believe wrote in about 90 A.D. tells us about these ten future kings who have not come into being yet. He says when they do, they just come to power for a brief period, and they align with the antichrist-beast. (If you read the section devoted to the antichrist, you will see without question that he is the final world ruler, prophesied from about 570 years B.C. or nearly 2600 years ago.) He is defeated by Christ Jesus as described in the last part of Revelation 19.

"[16] And the ten horns which you saw on the beast, these will hate the harlot, make her desolate and naked, eat her flesh and burn

her with fire. [17] For God has put it into their hearts to fulfill His purpose, to be of one mind, and to give their kingdom to the beast, until the words of God are fulfilled. [18] And *the woman whom you saw is that great city which reigns over the kings of the earth*." (Revelation 17:16-18)

The destruction of this great city (which is an entire nation, an entire land) is clearly the will of God. I believe it is naive to think that only one city in this very wealthy nation will be destroyed. As noted, Rome, the city, was referred to in Scripture to describe the entire Roman empire. Referring to a place as "the great city" that did not exist in the time of John the Apostle but which he foresaw by the Holy Spirit would be a similar usage. (Refer to appendix 6 for more clarity that *many cities* are destroyed.) A complete understanding of this doomed end-time "Babylon the Great" indicates that it is the focus of world trade. We see this as we examine **Revelation 18:3: " ...and the merchants of the earth have become rich through the abundance of her luxury."** Merchants from all over the earth sell their goods to all the people of this land, not just one city in the land.

The people of this place, Babylon the Great, think to themselves that they are safe, for they are rich and live in luxury. Moreover, they have a haughty attitude. See how Scripture describes their attitude in Revelation 18:7 and what is in store for them in verse 8: "[7] **In the measure that she glorified herself and lived luxuriously, in the same measure give her torment and sorrow; for she says in her heart, '*I sit as queen, and am no widow, and will not see sorrow.*' [8] Therefore her plagues will come in one day—death and mourning and famine. *And she will be utterly burned with fire,* for strong is the Lord God**

who judges her." (Revelation 18: 7-8) The attitude of the people of this place is that they are secure and untouchable. **"[25] He will cause deceit to prosper, and he will consider himself superior.** ***When they feel secure, he will destroy many*** (again, America) **and take his stand against the Prince of princes." (Daniel 8:25)** The smoke of the fire with which this place is burned is such that those who see it, even those far out to sea, will keep far off for fear of "the smoke of her burning" and her torment.

All the Merchants of the World Sell Their Goods Here

[15]"The merchants of these things, who became rich from her, ***will stand at a distance because of the fear of her torment,*** **weeping and mourning, [17]for in one hour such great wealth has been laid waste!' And every shipmaster and every passenger and sailor, and** ***as many as make their living by the sea, stood at a distance,*** **[18]and were crying out as they saw the smoke of her burning, saying, 'What city is like the great city?' (Revelation 18:15, 17-18)** The observers of the destruction of this place find this event almost incomprehensible, so great is this place. These images and descriptions suggest the possibility of a thermonuclear event, especially since people must "stand at a distance." (I recall to mind that the U.S. Navy moved their ships 50 miles out to sea when the Japanese nuclear plant Fukushima disaster occurred on March 11, 2011.)This place, Babylon the Great, is critical to world commerce. Its destruction causes lamenting in much of the rest of the world, not because they grieve at the loss of life, but because no one buys their goods any longer. They lament their own economic loss.

[9] "The kings of the earth who committed fornication and lived luxuriously with her will weep and lament for her, ***when they see***

the smoke of her burning, [10] ***standing at a distance for fear of her torment*, saying, 'Alas, alas, that great city Babylon, that mighty city! For in one hour your judgment has come.'** [11] **"And the merchants of the earth weep and mourn over her, *because no one buys their cargoes any more*— (Revelation 18:9-11)**

This nation is described as influencing multitudes, nations and peoples and tongues. This "harlot" is so influential that she influences the kings (and by extension, their peoples) of the earth to commit fornication (see verse 9 above). This means all kinds of sexual immorality are promoted by this harlot's influence. Think about how America shapes the cultures of all peoples in the world through our movies, television shows, music, and culture. Revelation 17:15 tells us: [15] **Then he said to me, "The waters which you saw, where the harlot sits, are peoples, multitudes, nations, and tongues."**

"Come Out of Her"

Never in history has there been a nation as rich and self-indulgent as America. God's saints are warned to flee this place before the attack on "the harlot" occurs. The question we must ask is this: Is this just one city, or is the impending doom for the people of this place far more widespread? (Continue in appendix 6 for compelling evidence that the destruction encompasses far more than one city.) What events lead up to this destruction? Will we know when the time to come out of her is near? We are told to "come out of her." Where do we go? We are told, "Come out of her, my people, lest you share in her sins, and lest you receive of her plagues." (Revelation 18:4-5). These rich, prosperous people are going to be destroyed at the hands of the beast and ten other nations because of the judgement of God. They have lived luxuriously and indulged themselves and influenced the world to immorality. They thought themselves to be safe, free from the worry of being attacked by other people. But at the end of time, the final world ruler, the antichrist, will align with ten nations and together they will destroy these people and this land.

In chapter five of this book, we examined Daniel chapter 8 which gave us insight as to what to look for to recognize the antichrist-beast. We learned that Iran (Persia) will be prominent in end time events that lead up to this individual being revealed. What follows will be difficult to understand if you do not read chapter five first, in which we discuss the goat prophesied about in Daniel. Additionally, while possible, it does not seem likely that America is the goat in the prophecy in Daniel 8. If America is the goat, she is broken (ruined) and four other nations arise from it but not with its power, who would those be? I admit I do not know, but what seems clear *is that these events occur at the end of time*, not 300 years before Christ. In seeking to understand, let's go back once again to Javan. According to Scripture, Javan, one of Noah's grandsons, became the people groups of the coastlands of the Mediterranean Sea and formed nations. The nations they formed would be the nations of Europe. Iran (Persia, the ram) already is a sponsor of terrorism and suicide bombings in Iraq and elsewhere. There are great tensions between the Sunni and Shia Muslims in Iran and Iraq. Former U.S. President Obama withdrew the U.S. troops from Iraq (Iran's western neighbor). It does not take a great leap of imagination to think that the removal of the U.S. troop presence from Iraq opens the door for the westward aggression by Iran described in Scripture in Daniel 8 at the end of time.

Biblical Precedent for God's Deliverance of His People

As previously observed, we know from Scripture that Christians are not destined for wrath and that Jesus will rescue us. We read in 1 Thessalonians that Jesus "rescues us from the wrath to come," and that this is because "God has not destined us for wrath" (1 Thessalonians 1:10, 5:9).

Jesus also told us in Luke 21 to "**keep on the alert at all times,** ***praying that you may have strength to escape all these things that are about to take place*****, and to stand before the Son of Man." (Luke 21:36)** In this particular case however, God's people are warned to "come out of her," seemingly suggesting they come out of this place called "Babylon the Great." We are assured God has not destined us for wrath. But we are also warned by Jesus to keep on the alert at all times, praying to escape all these things that are about to take place. Jesus told us (in Matthew 24:29-31) that He sends His angels to gather the elect...after the tribulation of those days. God would not warn us in His Word to "come out of her" *if we were not going to be present and need to come out when these things happen.* We must be people who pray and ask Him for insight and direction. I see a precedent in Scripture where God prepared in advance a deliverance for his people, in the midst of famine. In Genesis, God's people could have suffered alongside the people around them when a famine struck the land, but God prepared in advance for his people through Joseph. Because he revealed to Joseph a special knowledge of the future that there would be famine and that he would need to set aside extra provisions during the years of plenty, God's people were able to come and receive grain and provisions from Joseph once the famine began. The potential social anarchy and lawlessness that would prevail if there were a widespread attack on America is beyond most individuals' ability to address, even significantly wealthy ones. It would require a community effort to survive and protect one's family. We may have to obey Scripture and do something to escape, rather than mistakenly believing that God "gathers us up" right before everything occurs. The "rapture" occurs at the Lord's return, when the seventh angel sounds.

My hope is that reviewing these Scriptures will serve to motivate Christians to be on the alert, to be sober-minded, not given to worldly pursuits, but to keep our hearts set on things above and *be determined to persevere and be steadfast in our faith in Jesus knowing that our reward is sure and eternal.* Those who fix their hope on Jesus' return will purify themselves. Proverbs 30:24-27 resonates with me regarding these times and what we may be facing: **"Four things on the earth are small, yet they are extremely wise: ants are creatures of little strength, yet *they store up their food in the summer*; coneys (rock badgers) are creatures of little power, yet *they make their home in the crags*; locusts have no king, yet *they advance together in ranks*. The spider skillfully grasps with its hands, And it is in kings' palaces." (Proverbs 30:24-27)**

The first part of **Psalm 127:1** says: **"Unless the Lord builds the house, they labor in vain who build it. *Unless the LORD guards the city*, The watchman stays awake in vain."** Scripture makes it clear that at some point God not only ceases to "guard the city," but He puts it in the hearts of others who do His will to burn up "the city with fire". He tells His people to "come out of her." I believe the challenges we face are so great that we must rely on the Lord to see us through them. We must pray and seek His guidance. I believe we will need the strength that is found in the Christian community, like the locusts, in ranks. Like the ants, we need to "store up food in the summer" while there is no crisis or emergency. And like rock badgers, we may need homes in the crags (in the hills, the mountains, but away from the cities). Clearly, for the people who live in the great city called "Babylon the Great" in the end time, *the Lord does not guard the city*. Instead, He puts it into the hearts of ten kings and the beast-antichrist to destroy it and its inhabitants with fire. Let me conclude by saying that I am still puzzling over the message that the Lord intends for believers in this age from Revelation chapter 18:4 where we read: ***"Come out of her, my people*, lest you share in her sins, and lest you receive of her plagues." (Revelation 18:4)**

Does this mean we must flee? Yes, away from the great city. But is this a warning for multiple cities, or just one city? There are other Scriptures that point *to multiple cities*. (I have compared the parallels between ancient Babylon to the end-time Babylon the Great in Appendix 6.) Regardless, Christians are not appointed to suffer God's wrath. We are, however, told to persevere and endure suffering if we are called to. **Proverbs 22:3** says, **"A prudent man sees the evil and hides himself."**

It is naïve to think that our nation cannot fall. What you will read next is but one example of a credible threat to our continued existence. This report predicted that 90% of our people would die within a year if this should occur. While it does not describe thermonuclear war, it does demonstrate our vulnerability to attack. Now in the age of artificial intelligence, hostile nations can use their advanced technology to evaluate our vulnerabilities.

U.S. Government commissioned reports which are available to all (as of this writing) from the internet state that Iran is considered a threat to attack the United States with a nuclear weapon and cause an electromagnetic pulse (EMP). (An EMP could so weaken the U.S. and cause such chaos that it might be the precursor to the launch of nuclear weapons against America by the ten kings (nations) in alliance with the antichrist.) The contents of these reports raise serious concerns for all U.S. citizens. A link to these reports is below. An excerpt from the executive summary reads:

- "Several potential adversaries have or can acquire the capability to attack the United States with a high-altitude nuclear weapon-generated electromagnetic pulse (EMP). A determined adversary can achieve an EMP attack capability without having a high level of sophistication.

- An EMP is one of a small number of threats that can hold our society at risk of catastrophic consequences. An EMP will cover a wide geographic region within the line of sight of the nuclear weapon. It has the capability to produce grave damage to critical infrastructures and thus, to the very fabric of US society, as well as to the ability of the United States and Western nations to project influence and military power.

- The common element that can produce such an impact from EMP is primarily electronics, so pervasive in all aspects of our society and military, coupled through critical infrastructures. Our vulnerability is increasing daily as our use of and dependence on electronics continues to grow. The impact of EMP is asymmetric in relation to potential protagonists who are not as dependent on modern electronics.

- The current vulnerability of our critical infrastructures can both invite and reward attacks if not corrected. Correction is feasible and well within the Nation's means and resources to accomplish."
- (See the link at www.empcommission.org ; www.**empcommission**.org/docs/A2473-**EMP_Commission**-7MB.pdf ; The 62-page executive summary is available at http://www.empcommission.org/docs/empc_exec_rpt.pdf)

This report postulates the launch of a nuclear warhead-tipped missile from the deck of a ship or tanker just outside the borders of our international waters, off our coast. The warhead would be detonated at a high altitude over the U.S., causing an electromagnetic pulse. This pulse or "EMP" has been known about by scientists for decades since it was first observed when the U.S. did atmospheric testing of nuclear bombs in the 1950's, before the above-ground nuclear test ban treaty with the Soviets. The report was commissioned by Congress and delivered to Congress in 2008, and it has also been written about in the Wall Street Journal. According to the report, which is available for download from the web and runs 208 pages, the detonation of a single nuclear device high above the U.S. would result in the complete failure of our nation's electric power grid. It would not be possible to restore power for a year or longer. The results would be to thrust our country back into the equivalent of the 1800's but without the ability to feed our population. The projections call for the death of 90% of our population within one year. It would knock out electric power from the middle of Canada to the middle of Mexico, and from the East Coast to the West Coast. Even a small detonation over the East Coast would have the same lasting effects and knock out power to the majority of the

U.S. population because the U.S. population is heavily concentrated east of the Mississippi River.

I again share this because we need to realize that what Scripture says in Psalm 127:1 applies just as much to us in our age as it did when the Holy Spirit gave this truth to Solomon, that "Unless the LORD guards the city, The watchman stays awake in vain."

We deceive ourselves if we do not think we must rely on the Lord for his protection. This includes modern-day American Christians. We remember Jesus' words to us: **"Watch therefore, and pray always that you may be counted worthy to escape all these things that will come to pass, and to stand before the Son of Man." (Luke 21:36)**

What, then, should our response be to these warnings? We must pray. Pray for our nation and our governing authorities that we may continue to live quiet lives and be at peace. Pray that you will abide in Christ and be steadfast and persevere unto the end. Pray for your children, your friends and neighbors, that if they have not come to faith in Jesus Christ, that God will draw them to Himself, shine the light of the truth into their hearts and save them.

Appendix 6

Parallels Between Ancient Babylon and the End Time Mystery Babylon the Great

The Word in Revelation 17 and 18 reveals that in the end time, a people or a nation is called *a woman*, a great harlot: **"[5]and *on her* forehead a name was written, a mystery, 'BABYLON THE GREAT, THE MOTHER OF HARLOTS AND OF THE ABOMINATIONS OF THE EARTH'" (Revelation 17:5).** Before the end of this same chapter, the Word goes on to reveal that this **"woman whom you saw is the great city, which reigns over the kings of the earth." (Revelation 17:18)**

Knowing this information, let us examine parallels in Scripture between this people group in the end time and another people, ancient Babylon. God used the nation of Babylon under the rule of Nebuchadnezzar six hundred years before Christ to discipline Israel severely, conquering Jerusalem and carrying all the people except the poorest of the land into exile in Babylon for seventy years. But because Israel was the chosen people of God, he promised retribution against those who struck Israel. God was using Babylon to teach and correct his people, but it was not without consequences to Babylon. He sent a destroyer against Babylon because of what they did to His people Israel: "[1]**Thus says the LORD: 'Behold, I am going to arouse against Babylon And against the inhabitants of Leb-kamai The spirit of a destroyer'" (Jeremiah 51:1).** The Lord said He would rouse the spirit of a destroyer against Babylon and He did so. In the end time, the Lord says he will raise up ten kings and have them align with one (the beast or antichrist) who will rule the world to destroy this woman (a nation or people) called a harlot, a mystery, with the name *Babylon the Great* written on her forehead. Observe the language found in Revelation 17 and consider:

[12]*The ten horns* which you saw *are ten kings* who have not yet received a kingdom, but they receive authority as kings with the beast for one hour. [13]These have one purpose, and they give their power and authority to the beast. [16]And *the ten horns* which you saw, *and the beast*, these will hate the harlot and will make her desolate and naked, and will eat her flesh *and will burn her up with fire.*

***[17]For God has put it in their hearts to execute His purpose by having a common purpose*, and by giving their kingdom to the beast, until the words of God will be fulfilled. (Revelation 17:12–13; 16-17)**

Just as God has a purpose in the end time, which is to destroy a particular people group, Jeremiah 51 reveals the purpose of the Lord in the ancient time: "**[11]Sharpen the arrows, fill the quivers! The Lord has aroused the spirit of the kings of the Medes, *Because His purpose is against Babylon to destroy it;* For it is the vengeance of the Lord, vengeance for His temple" (Jeremiah 51:11).** Just as the Lord had declared in ancient times that He would destroy Babylon, He has declared that He will destroy "Mystery Babylon" in our time. Our question should be, *who* in our time is the harlot, "Mystery Babylon the Great" that these kings (and their nations) hate and burn up with fire? We learned in Revelation 17:18 that "the woman" is "the great city," the one that rules over other nations of the earth.

As we compare the fate of the ancient empire Babylon to the end time one, it is noteworthy that Jeremiah 51 elaborates to reveal that the destruction of ancient Babylon included *not just one city*, but the cities of the nation referred to as Babylon: [43]"***Her cities have become an object of horror,*** **A parched land and a desert, A land in which no man lives And through which no son of man passes" (Jeremiah 51:43).**

God in Jeremiah 51 instructs his people *to flee* ancient Babylon:

[2]***I will dispatch foreigners to Babylon that they may winnow her And may devastate her land;*** **For on every side they will be opposed to her In the day of her calamity. [5]For neither Israel nor Judah has been forsaken By his God, the LORD of hosts, Although their land is full of guilt Before the Holy One of Israel.** [6]***Flee from the midst of Babylon, And each of you save his life! Do not be destroyed in her punishment,*** **For this is the LORD's time of vengeance; He is going to render recompense to her. (Jeremiah 51:2,5-6)**

Now compare the language to that in Revelation 18 dealing with the destruction of the end time Mystery Babylon the Great, where we find the same message to come out:

[4]I heard another voice from heaven, saying, "*Come out of her, my people, so that you will not participate in her sins and receive of her plagues*; (Revelation 18:4)

The Lord has issued the same warning to His people in our time, to come out of her, or you will pay a very heavy price. If you do not come out of her, you will participate in her sins and receive of her plagues.

Jeremiah 51 speaks of *the cup* of ancient Babylon of which the nations have drunk: "[7]***Babylon has been a golden cup*** **in the hand of the LORD, Intoxicating all the earth. The nations have drunk of her wine; Therefore the nations are going mad" (Jeremiah 51:7).** Now read about *the cup* of the *end time Mystery Babylon* in Revelation: "[5]**for her**

sins have piled up as high as heaven, and God has remembered her iniquities. [6]Pay her back even as she has paid, and give back to her double according to her deeds*; in the cup which she has mixed, mix twice as much for her"* **(Revelation 18:5–8).** The description of the ancients drinking of the cup of ancient Babylon is echoed in the Scripture in Revelation when describing the cup of the end time Mystery Babylon, ***"a gold cup full of abominations*** **and of the unclean things of her immorality," (Revelation 17:4).**

Read the Scripture on the end time Babylon from Revelation 18 and the sudden coming destruction of it: **[7]To the degree that she glorified herself and lived sensuously, to the same degree give her torment and mourning; for she says in her heart, 'I SIT AS A QUEEN AND I AM NOT A WIDOW, and will never see mourning.' [8]For this reason *in one day her plagues will come*, pestilence and mourning and famine, *and she will be burned up with fire*; for the Lord God who judges her is strong. (Revelation 18:7,8)**

The phrase "I sit as a Queen and I am not a widow, and will never see mourning" betrays the haughty pride of this nation, which considers itself to be in a lofty position, safe from attack or disaster. We are told that because these people live sensuously, glorifying themselves, with pride and haughtiness, they bring upon themselves judgment from God. He will use these other nations to destroy them.

Likewise, Jeremiah 51 speaks *of the sudden judgement* from the Lord on ancient Babylon: "***[8]Suddenly Babylon has fallen and been broken;*** **Wail over her! Bring balm for her pain; Perhaps she may be healed" (Jeremiah 51:8).**

Jeremiah 51 says Babylon's judgement has reached to heaven: [9]**We applied healing to Babylon, but she was not healed; Forsake her and let us each go to his own country, *For her judgment has reached to heaven* And towers up to the very skies. (Jeremiah 51:9)** Compare this to the language about the end time Mystery Babylon in Revelation 18: [5]**for *her sins have piled up as high as heaven*, and God has remembered her iniquities. (Revelation 18:5)**

End time Babylon in Revelation is a woman, a *great harlot,* who *sits on many waters*: [1]**Then one of the seven angels who had the seven bowls came and spoke with me, saying, "Come here, I will show you *the judgment of the great harlot who sits on many waters*, (Revelation 17:1)** [15]**And he said to me, "The *waters which you saw* where the harlot sits, *are peoples and multitudes and nations and tongues.* (Revelation 17:15)** Likewise, Jeremiah 51 speaks of ancient Babylon by *many waters*: [13]***O you who dwell by many waters*, Abundant in treasures, Your end has come, The measure of your end.** [14]**The LORD of hosts has sworn by Himself: "Surely I will fill you with a population like locusts, And they will cry out with shouts of victory over you." (Jeremiah 51:13)**

Jeremiah 51 tells us the Lord will repay ancient Babylon: [24]**"*But I will repay Babylon and all the inhabitants of Chaldea for all their evil that they have done in Zion* before your eyes," declares the LORD.** [25]**"Behold, I am against you, O destroying mountain, Who destroys the whole earth," declares the LORD, "And I will stretch out My hand against you, And roll you down from the crags, And I will make you a burnt out mountain. (Jeremiah 51:24,25)** The Lord fulfilled his promise to overthrow ancient Babylon and destroy it. What does

Revelation say about pay back to the end time Babylon?

[6]"*Pay her back* even as she has paid, and give back to her double according to her deeds; in the cup which she has mixed, mix twice as much for her. (Revelation 18:6)

Jeremiah 51 says ancient Babylon will be desolate forever:

[26]"They will not take from you even a stone for a corner Nor a stone for foundations, *But you will be desolate forever*," declares the LORD. [27]Lift up a signal in the land, Blow a trumpet among the nations! Consecrate the nations against her, Summon against her the kingdoms of Ararat, Minni and Ashkenaz; Appoint a marshal against her, Bring up the horses like bristly locusts. [28]Consecrate the nations against her, The kings of the Medes, Their governors and all their prefects, And every land of their dominion. [29]So the land quakes and writhes, For the purposes of the LORD against Babylon stand, *To make the land of Babylon A desolation without inhabitants.* (Jeremiah 51:26-29) Revelation likewise declares destruction of end time Mystery Babylon: **[21]Then a strong angel took up a stone like a great millstone and threw it into the sea, saying, "*So will Babylon, the great city, be thrown down with violence, and will not be found any longer.* (Revelation 18:21)**

Jeremiah 50 and 51 *tell us of fire* that will come upon ancient Babylon: **[32]"The arrogant one will stumble and fall With no one to raise him up; *And I will set fire to his cities And it will devour all his environs[...]* [30]The mighty men of Babylon have ceased fighting, They stay in the strongholds; Their strength is exhausted, They are becoming like**

women; ***Their dwelling places are set on fire,*** **The bars of her gates are broken. (Jeremiah 50:32, 51:30)** Again paralleling ancient Babylon, Revelation 18 tells us end time mystery Babylon will be burned up with fire: **[8]"For this reason in one day her plagues will come, pestilence and mourning and famine,** ***and she will be burned up with fire*****; for the Lord God who judges her is strong. (Revelation 18:8)**

Jeremiah 50 tells us the end of ancient Babylon is *desolation,* not to be inhabited again: **[39]"Therefore the desert creatures will live there along with the jackals; The ostriches also will live in it,** ***And it will never again be inhabited Or dwelt in from generation to generation.*** **(Jeremiah 50:39)** Revelation 18 describes this promised desolation as the same fate for end time mystery Babylon:

[21]Then a strong angel took up a stone like a great millstone and threw it into the sea, saying, "So will ***Babylon, the great city, be thrown down with violence, and will not be found any longer.*** **[22]"And the sound of harpists and musicians and flute-players and trumpeters will not be heard in you any longer; and no craftsman of any craft will be found in you any longer; and the sound of a mill will not be heard in you any longer; [23]and the light of a lamp will not shine in you any longer; and the voice of the bridegroom and bride will not be heard in you any longer; for your merchants were the great men of the earth, because all the nations were deceived by your sorcery. (Revelation 18:21–23)**

In the midst of all this proclamation about ancient Babylon, Jeremiah 51 *reveals something hidden*, when it speaks not of Babylon, but *the daughter of Babylon*: **[33]For thus says the LORD of hosts, the God of Israel: "*****The daughter of Babylon*** **is like a threshing floor At the time**

it is stamped firm; ***Yet in a little while the time of harvest will come for her.*****" (Jeremiah 51:33)** (I believe by introducing "the daughter of Babylon, Scripture is pointing us to the mystery "Babylon The Great" of the end time.) Jeremiah 51 *immediately after introducing the daughter of Babylon,* says this: [37]**"*Babylon will become a heap of ruins, a haunt of jackals, An object of horror and hissing, without inhabitants.* (Jeremiah 51:37)** Revelation 18 describes a similar state for end time mystery Babylon: [2]**And he cried out with a mighty voice, saying, "Fallen, fallen is Babylon the great!** ***She has become a dwelling place of demons and a prison of every unclean spirit, and a prison of every unclean and hateful bird.*** **(Revelation 18:2)** Jeremiah 51 elaborates on the final end of ancient Babylon: [43]**"Her** ***cities*** **have become an object of horror, A parched land and a desert, A land in which no man lives And through which no son of man passes.**

Remember, the Lord instructed in Jeremiah 51 *for his people to flee ancient Babylon*: [45]**"*Come forth from her midst, My people*, And each of you save yourselves From the fierce anger of the Lord. (Jeremiah 51:45)** This same warning is found in Revelation 18 to flee end time Mystery Babylon: [4]**I heard another voice from heaven, saying, "*Come out of her, my people*, so that you will not participate in her sins and receive of her plagues; (Revelation 18:4)**

Jeremiah 51 tells of the reaction of heaven and earth to the destruction of ancient Babylon: [47]**Therefore behold, days are coming When I will punish the idols of Babylon; And her whole land will be put to shame And all her slain will fall in her midst.** [48]**"*Then heaven and earth and all that is in them Will shout for joy over Babylon,* For the destroyers will come to her from the north," Declares the Lord.**

(Jeremiah 51:47,48) Revelation 19 echoes this declaration of joy at the destruction of end time Mystery Babylon: [1]**After these things I heard something like *a loud voice of a great multitude in heaven, saying,* "Hallelujah! Salvation and glory and power belong to our God;** [2]**BECAUSE HIS JUDGMENTS ARE TRUE AND RIGHTEOUS; for *He has judged the great harlot* who was corrupting the earth with her immorality, and HE HAS AVENGED THE BLOOD OF HIS BOND-SERVANTS ON HER." (Revelation 19:1–2)**

Jeremiah 51 speaks of ancient Babylon and the slain of all the earth: [49]**Indeed Babylon is to fall for the slain of Israel, *As also for Babylon the slain of all the earth have fallen.* (Jeremiah 51:49)** As Jeremiah stated that for Babylon, the slain of all the earth have fallen, compare now the language in Revelation 18 when talking about end time Babylon: [24]**"And in her was found the blood of prophets and of saints *and of all who have been slain on the earth.*" (Revelation 18:24)**

Lastly, let us examine the final words on Babylon's fate from Jeremiah 51:

[60]**So Jeremiah wrote in a single scroll *all the calamity which would come upon Babylon*, that is, all these words which have been written concerning Babylon.** [61]**Then Jeremiah said to Seraiah, "As soon as you come to Babylon, then see that you read all these words aloud,** [62]**and say, 'You, O LORD, have promised concerning this place to cut it off, *so that there will be nothing dwelling in it, whether man or beast, but it will be a perpetual desolation.*'** [63]**"And as soon as you finish reading this scroll, you will tie a stone to it and throw it into the middle of the Euphrates,** [64]**and say, 'Just so shall Babylon sink down and not rise again because of the calamity that I am going to bring upon her; and they will become exhausted.' " Thus far are**

the words of Jeremiah. (Jeremiah 51:60-64) The parallels between Jeremiah 50 and 51 to the Scriptures of Revelation 17, 18, and 19 are unmistakable. While we know the retribution against ancient Babylon was swift and decisive, the destruction of end time Mystery Babylon The Great is yet to be fulfilled. It is clear from Revelation 17 that ten kings and the beast burn up another place with fire, and that place is the end time Mystery Babylon the Great. The destruction will not be limited to only one city in this nation in the end time. Just as it was with ancient Babylon, *the cities of this nation in the end time*, Mystery Babylon the Great, will be burned with fire. Does Scripture give a clear enough description for us to be able to identify this place that God has clearly marked for destruction? Where is this place? I believe the nation of America makes the most sense given the information we are given, but you can review Appendix 5 for a fuller explanation of the parallels.

Appendix 7

Scriptures Referenced by Chapter

Preface

2 Peter 1:20-21

Introduction

2 Timothy 3:16-17; 1 Thessalonians 5:21; Mark 13:7; Matthew 13:20-21;

Chapter 1

2 Peter 3:8; Isaiah 13:9; 1 Thessalonians 5:2, 4:16,17; Revelation 19:15, 20:4,7-8; 2 Peter 3:8,10; Genesis 2:16-17; Hebrews 4:4-9; Mark 13:37; Luke 21:34; Daniel 12:10; Mark 13:19; Revelation 13:7, 10; 3:10-11; 2:10; 2 Thessalonians 1:4-10; Philippians 1:28-29; Matthew 5:10; 1 Peter 3:14; Revelation 6:9-11; 7:9, 13-14; 1 Thessalonians 5:9; Matthew 24:6-13; Revelation 6:16-17; 11:16-18; 1:3; Luke 21:29-30; 2 Peter 1:20-21; Matthew 24:32-33; Revelation 6:8; Proverbs 1:32; John 16:33; Revelation 20:4-6; 11:15; 2 Peter 1:20-21; 3:3-4; Matthew 24:21-25; 29-31

Chapter 2

2 Peter 3:8,10; 1 Thessalonians 5:1-4; Matthew 24:32-33; 2 Thessalonians 2:2-3; Isaiah 13:9-11

Chapter 3

Daniel 12:9; Luke 21:24,32; Deuteronomy 12:5,11; Nehemiah 1:9; Psalms 74:7; Ezra 6:12; Psalms 122:6; Acts 17:11; Revelation 20:1-10;; Psalms 50:10; Revelation 19:20; 20:1-10;1:12,16,20; Matthew 11:14; 17:11; Isaiah 65:20,22,25; Revelation 20:6; Ezekiel 47:12; 45:7; 48:21;

46:16-17; Revelation 21:1-3, 23; 20:4-5; 1 Thessalonians 4:15-17; Revelation 20:11-15

Chapter 4

Luke 21:34-36; 1 Thessalonians 5:1-5; 2 Thessalonians 2:1-5; Matthew 25:1; 10-12, 10:10-11,13; 24:13; Hebrews 12:17; James 2:19; Matthew 4:17; Luke 13:2-5; Revelation 22:6-11; John 6:44; Daniel 12:4-10; 11:32-36; Proverbs 1:24-32; Hebrews 4:1,3,7; Leviticus 24:24; Revelation 6:8; 9:20-21; 16:9,11; Job 36:13; Revelation 11:18, 19:15, 14:13; Luke 18:24, 18:8; 1 Peter 4:17-19; 1 Thessalonians 1:4-5, 5:9; James 1:12; Revelation 20:4; 2 Thessalonians 2:6-7; Titus 3:5; 1 Corinthians 2:12-14; Luke 21:25-28; Luke 21:34-36; Matthew 10:33; Mark 13:24-27; Matthew 24: 13-14, 21-22, 27,29-31; 2 Timothy 2:12; Proverbs 1:32; Luke 21:24,32; Revelation 3:10, 15-17; 2 Timothy 2:15; Revelation 1:3; Matthew 13:20-21; 24:6-10, 29-31; 2 Peter 3:2-4

Chapter 5

Matthew 24:21-22; 1 Thessalonians 5:9; Daniel 7:25; Revelation 3:10; 6:8; 9:3-5; 4:1; 7:9, 13-14; 2 Thessalonians 2:1-2; 1 Thessalonians 5:2; 2 Thessalonians 2:6-7; 1 Thessalonians 5:21; 1:10; Revelation 6:16-17; Luke 19:16-17; 2 Corinthians 5:10; 2 Thessalonians 2:1; Matthew 25:1-13; 2 Thessalonians 2:4-10; Acts 2:41;Revelation 9:20-21; 1Corinthians 15:52; Revelation 11:15,18; Romans 4:22-24; Revelation 20:4-5, 16:11; 11:7; 13:1-8; 4:1-2; 1 Corinthians 15 51-53; Revelation 4:4; 2 Timothy 2:6-7; Titus 2:13; Acts 17:10-11; Revelation 19:11-21; 20:1-6; 1 Thessalonians 5:21; 4:17; Revelation 6:15-17; 11:15,18; 1 Thessalonians 5:9; Revelation 6:9-11; 2 Peter 3:5-7,10; 2 Thessalonians 2:1-2; Daniel 7:11-12; Revelation 20:5,11-12,15; 9:4; Ephesians 1:4-

6; 13:4; 2 Corinthians 1:21-22; Revelation 11:15-18; Exodus 9:26; 10:23; Revelation 14:9-13; James 1:12; 1 Peter 4:17-19; Revelation 3:10; 2 Thessalonians 1:4-10; Matthew 24:31; 1 Thessalonians 4:16; 1 Corinthians 15:51-52; Revelation 10:7; 11:15; 1 Thessalonians 5:9; Luke 17:33; 21:34-36; Matthew 24:29-31; 2 Thessalonians 2:1-5; Matthew 24:10-13, Revelation 12:5; 14:8;18:4; 15:1; 11:15,18; 1 Thessalonians 1:10; Revelation 7:9-10, 13-15; 9:20-21; 6:9-11; 7:9, 13-14; 1 Corinthians 15:42-44,51-53; Matthew 19:27-28; Revelation 14:9-13

Chapter 6

Matthew 24:11-13, 4-8; 2 Thessalonians 2:3-4; Revelation 13:11-15; Acts 2:17-21; Matthew 17:11-12; Daniel 12:4,9-10; 8:17,19; 12:26; Jeremiah 32:37; Isaiah 11:11; Ezekiel 37:16-22; Luke 21:32; Genesis 15:13,16; Exodus 12:41; Psalms 90:10; Genesis 6:3; Mark 13:20,32; Luke 21:29-31; Daniel 9:27; 12:11-12; 7:25; 8:1-27; Revelation 13:7; Mark 9:9-13; Matthew 17:10-13; 11:14; 24:29-31,3; 13:2-3; 10:10-16

Chapter 7

Daniel 7:17, 7:7-8, 11:31-36,45, 12:10; 1 John 2:18,22, 4:3; 2 John 1:7; 2 Thessalonians 2:1-7, 8-12; Daniel 10:7-14; Revelation 11:7,4; Romans 11:17; Revelation 1:20; Zechariah 4:1-4,11-14; Exodus 29:4,7, 40:15, 19:4-6; 1 Peter 2:5,9; 2 Corinthians 1:21-22; 1 John 2:20-27; Revelation 11:5-6,8-9,11-12,7; Matthew 29:14; Daniel 7:25, 8:24; Revelation 13:7, 11:7; Luke 12:4; Revelation 11:15, 13:1-10, 9:20-21; Job 36:13; Revelation 16:9,11; Psalms 81:12; Acts 14:16; Isaiah 2:12; Ezekiel 18:32; Acts 17:30-31; Revelation 7:9,13-14; Matthew 10:22; Hebrews 3:6,14; Revelation 13:11-17, 19:19-20; 2 Timothy 2:12; 2 Thessalonians 1:5; Daniel 2:28-45, 7:11,7-12,13-22,23-27, 11:31, 8:25,

11:36,41; Matthew 24:15-31; Daniel 8:22-25; Revelation 13:1-9, 17:7-13,16-17, 9:1,11, 18:4

Chapter 8

Jeremiah 25:11; 2 Chronicles 36:20-21; Daniel 9:1-23,24-27; Ezekiel 4:4-6; Daniel 12:4,9; Nehemiah 2:1-8; Daniel 12:11-12; Exodus 30:19-21; 2 Kings 24:10-14; Jeremiah 41:4-5, 52:30; Leviticus 25:1-5,8-11; Mark 13:1-2; 1 Chronicles 21:22-26; 2 Chronicles 3:1; Revelation 11:2; Luke 21:24,32

Chapter 9

John 18:36; Revelation 11:15, 20:1-10,11-2, 6:9-11, 19:11-14,19,7-9; ! Corinthians 15:52,53; Daniel 7:11-12; 1 Corinthians 6:2; Daniel 7:22,27; Revelation 19:15; Isaiah 65:18-25,17; Revelation 21:1-4; Ezekiel 43:4-5, 44:1-3,22; Hebrews 7:26-27; 8:4; Ezekiel 45:1, 33:23-24, 45:7, 46:16, 45:8, 47:9,12, 48:35; Zechariah 14:16-19; 2 Peter 3:10,8

Chapter 10

Leviticus 23:11; 1 Corinthians 15:20; Acts 2:1; 1 Corinthians 15:52; Leviticus 23:24; Matthew 24:29-31; Revelation 19:9; John 1:14

Chapter 11

Jeremiah 32:37-42; Ezekiel 11:17-20; Romans 11:2-5; Ezekiel 39:27-29; Exodus 10:1-2; 14:17-18; Romans 9:17; Jeremiah 31: 31-37; Joel 3:2; Zechariah 12:1-10; 14:16-17; Romans 11:25-29

Chapter 12

Hebrews 10:23-25

Appendix 1

Mark 16:16; John 3:16-18; Matthew 4:14-15; Romans 10:9-11; Mark 9:23-24; Ephesians 2:8-9; Romans 4:3; Hebrews 5:1; 7:27; 9:22; 1 John 1:6-10; 1 John 2:1-6; Hebrews 9:27-28; 1 Corinthians 1:23-24; 2:7-14; 1 John 1:8-10; 1 Corinthians 2:7-14, 6:9

Appendix 2

2 Peter 1:10-11,8-9; 1 John 5:13; Hebrews 11:6; Romans 4:3; Hebrew 11:17-19; Romans 4:2-8; 1 Corinthians 1:21-24; Hebrews 9:22; Romans 5:8-10, 6:23; Ephesians 2:1-9; 1 Corinthians 15:16-17; James 2:19; 1 John 3:4-10; Matthew 7:16-23; Romans 10:8-17; Hebrews 4:1,7,16; Matthew 4:17; Luke 13:1-5; John 3:16-17; Acts 2:38,40-41; John 3:36; Acts 4:12; 1 Timothy 2:5; John 5:12; 2 Peter 1:1-11; 1 Corinthians 13:13; John 13:35; 2 Corinthians 13:5; James 2:14-26; John 15:5,8; Galatians 5:22-23

Appendix 3

Daniel 12:11-12; Exodus 30:19-21; 2 Kings 24:10-14; Jeremiah 41:4-5, 52:28-30; Matthew 11:14, 17:11-13; Leviticus 25:1-5,8-11; Daniel 9:27, 12:11; Mark 13:1-2; 1 Chronicles 21:22-26; 2 Chronicles 3:1; Revelation 11:2; Luke 21:24,32

Appendix 4

Revelation 6:12; Joel 2:31; Matthew 24:6-8; Joel 2:10-11; Isaiah 13:9-10; Matthew 24:29,31; Joel 2:2-11; Revelation 19:11-14; Joel 2:30-32

Appendix 5

2 Thessalonians 2:3,8; Revelation 17:12-13, 16-18, 14; 19:16-18; 18:3,

7-8, 9-10; 17:15; 18:11,15-18,4-5; 1 Thessalonians 1:10; 5:9; Luke 21:36; 1 Thessalonians 4:13-18; 1 Corinthians 15:51-52; Proverbs 30:24-27; Psalms 127:1; Proverbs 22:3; 27:12; Luke 21:36

Appendix 6

Revelation 17:5,18; Jeremiah 51:1; Revelation 17:12-13, 16-17; Jeremiah 51:11; Revelation 17:18; Jeremiah 51:43, 2,5-6; Revelation 18:4; Jeremiah 51:7; Revelation 18:5-8; 17:4,2; 18:7-8; Jeremiah 51:8-9; Revelation 18:5; 17:1, 15; Jeremiah 51:13-16, 24-25; Revelation 18:6; Jeremiah 51:26-29; Revelation 18:21; Jeremiah 50:32; 51:30; Revelation 18:8; Jeremiah 50:39; Revelation 18:21-23; Jeremiah 51:33,37; Revelation 18:2; Jeremiah 51:43; Revelation 18:4; Jeremiah 51: 47-48; Revelation 19:1-2; Jeremiah 51:49; Revelation 18:24; Jeremiah 51:60-64

About the Author

Robert Hart is an elder in his evangelical church in Atlanta, Georgia, an occasional preacher, and a long-time teacher of God's Word. As a seasoned and dedicated student of the Scriptures for over five decades, Robert Hart brings a wealth of knowledge and insight to the topic of popular end time beliefs.

Mr. Hart is a graduate of the University of Georgia, and has enjoyed a successful career as a businessman and is now enjoying traveling, speaking, and writing, as well as occasionally painting in his retirement. His faith and love of the Lord and passion for the Word of God, especially those regarding Bible prophecy coupled with his extensive biblical knowledge, has led him to explore the origins and impact of popular beliefs throughout history.

Beyond his scholarly pursuits, he treasures his role as a husband of forty-two years to his beloved wife Nancy, and as a proud father of two grown children and doting grandfather to three grandchildren. His close friends know him as Bob, but his wife and grandchildren call him Bobby. His personal experiences and deep-rooted faith provide a unique perspective in his writing, as he navigates the complex world of popular beliefs with a discerning eye and a compassionate heart.

With his engaging writing style and well-researched approach, Bob invites readers on a journey of discovery, challenging conventional wisdom and providing fresh insights into eschatology. Whether in the pulpit, the classroom, or the pages of this manuscript, Bob is passionate about sharing the Word of God and encouraging readers to think critically about the beliefs that shape our lives.

www.ingramcontent.com/pod-product-compliance
Lightning Source LLC
Chambersburg PA
CBHW062113020426
42335CB00013B/944
9798988360308